The Quality of Eligible Collateral, Central Bank Losses and Monetary Stability

T0326456

European University Studies

Europäische Hochschulschriften
Publications Universitaires Européennes

Series V
Economics and Management

Reihe V   Série V
Volks- und Betriebswirtschaft
Sciences économiques, gestion d'entreprise

Vol./Bd. 3300

PETER LANG

Frankfurt am Main · Berlin · Bern · Bruxelles · New York · Oxford · Wien

Philipp Lehmbecker

The Quality of Eligible Collateral, Central Bank Losses and Monetary Stability

An Empirical Analysis

PETER LANG
Internationaler Verlag der Wissenschaften

Bibliographic Information published by the Deutsche Nationalbibliothek
The Deutsche Nationalbibliothek lists this publication in the Deutsche Nationalbibliografie; detailed bibliographic data is available in the internet at <http://www.d-nb.de>.

Zugl.: Bremen, Univ., Diss., 2007

D 46
ISSN 0531-7339
ISBN 978-3-631-58076-9

© Peter Lang GmbH
Internationaler Verlag der Wissenschaften
Frankfurt am Main 2008
All rights reserved.

Printed in Germany 1 2 3 4 5   7

www.peterlang.de

Contents

List of Tables

List of figures

List of abbreviations

BIS	–	Bank for International Settlements
CPI	–	Consumer price inflation
ECB	–	European Central Bank
ECCB	–	Eastern Caribbean Central Bank
ESCB	–	European system of central banks
Fed	–	Federal Reserve Board
GAAP	–	Generally accepted accounting principals
GDP	–	Gross domestic product
GNI	–	Gross national income
IAS	–	International accounting standards
IMF	–	International Monetary Fund
IOU	–	I owe you – A certificate of debt
JGB	–	Japanese government bond
LOLR	–	Lender of last resort
NCB	–	National central bank
NPL	–	Non-performing loan
OECD	–	Organisation for economic cooperation and development
OLS	–	Ordinary least squares
QEC	–	Quality of eligible collateral
SNB	–	Swiss National Bank

Acknowledgements

Though only my name appears on the cover of this dissertation, many people have contributed to its production. I owe my gratitude to all those people who have made this dissertation possible.

My first thanks go to a person who is no longer here – Professor Otto Steiger. His kindness, enthusiasm, support and, not least, his theory made all the difference in my academic career. Otto Steiger was amazing for the breadth of his intellectual curiosity. From our first intentional meeting in 1999 until some months before his untimely death, Otto Steiger's conversations and emails were rich and stimulating. Otto Steiger was a mentor in the fullest sense of the word, and I am very fortunate for having known him.

My deepest gratitude is to my advisor, Professor Martin Missong. I have been very fortunate to have an advisor who gave me the freedom to explore on my own. Professor Missong has been always there to listen and give advice. I am deeply grateful to him for the long discussions that helped me sort out the technical details – especially in the empirical part – of my work. I am very proud of being Martin Missong's first advisee to graduate.

My thanks also go to the members of my board of examiners, Professor Gunnar Heinsohn, Professor Jörg Freiling, and Professor Peter Kalmbach as well as Liv Neumann and Fabian Paetzel. I am also thankful to Professor Missong's staff who were always very helpful and friendly. Kudos to Liv Neumann and Heidrun Sobing! I am also grateful to Henner Gratz for helping considerably with realizing the database behind the online questionnaire.

Next, I would like to thank Professor Thomas Lux from the University of Kiel for giving me the chance to embark on the research question of my choice during my master's thesis. The work on my master's thesis served as a good basis for my dissertation.

The data for this study were provided by experts in central banks all over the world. I am extremely grateful for their generosity without which this dissertation would not have been possible.

I have to thank Torben Heinze for holding me to a high research standard. He helped me through the gruelling process of writing and editing drafts in the last two years and provided many valuable comments that improved the presentation and contents of this dissertation – I salute his bravery – but he shall be absolved from the final product. In addition, I wish to thank Ulrich Stolzenburg for his help with calculations of White's heteroskedasticity consistent standard errors and stimulating discussions during our studies at the University of Kiel.

My family has aided and encouraged me throughout this endeavour. I have to give a special mention for the support given by my aunt and uncles, Gesine and Peter Liesegang as well as Wolfgang Lehmbecker. I warmly appreciate their generosity and understanding. I am also grateful to my sister, Annika

Lehmbecker, who took over a lot of my responsibilities in Bremen while I was in Strasbourg and my grandma, Agnes Riegel, who provided me with endless amounts of chocolate and encouragement. They have been a great motivation.

My parents, Brigitte and Hartwig, receive my deepest gratitude and love for their dedication and the many years of support during my studies. They have breathlessly awaited this dissertation, and they deserve full credit for it.

Last, but not least, I would like to thank Charlotte for her understanding and love during the past few years. Her support and encouragement was in the end what made this dissertation possible.

1 Introduction

Monetary stability is the overriding goal of central banks and represents a condition for continuous economic growth.[1] Corresponding to the significance of monetary stability a great many of empirical studies have been undertaken to identify determinants of inflation. Based on the works of Nobel laureates Kydland and Prescott, the central banking literature regards central bank independence and a transparent monetary policy as best suited to achieve and safeguard monetary stability. The existing empirical literature, however, failed in establishing a solid ground for this consensus in the central banking literature.[2] This survey will shed some new light on the empirical evidence on monetary stability and its determinants. In addition this thesis expands the current research agenda by considering two factors that have so far been neglected in the central banking literature: Central bank losses and the quality of eligible collateral.

The use of collateral is pervasive: More than two thirds of all credit contracts in developed countries are secured by collateral.[3] Yet, only in exceptional times does collateral make the headlines.[4] However, if it does – as in the recent crisis in the international banking system – even central banks need to act vigorously in response to prevent the whole system from collapsing.[5] In recent years collateral has also become a subject of mainstream economic analysis.[6] But collateral also plays a vital role in the theory of Property Economics developed by Heinsohn and Steiger.[7] In the academic literature on the theory of the central bank, however, collateral has received only very little attention.[8] This dissertation aims at joining the theory of the central bank and Property Economics by investigating to what extent the quality of eligible collateral is able to explain inflation. In doing so, three hypotheses derived from the theory of Property Economics are tested.

Like collateral, central bank losses have so far been largely ignored as a possible determinant of monetary stability. This is a bit surprising given the

---

1   Cf. Levine (1997).
2   See the overview of the literature on central banking provided in section 2.1.
3   Cf. Bigus et al. (2004).
4   See, for instance, the August 18th issue of the Economist, Economist (2007a).
5   Though many observers were somewhat waiting for the subprime bubble to burst even big players like Goldman Sachs estimated the likelihood of such crisis to be "[ ] 25 standard deviations away from normal. In terms of probability (where 1 is a certainty and 0 an impossibility), that translates into a likelihood of 0.000...0006, where there are 138 zeros before the six." See Economist (2007b).
6   See the overview of the literature on collateral in economic analyses provided in section 2.4.
7   See Heinsohn & Steiger (1996; 2002; 2006 and 2007b).
8   Cf. BIS (2001) p. i.

strict standards established for related parameters, like capital adequacy, within the scope of banking supervision after Basel II. However, a growing literature on central bank capital and central bank losses argues that financially weak central banks cannot safeguard monetary stability.[9] The theory of Property Economics is consistent with this thesis, whereas the literature following Kydland and Prescott remains silent on this issue.

This dissertation provides the first comprehensive dataset suitable to assess the significance of central bank losses and the quality of eligible collateral for monetary stability. Data have been collected using an online questionnaire that was answered by central bank officials. This survey delivers new conclusions regarding determinants of the interrelation between the institutional framework of monetary policy and inflation. The results of this survey provide valuable policy advice, especially for less-developed and transition countries, towards a more stable economic development.

Based on this survey's findings it is argued that the literature following Kydland and Prescott, in its search for mechanisms that keep money scarce and inflation low, focuses on rather vague constructs like central bank independence and transparency: In addition to problems of measurement, evidence on central bank independence relies primarily on data for the 1960s, the 1970s and the 1980s. Monetary stability, however, represents a current challenge and thus deserves more up-to-date evidence. This survey uses such evidence to assess the explanatory power of central bank independence and transparency against the one of the quality of eligible collateral. This quality, it will be argued, can be measured directly and provides a more tangible mechanism, which ultimately relies on the scarceness of property to achieve monetary stability.

The dissertation proceeds as follows: Chapter two gives an overview of the literature on central banking and those issues in mainstream economic analysis related to this survey's research question: Central banks, central bank losses, collateral and money. In chapter three hypotheses on the effects of the quality of eligible collateral and central bank losses on inflation are generated based on the theory of Property Economics. The questionnaire used to collect data and the construction of an index of the quality of eligible collateral are described in chapter four. Results of regression analyses are presented in chapter five and interpreted in chapter six. Chapter seven concludes by discussing the theoretical implications of this study and by revealing opportunities for future research.

---

9   See the overview of the literature on central bank losses provided in section 2.3.

2 Review of the literature

The survey at hand investigates to what extent the quality of eligible collateral is able to explain cross-country differences in average inflation. An evaluation of this potential explanation of inflation calls for an overview of the state of the art dealing with the issue of inflation. The literature on monetary policy has witnessed major developments during the last thirty years. The discourse on the characteristics of an optimal monetary policy was strongly influenced by the debate on *rules versus discretion*.[10] Yet this influence has not been limited to academic research alone affecting also actual central bank policies. During the 1980s the paradigm of an independent central bank was developed. Central banks' monetary policy should be free from political pressures to be able to achieve the goal of price stability. The early 1990s saw just another innovation in monetary policy as inflation targeting was introduced in a number of countries. When more and more central banks became independent from their respective governments it became evident that the traditionally highly opaque monetary policy of many central banks would have to be adjusted to allow for greater central bank accountability: "Reasons of democratic legitimacy thus provided a political economy justification for greater transparency."[11] Section 2.1 reviews the literature on monetary policy frameworks.

The subjects of another ongoing debate in the field of the theory of money and central banking relate to the questions, what qualities money should possess and if a central bank is required to guarantee an efficient functioning of markets. These issues clearly matter for this survey's research question as there is no eligible collateral without a central bank and since the quality of eligible collateral potentially has a bearing on the quality of money. In the first half of the nineteenth century a very similar debate on central banks' raison d'être was already part of the agenda. At that time a central bank was a new and rather unknown institution. Before that time – in the era of the so called free banking – one had managed to do without a public supervision of the issuance of money. The dominating question, thus, was whether a central bank would represent an indispensable or only an unnecessary or even a harmful public interference with economic processes. Hayek and Friedman have revived this debate in the last decades.[12] Section 2.2 traces the debate's main arguments and appraises the significance of insights gained over the last decades.

Section 2.3 offers an introduction to the relatively young literature on effects of and remedies for central bank losses. Central bank losses might force the

---

10 Cf. Bofinger *et al.* (1996) p. 137 f.
11 See van der Cruisen & Demertzis (2005) p. 2.
12 Cf. Goodhart (1985) p. 1- 12.

central bank – in case government denies financial assistance – to print its way back to profitability, i.e. the central bank would have to follow a monetary policy leading to higher inflation in order to gain greater seigniorage revenues. This issue is of special interest for this survey's research question as collateral's primary objective is the limitation of losses from credit operations.

The macro- and microeconomic literature on collateral are reviewed in section 2.4 to give an idea of collateral's role in economic theory and, more importantly, to assess whether this literature has anything to say about the quality of collateral eligible for central banks. Section 2.5 offers an account of the neoclassical theory of the emergence of money. This section helps to distinguish between the conventional theories on money and Property Economics respectively. Property Economics derives basic concepts of economics like money, interest and markets from the special characteristics of property-based economic systems. However, a thorough comparison of the two theories is omitted as doubts of a general nature exist regarding the usefulness of such endeavours.[13]

2.1 The 'rules versus discretion' debate and its proposals

The debate on rules versus discretion led to major changes of monetary policy frameworks over the past two decades. Many if not most central banks during the 1980s were regarded as mere divisions of the treasury, which often had the last word concerning decisions relevant for monetary policy.[14] Communication with the public regarding policy targets etc. was considered as somewhat undesirable – even by major central banks like the US Federal Reserve Board (Fed).[15] Nowadays this picture has changed completely as a look at, for instance, the European Central Bank's (ECB) homepage reveals: The keywords independence and transparency feature most prominently just after the declaration of the European System of Central Banks' (ESCB) primary objective: maintaining price stability.[16]

> "The independence of the ECB is conducive to maintaining price stability. Theoretical analysis and empirical evidence show this."[17] "Today, most central banks, including the ECB, consider transparency as crucial. This is true especially for their mone-

---

13 Cf. Kuhn (1970) and Lakatos (1970) p. 93-138.
14 This conclusion suggests itself after a cursory inventory of the data for 72 countries on central bank independence in Cukierman *et al.* (1992a).
15 Cf. Cukierman & Meltzer (1986).
16 See the ECB homepage under http://www.ecb.de/ecb/orga/tasks/html/index.en.html.
17 See the ECB homepage under http://www.ecb.de/ecb/orga/independence/html/index.en.html.

tary policy framework. The ECB gives a high priority to communicating effectively with the public."[18]

Geraats, summarising these developments, regards central bank independence and transparency as the new paradigm in monetary policy.[19]

These changes stand in contrast to the original idea of introducing a rule bound monetary policy to put an end to high inflation, which has never really been considered by central banks. Mishkin reviews those monetary policy frameworks that are actually in place.[20] His work shows that actual frameworks have only very little – if anything at all – in common with originally proposed rules such as Friedman's "k percent rule", which represents one of the few explicitly mentioned rules.[21] Correspondingly criticisms questioning the idea of a monetary policy bound by rules have been part of the debate almost right from the start.[22]

The seminal paper launching this debate is Kydland & Prescott's "Rules Rather than Discretion: The Inconsistency of Optimal Plans".[23] A monetary policy bound by a fixed rule is justified on the grounds of a general dynamic time inconsistency of monetary policy. An announced monetary policy is only optimal as long as economic agents have not yet adjusted their plans accordingly. As soon as, for instance, wages have been fixed by corresponding contracts another monetary policy leading to a higher rate of inflation would become optimal.[24] Based on the analysis by Kydland & Prescott, Barro & Gordon published one of macroeconomics most reproduced models, the *natural rate model*.[25] This model is based on the following assumptions: All agents know how the economy works, the goals of government or central bank coincide with those of private agents, and all agents form rational expectations.[26] Despite these virtually ideal conditions a high rate of inflation prevails in this model unless the government ties monetary policy credibly to a certain rule.

The term natural rate model stems from a thesis according to which monetary policy has no effect on unemployment in the long run. Empirical work by Lucas established the idea that a natural rate of unemployment exists, which in

---

18 See the ECB homepage under http://www.ecb.de/ecb/orga/transparency/html/index.en.html.
19 See Geraats (2002) p. 532.
20 Cf. Mishkin (1999).
21 Cf. Barro & Gordon (1983a), see also Bofinger *et al.* (1996) p. 121 ff.
22 Cf. Taylor (1983).
23 Cf. Kydland & Prescott (1977).
24 Cf. Blinder (1998) p. 39-66 as well as Bofinger *et al.* (1996) p. 128 ff.
25 Cf. Barro & Gordon (1983a).
26 In a precursory model to the one of Barro & Gordon Sargent & Wallace (1975) p. 254 point out the importance of the assumption of rational expectations for the conclusions derived from this model.

the long run is only affected by structural factors.[27] In the short run, however, a certain negative (positive) interrelation between the level of unemployment (economic activity) and the rate of inflation prevails. A level of inflation above the one expected by economic agents would cause unemployment to decrease or, equivalently, economic activity to increase. The microeconomic explanation behind these interrelations is that producers of goods interpret the rise in the price of 'their' good as a real increase in demand for 'their' good – being unable to distinguish whether all prices rise or only 'their' good's price – and raise production accordingly.[28] Kydland & Prescott presented this trade-off between inflation and unemployment in an example to support their more general theory.[29] According to this theory a discretionary policy is always inferior to a rule bound policy in the long run as the former might increase economic instability.[30] A discretionary policy is defined as taking the decision concerning the optimal policy in each period anew while in a rule bound setting this decision is only taken once and for all future periods. Fischer reaches similar conclusions regarding monetary policy's effect on unemployment without, however, taking recourse to a natural rate hypothesis.[31] In Fischer's model a decrease of unemployment after an inflationary policy is due to sticky wages. These are fixed in nominal terms and are adjusted only once per period/year.[32] The irrelevance of the natural rate hypothesis for Fischer's model is of some importance since Friedman claims that the natural rate hypothesis fits the US post war experience but not the one of Europe.[33]

All these models have in common that the central bank is always tempted to boost the economy in the short run by unexpected – surprise – inflation. The resulting increase in economic activity and decrease of unemployment is – according to respective assumptions – welcomed by both private economic agents and central bankers. Economic agents know the goals and conditions under which the central bank takes its decisions regarding monetary policy. Therefore, economic agents adjust their expectations of future inflation accordingly and expected inflation under rational expectations turns out to be always higher than it would be if the central bank were able to commit credibly to a policy of zero inflation. In addition, monetary policy only has a positive effect on economic activity if actual inflation exceeds expected inflation. If one compares discretionary monetary policy and a credibly rule bound one, i.e. a policy devoid of incentives not to act according to the rule, with regard to overall welfare, the

---

27 See Lucas (1973).
28 Cf. Lucas (1973) p. 326-330.
29 Cf. Kydland & Prescott (1977).
30 Cf. Kydland & Prescott (1977) p. 477-480.
31 Cf. Fischer (1977).
32 See Fischer (1977) p. 191.
33 Cf. Friedman (2003) p. 113.

rule bound monetary policy comes out on top. The reason for this finding is that a credibly rule bound monetary policy allows policy makers to keep inflation at low levels whereas a discretionary monetary policy allows for a reduction of unemployment below its natural rate but at the cost of potentially excessive inflation rates. The finding of a superiority of a rule bound monetary policy rests on some technical preconditions. The result presupposes a sufficiently low preference for current consumption versus future consumption as well as a sufficiently high inflation aversion relative to agents' unemployment aversion.[34] The problem of time-inconsistency of monetary policy not credibly bound by some rule – as formulated by Kydland & Prescott – triggered a broad discussion on the issue of how to remedy or at least mitigate the time-inconsistency problem.

Barro & Gordon were also among the precursors regarding proposed remedies for the presumed time-inconsistency of a discretionary policy.[35] A central bank's reputation or credibility was supposed to make up – at least partially – for a rule bound monetary policy. The reputation of a central bank is said to have an effect on economic agents' formation of inflation expectations: The stronger the public's confidence in a central bank that promises to fight inflation effectively and with all means, the smaller expectations of inflation and therefore actual inflation would turn out to be. A central bank creating surprise inflation with the aim of pushing unemployment below its natural rate would thus jeopardise such a reputation. If economic agents become aware of the game the central bank is playing, agents will – assuming rational expectations – presume that the central bank will always induce agents to increase employment. The corollary of such monetary policy would be rising inflation expectations, ultimately resulting in higher actual inflation. Thus, the central bank would lose its reputation or credibility. This argument also forms the basis of the thesis that a central bank's reputation remains untouched as long as no deviation from the announced policy occurs, i.e. no surprise inflation. However, as announcements based on discretionary monetary policies are defined to be not entirely credible, a central bank's reputation has to be regarded as an at best partial compensation for a rule bound monetary policy.[36] The following two subsections illustrate the main proposals to create and maintain such credibility.

2.1.1 Transparency as means to build reputation

Cukierman & Meltzer advanced the reputation approach of Barro & Gordon by modelling a central bank's credibility as dependent on the public's learning curve.[37] Moreover, in their model the central bank has private information

---

34 Cf. Barro & Gordon (1983b).
35 Cf. Barro & Gordon (1983b).
36 Cf. Barro & Gordon (1983b).
37 Cf. Cukierman & Meltzer (1986) and Barro & Gordon (1983b).

regarding its goals. This entails that economic agents are unable to infer reliably the central bank's goals from policy results. The greater the central bank's control of inflation, however, the faster and more reliable economic agents' conclusions regarding central bank's goals would be. It follows from this argumentation that central banks might deliberately choose monetary policy instruments, which allow only for a less than optimal control of inflation, since such an imprecise control of inflation offers the advantage – from the central bank's point of view – of obscuring potentially desirable surprise inflation. The use of suboptimal monetary policy instruments might therefore lessen or even completely avoid any damages to a central bank's reputation that would otherwise result from surprise inflation.[38] Studying the Federal Reserve Board Goodfriend came across such behaviour: Neither the precise goals of monetary policy nor the Board's decision process were transparently communicated to the public.[39] Moreover, statements of central bank officials are often ambiguous. The papers by Barro & Gordon, Cukierman & Meltzer and Goodfriend marked the beginning of a debate on advantages and disadvantages of a transparent monetary policy.

At the beginning of the 1990s the idea that an improved reputation could primarily be achieved by a more transparent form of monetary policy was taken up by a couple of central banks: Australia, Canada, Finland, Israel, New Zealand, Spain, Sweden and the United Kingdom were the first to introduce a new framework for monetary policy – inflation targeting.[40] The concept of inflation targeting comprises publicly announced targets for future inflation and a commitment to low and stable inflation rates as primary and overriding goal. Furthermore, inflation targeting entails an increased communication with the public: Targets for future inflation are not only announced but the central bank explains in publications and official speeches – often substantiated by econometric analyses – why the announced target was chosen. Precisely this form of public relations in connection with an inflation target, the degree to which it was achieved everybody can easily verify on the basis of the announced target, renders it virtually impossible for a central bank to shirk itself from the responsibility for actual inflation. In doing so inflation targeting not only offers the advantage of an increased credibility but also provides the possibility to rely on a discretionary policy and all conceivable indicators of inflation. Moreover, policy effectiveness is increased in the sense that agents' expectations are geared to central bank forecasts, allowing for a more direct influence on long term variables such as interest rates.[41] Considerable time lags with regard to policy measures' impact on inflation furthermore force the central bank to base its policies on long-term

---

38   Cf. Cukierman & Meltzer (1986).
39   Cf. Goodfriend (1986).
40   Cf. Bernanke & Mishkin (1997).
41   Cf. Woodford (2005).

considerations.[42] In addition theoretical foundations of inflation targeting are supported by empirical work: Mishkin & Schmidt-Hebbel review the literature on inflation targeting and conclude that inflation targeting has to be regarded as a success story.[43]

Similarly, but arguing more closely along the lines of the usual theoretical analyses, Svensson deems inflation targeting as a great progress in monetary policy.[44] He describes inflation targeting as inflation forecast targeting and ascribes its potential to the fact that in practice this would allow for relatively clear conclusions about the central bank's goals. Moreover, a high degree of transparency provides the public with a greater insight regarding the central bank's accountability for policy outcomes. The public could assess with greater certainty whether policy outcomes are mainly due to a central bank's monetary policy or are largely determined by factors outside its control. This in turn would present a strong incentive for the central bank to adhere to an announced low-inflation policy to avoid reputation losses.[45] Faust & Svensson augment the model of Cukierman & Meltzer to include not only the degree of control of inflation but also the degree of transparency as parameters of a central bank's monetary policy.[46] The results of the Faust & Svensson model are ambiguous. The model's results, however, do match the reality of the beginning of the 1990s insofar as central banks are predicted to be characterized by a very low degree of transparency while possessing a strong control over inflation. The results partly depend on the assumption that central banks' institutional setting and their degree of transparency are relatively fixed while the degree of inflation control can be changed rather discretionarily. Examples for such policies are seen in the Bundesbank's and Fed's policies of the 1990s. In the literature these two central banks have in fact often been described as actually practicing some kind of inflation targeting without, however, announcing this explicitly.[47]

Friedman claims that central bank transparency and especially an inflation targeting framework evade the problem of time-inconsistency by focusing the public debate on low inflation and leaving aside everything else, notably the development of real output.[48] He assumes that the public does not possess complete information on central bank's preferences for output versus inflation. This allows central banks to make "[ ] a commitment to low inflation believable by, keeping out of the discussion those considerations that would reveal that com-

---

42 Cf. Bernanke & Mishkin (1997) p. 98-103 and Mishkin (1999) p. 590-598.
43 Cf. Mishkin & Schmidt-Hebbel (2001).
44 Cf. Svensson (1999).
45 Cf. Svensson (1999).
46 Cf. Faust & Svensson (2002) and Cukierman & Meltzer (1986).
47 See for instance Bernanke & Mishkin (1997) p. 103 and 113 as well as Svensson (1999) p. 641.
48 Cf. Friedman (2003).

mitment to be qualified, and hence not completely credible in the usual sense."[49] Friedman argues that central banks employing an inflation targeting framework would have to follow the fastest disinflation paths to achieve low inflation if they did not care about output. As central banks usually announce a certain time frame for achieving the targeted low inflation they evidently put some weight on the development of output without, however, explicitly mentioning it in their explanations of monetary policy. Thus, keeping central banks' concern for real variables out of the discussion the commitment to low inflation in an inflation targeting framework becomes credible.

Cukierman also considers greater central bank transparency to be desirable.[50] He shows that central banks are not yet sufficiently transparent concerning their forecast models in general and regarding the weightings assigned by a central bank to the output goals in its loss function, which a central bank is assumed to minimise in models following Barro & Gordon.[51] Cukierman argues that a new inflation bias might arise due to potentially asymmetric weightings of output goals: Central banks might be more concerned about negative departures from an output goal, i.e. recessions, than positive departures. This avoiding-recessions motive does not rely on some time-inconsistency à la Kydland & Prescott. It remains nonetheless questionable whether this new inflation bias can explain high inflation rates in the range of, say, 7% or higher.[52] An asymmetric weighting of positive and negative departures from some output goal cannot simply be equated with an inflationary policy. The new 'inflation bias' does, however, explain why zero-inflation represents a very rare phenomenon. The measurement of inflation still remains an insufficiently exact science. Many central banks therefore prefer to display more than 1% inflation in order to avoid finding out later that 1% inflation was in fact already a small deflation. The Eurosystem argues along similar lines justifying its inflation goal of less than 2 percent.[53] Thus, policies that aim at avoiding deflation should not be confused with some alleged asymmetrical weighting of departures from central bank's output goals.

The main empirical study on central bank transparency's effect on inflation was conducted by Chortareas et al.[54] Their results support the thesis that the more detailed the explanations of central bank's forecasts are the lower the inflation rate will be. A better explanation of a central bank's monetary policy is by the way a fairly old request, which renders the rather late empirical treatment of this relationship quite surprising.[55] In addition to the detail of central bank

49 Cf. Friedman (2003) p. 120 f.
50 Cf. Cukierman (2002).
51 Cf. Barro & Gordon (1983a; 1983b).
52 Cf. Cukierman (2002).
53 Cf. Reischle (2004).
54 Cf. Chortareas et al. (2002b).
55 See Taylor (1982) p- 83 and 85.

forecasts' explanations Chortareas *et al.* study the transparency in decision taking by the central bank as determinant of inflation. They do not find, however, any significant correlation between transparency in decision taking, i.e. the publication of minutes of monetary policy committees, and inflation.[56] Chortareas *et al.*'s results thus confirm central bank transparency's negative effect on inflation and they even show in their data analyses that the sacrifice-ratio, i.e. the economic costs of disinflation, is smaller the more transparent the monetary policy is. This, however, raises the question why the degree of transparency in monetary policy for a great many central banks still has to be described as low.[57]

Posen regards central bank transparency as determinant of inflation but criticises Chortareas *et al.*'s paper for employing average inflation as dependent variable.[58] According to Posen the theoretical literature on central bank transparency focuses on inflation expectations and thus on the persistence of inflation. Geraats– inspired by the findings of Chortareas *et al.* – develops a model in which transparent central banks might force opaque central banks to become transparent.[59] In her model central banks with a low inflation target choose to publish their forecasts while central banks with high inflation targets due to respective output goals would choose to leave the public in the dark concerning its target levels. If central banks are free to choose their regime, i.e. either transparency or opacity, choosing transparency would represent a signal that the respective central bank has a low inflation target. Opaque central banks might thus be punished by the market in the sense that inflation expectations could be substantially higher for opaque central banks compared to transparent ones. Such market feedback might eventually force all central banks to become transparent.

Van der Cruisen & Demertzis analyse the effect of central bank transparency on the relationship of inflation and inflation expectations.[60] Their analysis is based on the idea that changes of the institutional framework of a central bank affect first of all inflation expectations of private agents. Thus, any effect of such changes can only be the result of changes in the way private agents form their inflation expectations. Previous attempts to measure the effect of central bank transparency on inflation, therefore, remained indirect in the sense that these lack a proper theoretical foundation.[61] Van der Cruisen & Demertzis' results are based on four transparency indices compiled for nine industrial countries for the period 1998 to 2003. They find that most of the surveyed banks increased their transparency and that more transparent central banks experience a weaker link between inflation and inflation expectations. More transparent

---

56 Cf. Chortareas *et al.* (2002a).
57 Cf. Chortareas *et al.* (2002b).
58 Cf. Posen (2002).
59 Cf. Geraats (2005).
60 Cf. van der Cruisen & Demertzis (2005).
61 See also Posen (2002).

central banks are expected to be better able to react to shocks due to better communication with the public. Thus, more transparent central banks should be better in tying inflation expectations to their inflation targets irrespective of actual inflation. This interpretation of their results, however, ignores the fact that reported significance levels of coefficients as well as coefficient signs are often not of the desired distinctness and do not possess the expected sign respectively. In other words, it is far from clear that the results presented in van der Cruisen & Demertzis have to be interpreted in favour of central bank transparency as foolproof way to achieve price stability.

Whether a central bank's credibility in fighting inflation depends on its institutional structure, i.e. central bank independence, or on the actual conduct of monetary policy is analysed by Goldberg & Klein.[62] They employ high frequency-data to assess if monetary policy decisions possess an effect on the evolution of market participants' perceptions regarding inflation aversion. Goldberg & Klein find evidence that the ECB's credibility was influenced by its monetary policy during the first years of its existence. They interpret this as evidence for the thesis that the ECB's communication with the public strengthened its credibility.

Posen distinguishes six different perceptions of central bank transparency, of which only two are supported by empirical analyses: The publication of medium term inflation targets contributes to a decrease of inflation persistence and the explanation of decisions concerning a central bank's main interest rate reduces the volatility of financial markets.[63] Posen regards the empirical fact that central banks become more transparent as a good development: More transparency is mostly better and especially inflation targeting enables central banks to use the advantages of transparency more effectively. There is, however, no evidence that an increased central bank transparency implies a stronger accountability on the side of the central bank. Most notably, the newly gained independence of many central banks – even with regard to the specification of monetary policy goals – did not increase central banks' accountability although these central banks became significantly more transparent.[64]

A review of the substantial theoretical but still scant empirical literature on central bank transparency by Geraats reaches a similar conclusion.[65] Though it is often argued that a newly independent central bank necessitates – for reasons of democratic legitimacy – an increased transparency to guarantee the central bank's accountability vis-à-vis the public, this argumentation is not supported by empirical findings in economic literature. Nonetheless central bank transparency tends to be advantageous as most surveys reveal. However, Geraats concludes

---

62 Cf. Goldberg & Klein (2005).
63 Cf. Posen (2003).
64 Cf. Posen (2003).
65 Cf. Geraats (2002).

that despite a lot of progress in the theoretical literature a "[   ] consensus on the economic desirability of transparency of monetary policy [   ]" is still missing.[66]

Little remains to be added to Geraats' conclusion. More transparency is generally a good thing for central banks' monetary policy and transparency strengthens central banks' influence on inflation expectations. But transparency of monetary policy alone does not imply central bank accountability in the sense that a well informed public controls an independent central bank. Unsurprisingly, a central bank that acts as announced and successfully fights inflation is generally considered the best method to build and preserve credibility while central bank independence is seen as second best solution to achieve higher credibility.[67] This raises questions on the optimal degree of central bank independence and to what extent central bank independence is able to limit central banks' alleged inflation bias. The answers given in the central banking literature are the subject matter of the following section.

2.1.2 Central bank independence: Safeguard against political pressure

The two papers by Barro & Gordon represent the origin of the discussion on central bank independence.[68] Their central thesis is that governments tend to force central banks to issue as much currency as possible. The thus increased central bank profits would help government to finance a good portion of its budget. Due to higher inflation the value of government debt would shrink and a decrease of unemployment levels could be beneficial for government's chances in the next elections. As an increased issuance of money causes inflation, governments are generally to be regarded as possessing an inflationary tendency. Accordingly inflation rates should be lower in those countries where central banks are able to conduct monetary policy independently from governments.[69]

Cukierman et al. were among the first to empirically test whether central bank independence has any effect on inflation.[70] They employ two different central bank independence indices. An index based on the formal legal dimension of central bank independence possesses a statistically significant negative correlation with the level of average inflation among developed countries. This legal independence index possesses, however, no effect on inflation among developing countries. A second central bank independence index, which is based on the frequency of turnover of central bank governors, exhibits a statistically significant positive correlation with average inflation among developing countries and none among developed countries. There exists thus no unitary index with

---

66 See Geraats (2002) p. 562.
67 Cf. Blinder (2000).
68 Cf. Barro & Gordon (1983a; 1983b).
69 Cf. Berger et al. (2001).
70 Cf. Cukierman et al. (1992a).

which central bank independence could be measured. The difference in crucial factors for central bank independence might be due to a somewhat less binding interpretation of the texts of law in developing countries compared to developed ones.[71] In view of the empirical observation that more independent central banks tend to be in politically more stable countries the survey by Cukierman *et al.* supports these results: Political instability promotes a government practice that relies considerably on central bank seigniorage income to finance the government's budget.[72] Their argument is based on the idea that an inefficient tax system constrains government's collection of revenues and that such inefficiency might be welcomed by political opponents, particularly in politically more instable countries. This constraint on government finances would thus force governments – other things being equal – to rely more heavily on seigniorage revenues, which should of course affect inflation.

Another very influential empirical paper stems from Alesina & Summers who investigate the effect of central bank independence on the level and variability of several macroeconomic variables.[73] They find cross-country evidence for 16 developed countries and the period 1955 to 1988 that the level of inflation and its variability are both negatively correlated with central bank independence indices while central bank independence has no effect on real variables. This suggests, they argue, that money is neutral and thus central bank independence reduces inflation without causing costs in terms of real macroeconomic performance. Furthermore, Alesina & Summers challenge the idea of the superiority of a rule based monetary policy as it is obviously possible for countries to achieve low and stable inflation without a rule based policy by granting independence to their central banks.[74]

Loungani & Sheets explore the interrelation of central bank independence and inflation for a sample of twelve countries in transition from a socialist to a market based economic system.[75] They construct an index measuring how close transition countries central banks match the independence of the pre Eurosystem Bundesbank. The Bundesbank is chosen as a benchmark since it is widely regarded as the ideal of an independent central bank due to its pre-eminent success in fighting inflation.[76] Greater resemblance to the Bundesbank is found to be negatively correlated with inflation. Loungani & Sheets, however, refuse expressly Barro and Gordon's claim that central bank independence is supposed to merely represent a safeguard against surprise inflation as they find a negative correlation between economic growth and inflation for their sample of transition

---

71   Cf. Cukierman *et al.* (1992a) p. 376.
72   Cf. Cukierman *et al.* (1992b).
73   Cf. Alesina & Summers (1993).
74   Cf. Alesina & Summers (1993).
75   Cf. Loungani & Sheets (1997).
76   Cf. Loungani & Sheets (1997) p. 386.

countries.[77] This raises the question why a central bank should be independent from political pressures if government itself can be expected to have an interest in low inflation.

Similarly, McCallum believes that central bank independence can be crucial for the attainment of low inflation.[78] He challenges, however, Barro and Gordon's assumption that central banks – unable to see things the way others see them – would time and again provoke surprise inflations to push unemployment below its natural level.[79] Akin to McCallum Blinder argues that many countries have witnessed successful disinflations without granting more independence to their central banks: "As in the Nike commercial, they [the central banks] just did it."[80] Blinder's justification of central bank independence is that, given long time lags in monetary policy, central bankers possess a longer time horizon compared to politicians and thus deliver better results, particularly in the case of disinflation. Barro & Gordon's credibility justification he rejects vigorously: "Much fascinating theory to the contrary, I do not know a shred of evidence that supports it."[81] Forder offers a review of literature that challenges the typical rationalisation of central bank independence, Barro & Gordon's credibility theory.[82] Forder himself feels that "[ ] much of the advocacy of central bank independence is attributable to cynicism about democracy."[83] He argues that Barro & Gordon's thesis has at its centre simply a central bank governor, not an elected governor or politician. Thus, elections have no role in the time-inconsistency problem, and hence establishing politically independent central banks should hardly solve the time-inconsistency problem.[84] Forder thus rejects proposed remedies to the problem of time inconsistency, like central bank independence, 'conservative' central bank governors and contracts between central bank governors and the government, on these grounds.[85]

Posen examines the thesis that a central bank's independence enhances its credibility at such a rate that inflation expectations sink fast enough to allow for disinflations with relatively small output losses.[86] His results suggest rather the contrary: Independent central banks cause higher costs of disinflation than

---

77 Cf. Loungani & Sheets (1997).
78 Cf. McCallum (1997).
79 Cf. McCallum (1997) p. 103-108. See also Fuhrer (1997) who provides evidence supporting McCallum's argument.
80 See Blinder (1998) p. 43.
81 See Blinder (1998) p. 45.
82 Cf. Forder (2000).
83 See Forder (2000) p. 183.
84 See Forder (2000) p. 168.
85 Cf. Forder (2000). On the issues of 'conservative' central bank governors and contracts between central bank governors and the government see the discussion below on the papers by Rogoff (1985) and Walsh (1995).
86 Cf. Posen (1998).

relatively dependent central banks. Obviously, it is not possible for a central bank to attain a higher credibility simply by implementing institutional reforms. Increased central bank credibility is rather the result of a long-lasting process, characterized by announcements which are matched by respective actions and results. Unfortunately, this claim gives no clue as to what causal mechanism could explain why central bank independence should lead to lower inflation.[87] Indeed Blinder notes that it is the duty of every independent central bank to establish credibility to provide the usual checks and balances of democratic societies.[88] He does not explain, however, why a central bank's independence should have an effect on its credibility. Berger et al. review the empirical literature that investigates central bank independence's influence on inflation.[89] The results of those 35 studies covered are rather ambiguous: Less than every second study finds a robust negative correlation in the spirit of Barro & Gordon's predictions. At least nine studies cannot detect any correlation between central bank independence and inflation. Many of these studies use different central bank independence indices. Though Cukierman et al.'s legal-index represents the dominant one being employed by 30 of 35 studies.[90] Overall the results of Cukierman et al. are essentially confirmed by these studies, i.e. formal central bank independence possesses a negative effect on inflation among developed countries while this holds not true among developing countries. Among the latter political instability possesses a positive effect on inflation.[91]

There are also several studies questioning the robustness of the presented results on the effects of central bank independence. Fujiki reviews and reexamines several analyses that employed some index of central bank independence.[92] He argues that results presented by, for instance, Cukierman et al. and Alesina & Summers do not provide a reliable foundation for policy proposals.[93] Their results are found to be not robust to the inclusion of control variables and depend on the periods covered and the samples employed – in particular there is no significant correlation between central bank independence and inflation in the period 1980 to 1989. Fujiki thus challenges the robustness of Alesina & Summers results.[94] Similarly, Fuhrer examines hypotheses about central bank independence and inflation presented in the literature and reconsiders the empirical evidence provided by Alesina & Summers and Cukierman et al.[95] Fuhrer finds that

---

87 Cf. Posen (1998). See also Blinder (1998) p. 62-66 and Berger et al. (2001) p. 28 f.
88 Cf. Blinder (1998).
89 Cf. Berger et al. (2001).
90 Cf. Berger et al. (2001) and Cukierman et al. (1992a).
91 Cf. Cukierman et al. (1992a; 1992b) and Berger et al. (2001) respectively.
92 Cf. Fujiki (1996).
93 Cf. Fujiki (1996). See also Cukierman et al. (1992a) and Alesina & Summers (1993).
94 Cf. Fujiki (1996).
95 Cf. Fuhrer (1997). See also Alesina & Summers (1993) and Cukierman et al. (1992a).

the beneficial effect of central bank independence on inflation in the Cukierman *et al.* sample disappears if covered decades are assessed separately or if some index of central bank independence is not the sole explanatory variable. As soon as other explanatory variables are included in the statistical model central bank independence becomes insignificant. In other words, Fuhrer's reappraisal of empirical studies casts substantial doubt on the robustness of the correlation between inflation and central bank independence as presented by Alesina & Summers and Cukierman *et al.*[96]

Fry develops a thesis of fiscal dominance in developing countries: A developing country's fiscal situation largely determines its central bank's activities and its degree of independence.[97] He tests this thesis employing a measure for central bank independence that relies on a central bank's degree of neutralisation of government's credit demands. Fry shows that according to this measure usual measures, i.e. Cukierman *et al.*'s legal index and governor turnover, do not work for developing countries.[98] Fry finds in a sample of seventy developing countries that larger government deficits and a larger government share in the domestic credit market correlate negatively with central bank's neutralisation of credit to government. He interprets these findings as supporting his thesis that a country's fiscal situation is a good measure of its degree of independence. Chortareas *et al.* who test for the effect of central bank transparency on inflation employing the data set on monetary policy framework characteristics provided by the Bank of England include Fry's measure of fiscal dominance in their regressions.[99] They find that Fry's result also holds true in this larger sample and using more standard methods of data analysis.

Romer investigates the effect of a country's openness to trade on inflation in a monetary policy framework like the one proposed by Barro & Gordon, i.e. time inconsistent monetary policy.[100] His model predicts that a country's degree of openness positively affects the costs of high inflation, due to depreciation of exchange rates. Thus, more open countries should tend to have lower inflation. Romer, testing this prediction in a sample of 114 countries for the period 1973 to 1992, finds a robust and statistically significant negative relationship between openness and inflation among developing countries.[101]

The evidence on determinants of average inflation delivered by – among others – Cukierman *et al.*, Romer and Posen is reconsidered in the study by

---

96 Cf. Fuhrer (1997). See also Alesina & Summers (1993) and Cukierman *et al.* (1992a).
97 Cf. Fry (1998).
98 Cf. Fry (1998) and Cukierman *et al.* (1992a).
99 Cf. Chortareas *et al.* (2002b).
100 Cf. Romer (1993).
101 Cf. Romer (1993).

Campillo & Miron.[102] The methodology they employ is largely analogous to Cukierman et al.'s and is also based on the same sample of 62 countries – albeit comprising a shorter period, 1973 to 1994. The difference to previous papers merely consists in the inclusion of additional control variables like GDP per capita in the same model. Thus, for the first time in the empirical literature on determinants of average inflation competing concepts, i.e. right-hand side variables, are compared directly. Campillo & Miron find that central bank independence, the exchange rate regime and financial sector inflation aversion possess no effect on average inflation while political stability and a country's openness to trade both possess a statistically significant negative effect on average inflation. Furthermore, they find that GDP per capita possesses a statistically significant positive effect on average inflation in their basic model. However, their correlation matrices reveal a statistically significant negative correlation between average inflation and GDP per capita.[103] Therefore, their results need to be interpreted cautiously as their basic model with nine independent variables is obviously delivering partly inconsistent results. Nevertheless, their contribution is of utmost importance as it sheds light on the robustness of previous survey's results leading to the "inescapable" conclusion that central bank independence possesses no effect on inflation.[104]

Jácome tests for central bank independence's effect on inflation among a sample of fourteen Latin American central banks to assess the impact of central bank reforms during the 1990s.[105] His data are based on what he describes as best practices on central bank independence and accountability. These summarise the International Monetary Fund's (IMF) agenda in the course of technical assistance provided during the 1990s to reform central bank charters. Jácome's index of central bank independence includes measures of limits on lender of last resort emergency credits and whether government guarantees the central bank's financial soundness. He finds that central bank independence – measured with his index – is weakly correlated with average inflation and that the mentioned factors are largely responsible for this result.

A recent review of the empirical literature on central bank independence is offered by Arnone et al.[106] They provide a useful overview of all major surveys conducted so far on the relationship between central bank independence and inflation. Detailed accounts of these surveys' results suggest that central bank independence's effect on inflation is not robust to the inclusion of control variables such as openness to trade, political stability and GDP per capita. In other

102 Cf. Campillo & Miron (1997). The empirical papers mentioned are Cukierman et al. (1992a), Romer (1993) and Posen (1998).
103 See Campillo & Miron (1997) tables 9.2 and 9.5 on p. 344-346 and 351 respectively.
104 Cf. Campillo & Miron (1997) p. 356.
105 Cf. Jácome (2001).
106 Cf. Arnone et al. (2006a).

words, these variables are more significant than central bank independence in explaining inflation. Despite these results Arnone *et al.* conclude somewhat stupendously that "[ ] the evidence on the beneficial effects of CB [central bank] autonomy is more than substantial, but some technical issues remain for further research."[107] Arnone *et al.* also review papers by Stella and Ize on the role of central bank capital for central bank independence.[108] They consider the relationship between central bank financial strength and central bank indepen-dence as a promising area for empirical research. This literature, though mostly concerned with the issue of central bank financial independence, is covered in section 2.3 on effects of and remedies for central bank losses due to its particular relevance for this survey's subject matter.

Arnone *et al.* update measures of central bank independence for a set of developed and developing countries and emerging market economies.[109] They assess changes in central bank independence between 1992 and 2003. Their results suggest a significant increase in central bank independence, especially in developing countries. Somewhat surprisingly, Arnone *et al.* do not test whether this increase in central bank independence can help to explain the inflation performance of surveyed countries.

Blinder, finally, employs a questionnaire to find out what central bankers and monetary economists think about central bank credibility and different means to create it.[110] Among central bankers from 84 countries there is a consensus that its credibility is very important for a central bank, while the opinions of 53 American economists are more diverse. Central bankers generally agree that greater credibility lowers the costs associated with a disinflation. Similarly, scholars agree although their answers reflect generally greater scepticism. The best way for a central bank to attain credibility seems to be the creation of a tradition of honesty. Central bank independence is regarded only as second best approach for establishing credibility. A historic record of an effective fight against inflation is ranked third corroborating that a track record of matching deeds to words is more important with regard to the enhancement of central bank credibility than degrees of inflation aversion or central bank independence.[111]

Two additional proposals to overcome the time-inconsistency in the model of Barro & Gordon shall be discussed briefly for reasons of completeness: The papers by Rogoff and Walsh, which basically represent mere formal elabora-

---

107 Cf. Arnone *et al.* (2006a) p. 55.
108 Cf. Arnone *et al.* (2006a). See also Stella (1997; 2003; 2005) and Ize (2005).
109 Cf. Arnone *et al.* (2006b).
110 Cf. Blinder (2000).
111 Cf. Blinder (2000).

tions of two proposals that already appeared in Barro & Gordon's paper.[112] Rogoff suggests the installation of a conservative, i.e. inflation averse, central banker as central bank governor to counter the alleged inflation bias. An empirical test of this proposal is, however, missing as it is currently impossible to perform since personality research so far fails to provide the needed test for conservativeness. Walsh's proposal of a contract between central bank officials and the government that punishes central bank officials in some form if inflation targets are missed failed as well. The Reserve Bank of New Zealand remains the only central bank to have experimented with such contracts. This neglect might be explained by the arguments put forward by McCallum and Blinder who question government's interest to actually enforce contract penalties in case of surprise inflation.[113]

The insights of the literature on central banking following Kydland & Prescott can be summarised as follows: In this literature exists a consensus regarding what central bank goals ought to have priority. There also exists a consensus with regard to the characteristics of the institutional framework. A central bank should be independent and implement a transparent monetary policy in order to best suit the goals of monetary stability and a stable financial system.[114] The consensus on the institutional framework, however, is not unequivocally supported by the empirical evidence:

i)   Greater transparency can generally be viewed as beneficial even in light of the scant empirical evidence since it is regarded as strengthening central banks' influence on inflation expectations. But central bank transparency alone does not help to strengthen a central bank's accountability in the sense that a well informed public could control a central bank unrestrained by democratic checks and balances. Moreover, a consensus regarding the theoretical underpinning of why transparency could help to achieve monetary stability is still missing.

ii)   A central bank's degree of independence seems to have an effect on monetary stability, but the concept of independence so far withholds itself from measurement by one index alone. Indices of legal central bank independence are used to assess the degree of a central bank's independence in developed countries whereas central bank independence in developing countries is assessed with measures of 'actual' independence like the turnover rate of central bank governors and central bank's degree of neutralisa-

---

112 Cf. Rogoff (1985) and Walsh (1995) as well as Barro & Gordon (1983a) footnote 19 on p. 607.
113 Cf. McCallum (1997) p. 108 f. See also Blinder (1998) p. 44-48.
114 Cf. Cukierman (2002) p. 15, Berger et al. (2001) p. 3 f. and Mishkin (1999) p. 580.

tion of government's credit demands. This makes a comparison of existing findings even more difficult.[115]

iii)   If a significant correlation between central bank independence and inflation is found, such correlation is typically not robust to the inclusion of control variables and periods covered. Unfortunately, the most influential surveys suggesting that central bank independence possesses an effect on inflation did not test for the robustness of their results.[116] The evidence, however, on the missing robustness of these surveys' results is substantial.[117]

iv)   Surveys on the effects of central bank independence cover only the period 1950 to 1995. More recent data to test for the effect of central bank independence on inflation exist, but are surprisingly either not used – Arnone *et al.* update the Cukierman *et al.* index only to establish that legal central bank independence increased substantially in the last 15 years – or ignored as in the case of data provided by the Bank of England, despite being considered as the most comprehensive survey on monetary policy framework characteristics to date.[118]

v)   There exists no empirical evidence to view central bank independence as a means to increase central bank credibility. Posen finds that independent central banks cause higher costs of disinflation than relatively dependent central banks.[119] This finding directly contradicts Barro & Gordon's thesis that central bank independence could raise central bank credibility.

vi)   Central banks do not have to be bound by rules to achieve monetary stability, i.e. low inflation. During the 1980s the Fed and the Bundesbank – among others – brought inflation down without any changes in their degrees of independence or transparency and without any officially rule based monetary policy. This directly contradicts Kydland & Prescott's thesis of a general time inconsistency of monetary policy.[120]

vii)   Fighting inflation successfully and acting as announced is generally considered to represent the best way for central banks to build and preserve

---

115 Cf. Cukierman *et al.* (1992a) for the governor turnover variable and Fry (1998) for the fiscal dominance measure.

116 Cf. Alesina & Summers (1993) and Cukierman *et al.* (1992a).

117 Cf. inter alia Fujiki (1996), Fuhrer (1997) and Campillo & Miron (1997).

118 Cf. Arnone *et al.* (2006b) and Cukierman *et al.* (1992a) as well as Fry *et al.* (2000). Neither of the two comprehensive reviews on central bank independence, Berger *et al.* (2001) and Arnone *et al.* (2006) even mentions the Bank of England's survey by Fry *et al.* (2000).

119 Cf Posen (1998).

120 Cf. Blinder (1998).

credibility, whereas central bank independence is seen only as second best solution to achieve higher credibility.[121]

Therefore, the current consensus on central banks' institutional framework, central bank independence and transparency, has to be regarded as standing on shaky ground. Nonetheless, it is not so much the practical consequences of this consensus that have to be criticised – after all there are no significant disadvantages to be expected from greater central bank independence, not to mention central bank transparency. Rather advocates of the theory of central banking following Kydland and Prescott as well as Barro and Gordon must be criticised for holding on to an incomplete theory. This finding is somehow implicit in many recent contributions. As genuine alternatives seem missing – or are largely ignored as Fry's thesis of fiscal dominance – this situation should not come as a surprise. According to Lakatos and Kuhn adhering to a falsified theory represents the only rational approach as long as there is no better theory at hand.[122] Yet, as soon as a potential alternative is found a failure of the established theory – Kydland and Prescott's time-inconsistency – is accepted. The paper by Cukierman represents an interesting example for this argument.[123] Other alternative explanations have been phrased, like Posen's thesis of a strong financial sector that affects inflation, but so far could also not be corroborated.[124] Correspondingly one can assume that important insights in the field of central bank theory still await their discovery. For this reason the third chapter of this survey presents an alternative to a central banking theory à la Barro & Gordon, the theory of property economics by Heinsohn and Steiger. This relatively recent theory ascribes great importance to the quality of eligible collateral for monetary stability, an issue not addressed in the covered literature.[125]

2.2 A central bank's raison d'être

A major debate in the theory of central banking is the question if a central bank is required to guarantee an efficient functioning of markets. In the first half of the nineteenth century a very similar debate took place. At that time a central bank was a new and rather unknown institution. Before that time – in the era of the so called free banking – one had managed to do without a public supervision of the issuance of money. The dominating question, thus, was whether a central

---

121 Cf. Blinder (2000) who shows that transparency is regarded only as fourth best means to achieve central bank credibility. See also Posen (1998).
122 Cf. Lakatos (1970) p. 93-138 and Kuhn (1970).
123 See Cukierman (2002) p. 31.
124 Cf. Posen (1998) and Berger et al. (2001) p. 23 f.
125 In fact, this is somewhat surprising since at least Robert Barro is aware of the importance of collateral for economic analysis. See Barro (1976).

bank would represent an indispensable or only an unnecessary or even a harmful public interference with economic processes. Hayek and Friedman picked up this issue reviving this debate in the last decades.[126]

Arguments of early central bank theorists as well as many of today's reasoning rely on the Bank of England's history.[127] The Bank of England is typically described as archetype of a central bank, yet was founded as a private bank in 1694 to facilitate government's raising of credit before becoming the first genuine central bank.[128] The Bank of England as a public institution served as a blueprint for many other European central banks.[129] Goodhart gives an account of the evolution of central banks in Europe.[130] The first public banks were established to achieve a standardisation of banknote issue. These banks were the banker of government, held large parts of a country's gold reserves and thus occupied an outstanding position. For these reasons other commercial banks began to hold reserves at these special banks. Such a bank was usually chosen to act as banker's clearing house and served as a source of additional liquidity by discounting bills. These banks were thus virtually growing into their function as central bank. The consequences of these developments were, however, not discussed in detail at that time. It should be stressed that these banks neither possessed a monopoly on banknote issue nor were they conducting monetary policy as it is common today. Due to their special position in the market these banks finally became the banker's bank, i.e. the lender of last resort (LOLR).[131]

Later, according to Goodhart, the opinion gained prominence that the role as banker's bank implicates a certain responsibility concerning public interest: A banker's bank not only has to guarantee a stable banking system but also has to provide for stability on the macroeconomic level.[132] One had been conscious about the fact that a LOLR implies a kind of insurance for commercial banks. To meet the moral hazard problem, which accompanies the establishment of a LOLR, the banker's bank was given the right to control its counterparties, i.e. commercial banks.[133] Thus, central banks ultimately assumed the function of

---

126 Cf. Goodhart (1985) p. 1- 12 and Friedman & Schwartz (1986) for an overview of the debate. On the literature that views a central bank as unnecessary see White (1984).

127 See for instance Goodhart (1999).

128 Cf. Santoni (1984) for an account of the Bank of England's history.

129 Cf. Goodhart (1985) p. 90-139.

130 Cf. here and in the following Goodhart (1985). Freixas *et al.* (2002) define LOLR as discretionary provision of liquidity by the central bank to financial institutions. In addition, such provision of liquidity has to represent a response to a shock, which entails a rising demand for liquidity that cannot be provided by private participants in the money market.

131 Cf. Goodhart (1985).

132 Cf. here and in the following Goodhart (1985).

133 Cf. Goodhart (1985). The moral hazard problem consists here in the possibility of commercial banks signing very risky contracts without creating sufficient reserves for

banking supervision to prevent unduly risky behaviour on the part of commercial banks to safeguard the stability of the banking system. Since then controlling commercial banks for the sake of payment system's stability is regarded as central banks' primary and most important function. These developments also account for a major change in central bank forerunners' status from private banks to public institutions since the profit-maximising behaviour of private-sector banks causes conflicts of interest inconsistent with the goals of a regulatory authority for the banking system. The problem is probably best illustrated by an example: The Bank of England was – shortly before becoming the world's first central bank – still geared to making profits when it was granted the right to control its competitors and even to issue instructions concerning their conduct.[134] Monetary policy, which nowadays receives most of the attention, is said to have played only a minor role as banknotes were still redeemable in precious metals. Goodhart thus concludes that a central bank's raison d'être lies in guaranteeing a stable payment system by providing a LOLR.[135]

Selgin & White review the literature on theories of monetary laissez faire, i.e. monetary systems without any public regulation.[136] Historical research is said to have found evidence suggesting that financial sector crises would be less frequent under laissez faire since LOLR institutions had encouraged risk taking by providing some kind of insurance to troubled banks. This has naturally raised the question of why central banks have been established and laissez faire removed in the first place.[137]

Santoni investigates whether the issuance of money under private or public control set different incentive structures for the Bank of England's monetary policy.[138] The Bank of England's money issue was from 1694 to 1793 and from 1821 to 1913 under private control, i.e. the owners of the Bank of England, who were predominantly net creditors, strictly followed the Bank of England's charter. The charter stated that only as many banknotes could be issued as were fully backed by the Bank of England's capital. Such a limitation of issue was reasonable as the Bank of England voluntarily offered to redeem its notes in gold. The Bank of England's owners were thus acting for reasons of pure self-interest since net creditors cannot approve an excess-issue of banknotes that would inevitably cause a debasement of that unit in which their claims are

---

potential losses. If such losses materialised the bank could be sure to be provided with the needed liquidity by the LOLR in order to safeguard the banking system's stability.

134 Cf. Goodhart (1985) p. 23-74.
135 Cf. Goodhart (1985).
136 Cf. Selgin & White (1994).
137 Cf. Selgin & White (1994). See also the discussion above in section 2.2 on a central bank's raison d'être.
138 Cf. Santoni (1984).

denominated.[139] During the years 1793 to 1821 and from 1913 on the Bank of England has been under government control. Governments, however, did not feel bound by the charter's limitation of the banknote issue and abolished the banknotes' redeemability into gold. Santoni observes that average inflation in England had been virtually zero during the years of private control of the banknote issue. Whereas average inflation is estimated to have been between 5% and 7% during the years of government control of banknote issue and thus distinctly higher than under private control. Yet, Santoni interprets this not as a general advantage of free banking vis-à-vis public control of banknote issue as advocates of free banking would do. He regards this comparison rather as evidence for the very general thesis that different incentive structures in monetary policy might give rise to different policy results.[140] The literature presented in the following is concerned with the LOLR.

Friedman & Schwartz justify the necessity for a LOLR as follows: In case a commercial bank exhibits liabilities that exceed its assets the bank's solvency is in danger. If the bank's equity is sufficient to offset this difference between liabilities and assets, the bank can continue its operations. Problems arise if the bank's depositors doubt the solvency of the bank and cancel their deposits. A commercial bank's liabilities are predominantly short term callable, i.e. they can be withdrawn very quickly.[141] In case deposits are withdrawn a commercial bank might therefore experience a liquidity problem that could easily exceed the magnitude of the described solvency problem. To be able to solve such liquidity problem the commercial bank has to liquidate its assets, i.e. to turn them into cash. The underlying assumption is that the considered commercial bank is solvent and should thus be able to liquidate its assets with the help of other commercial banks. For Friedman & Schwartz a liquidation of assets implies that a commercial bank grants a collateralised credit to the bank with a liquidity shortage, i.e. a credit secured by the debtor bank's assets.[142] The bank should thus be able to calm its depositors' fears about financial losses. Frequently, however, the following happens: An uninformed public assumes, when being informed about a commercial bank's solvency problem, that other – often similar – banks face the same problem. If agents act accordingly and withdraw deposits the respective banks have to liquidate assets. If too many commercial banks are affected in this vein, unaffected commercial banks are normally unable to provide the required liquidity. In such a case the banking system has to rely on an external

---

139 Cf. Santoni (1984) p. 17, especially footnote 25.
140 Cf. Goodhart (1985).
141 On bank runs see also Freixas *et al.* (2002).
142 Cf. Friedman & Schwartz (1986) p. 52.

source of liquidity, which can only be provided by a central bank.[143] This argument can already be found en detail in Walter Bagehot's Lombard Street.[144]

Goodhart elucidates the importance of Bagehot's three rules in case of a banking crisis, which he summarises as:"1. Lend freely. 2. At a high rate of interest. 3. On good banking securities."[145] According to Goodhart the concept of a LOLR is obscured by four myths. i) The identification of illiquidity and insolvency as well as a differentiation between the two is always possible. Goodhart argues that Bagehot's principles are still valid as an evaluation of assets of a commercial bank that asks for extra-liquidity is, as a general rule, not possible. This opinion is justified with reference to the short time horizon, in which decisions have to be taken by the central bank in such a case. Moreover, the crisis on the asset market, which usually triggers commercial banks' illiquidity, complicates any sound evaluation of asset values as such crises generally cause high market volatility. Thus, the decision over the granting of LOLR credit is to be based primarily on the quality of the "good banking securities" to be pledged, i.e. on the offered collateral's quality. A bank's financial power is to be regarded as merely subordinate in this respect.[146]

The objection that the described principles apply as well to open market operations and LOLR credits would thus be superfluous is not met well by Goodhart.[147] He suggests that LOLR credits should be regarded as bilateral agreements and distinguishes these agreements in this way from open market operations. If a commercial bank were to fall back on LOLR credits this would raise suspicion: Obviously, such a commercial bank is insolvent as the bank was unable to solve its liquidity problem on the interbank market. Following Bagehot's argumentation, however, a central bank would have to disregard concerns about a commercial bank's solvency as long as the latter is able to pledge good collateral. If the central bank were to refuse a commercial bank's demand for a LOLR credit although good collateral is offered, a panic among commercial banks would barely be avoidable.[148] Ultimately such a refusal would entail that commercial banks become defenceless against rumours of insolvency. Illiquidity usually causes rumours of insolvency, which can only be rebutted if the commercial bank has the chance to procure liquidity against good collateral. A system, however, which is unable to protect itself against rumours, is without much doubt highly fragile. In Bagehot's words: "The object is to stay alarm, and

---

143 Cf. Friedman & Schwartz (1986) p. 52-55.
144 Cf. Bagehot (1873) chapter XII, p. 79-101.
145 Cf. Goodhart (1999) p. 340.
146 Cf. Goodhart (1999).
147 Cf. Goodhart (1999) p. 343-348.
148 Cf. Bagehot (1873) p. 92-101.

nothing therefore should be done to cause alarm. But the way to cause alarm is to refuse some one who has good security to offer."[149]

ii) The second myth – according to Goodhart – is that the IMF cannot act as an international LOLR. He calls for an international LOLR and would like to see it implemented under the IMF's auspices. Yet, Goodhart lists several reasons why the IMF is currently not able to act as a LOLR: Acting as a LOLR entails the contingency to suffer losses. A central bank has to hold sufficient capital and reserves to be able to cover such losses. Nowadays losses from LOLR credits could reach magnitudes that would exceed capital and reserves and thus cause negative central bank capital. Therefore, the government behind the central bank and ultimately the taxpayer would have to cover losses from LOLR operations. Behind the IMF, however, there stands no such source of finance and – apart from that – the IMF is not allowed to offer credits to central banks let alone commercial banks but only to member governments.[150]

iii) The third myth according to Goodhart is that the LOLR is regarded as some kind of insurance and that accordingly moral hazard represents a prevalent problem tempting many to abolish a LOLR altogether. The consequences of a financial crisis with no LOLR in place, however, would in any case be far too fearsome to seriously consider doing without a LOLR.[151] Freixas et al. review the literature on LOLR and consider Bagehot's rule to lend only on good collateral as an attempt to reduce the moral hazard associated with LOLR.[152] Other ways to limit such moral hazard include the notion of a) constructive ambiguity, b) 'punishment' of management and proprietors, and c) concerted lending by the private sector. The idea behind a) constructive ambiguity is rather simple: The central bank provides LOLR credits in principle but not necessarily, i.e. commercial banks cannot be sure to be rescued and thus have to operate prudently. Moral hazard should b) be relieved if LOLR support is due to improper management and consequently management loses their posts and shareholders their money. Finally, c) lending by the private sector to troubled commercial banks and organised by the central bank could help to overcome moral hazard and market inefficiencies as the central bank can reassure potential creditors of the solvency of the troubled debtor.[153]

iv) The fourth and final myth concerns the necessity for a LOLR. Goodhart assumes that in case of a financial crisis doing without a LOLR would cause a total breakdown of the financial system, which the electorate would not

---

149 See Bagehot (1873) p. 97. See also the discussion of a LOLR in Friedman & Schwartz (1986).
150 Cf. Goodhart (1999) p. 347-352.
151 Cf. Goodhart (1999) p. 352-356.
152 Cf. Freixas et al. (2002).
153 Cf. Freixas et al. (2002).

condone. Hence, an announcement on the part of government to do without a LOLR would not be credible and thus suffer from time inconsistency.[154]

Prudential policy's raison d'être is discussed by Rochet.[155] He notes that LOLR policies were and still are effective in reducing panics in the banking sector but that provision of LOLR is criticised for causing moral hazard on the part of commercial banks in the literature on banking crises. Contrary to this literature Rochet regards "[ ] the commitment problem of political authorities, which are likely to exert pressure to bail out insolvent banks and delay crisis resolution[,]" as main cause for recent banking crises. In a model he shows that public supervision is necessary to prevent closures of too many banks while such supervision causes the closure of too few banks and thus overinvestment since governments cannot commit themselves to proper bank closure policies. Rochet thus argues in favour of an independent bank closure policy similar to what has been established for monetary policy.[156]

Rochet proposes to insure LOLR credits with funds from some deposit insurance scheme to protect the central bank and the government from any credit risk associated with such operations. He develops a model to ascertain the characteristics of an optimal contract for LOLR activities. This contract envisions i) an *ex ante* evaluation of each commercial bank's social costs and benefits associated with a bailout of that institution given a systemic shock; ii) Banks for which bailout benefits exceed costs receive liquidity assistance by the central bank; iii) Banks for which bailout costs exceed benefits receive no liquidity assistance; iv) political interventions are excluded making supervisory authorities solely responsible for the decision whether LOLR credit is provided or not; and v) LOLR liquidity assistance by the central bank is completely insured by some deposit insurance fund.[157]

Bowen observes that the frequency of banking crises has been increasing in the last 30 years.[158] He notes that there is no generally agreed definition of financial stability and that it is difficult to ascertain the causes and consequences of banking crises. With regard to Rochet's proposal to base the decision on whether liquidity assistance is provided to a troubled commercial bank on an *ex ante* assessment of the bank's exposure to liquidity shocks Bowen argues that such procedure is rather impractical as such exposure would depend on the specific source of the shock. In a similar vein, Peng challenges Rochet's proposal on the ground of potentially large differences of banks' overall exposures

---

154 Cf. Goodhart (1999) p. 356-358.
155 Cf. Rochet (2005).
156 Cf. Rochet (2005).
157 Cf. Rochet (2005).
158 Cf. Bowen (2005).

between *ex ante* and *ex post* assessments. Moreover, significant changes for the worse in the assessment of a bank's exposure could cause a run on that bank.[159]

Observing recent incidents of bank failures, Goodhart notes that insolvencies of banks were often resolved by a voluntary levy on certain commercial banks organised by the central bank.[160] In the future, however, growing competition among, and variety within the financial sector should make it impossible to organize such crisis management.[161] This implies that large future rescues have to be financed by government funds. Goodhart notes that "An optimal regulator will be a regulator who fails from time to time in the exercise of her duty, because the alternative is too expensive."[162] He argues that the 1995 collapse of the Barings Bank must not be interpreted as showing a need for more and better banking supervision but that such supervision would not be efficient and too expensive.

Begg *et al.* examine the ECB's capability to accomplish the tasks conferred to it, i.e. to safeguard a stable currency and a stable financial system.[163] They criticise that a LOLR is missing just like a common banking supervision.[164] The Eurosystem's decentralised organisation reminds Begg *et al.* of the first Federal Reserve Board, which was replaced in 1935 by today's Fed with its centralised organisation due to the former's obvious design deficiencies. They note that national central banks in the Eurosystem possess a certain freedom to accept rather dubious assets as eligible collateral and that it is not clear, i.e. regulated, which institution would have to cover potential losses from such operations. Finally Begg *et al.* argue that a European LOLR, which is still to be set up, should provide liquidity to troubled banks in a banking crisis without the usually demanded good securities, i.e. collateral. Beforehand, they insist, an obligatory arrangement must be found – especially in light of the Eurosystem's decentral organisation – that governs, who has to cover potential losses from such rescue mission.[165] Dornbusch suggests that LOLR operations should generally be financed by the treasury.[166]

Institutional weaknesses of the Eurosystem are also discussed by Spethmann & Steiger.[167] They show that the ECB does not issue currency: The ECB's balance sheet for 2001 exhibits a zero under the item 'banknotes in circulation'.

---

159 Cf. Peng (2005).
160 Cf. Goodhart (1995).
161 See also Freixas *et al.* (2002).
162 Cf. Goodhart (1995) p. 5.
163 Cf. Begg *et al.* (1998).
164 Cf. Begg *et al.* (1998) p. 41.
165 Cf. Begg *et al.* (1998) p. 38.
166 Cf. Dornbusch (2001).
167 Cf. Spethmann & Steiger (2005).

"In the history of central banking, the ECB was until the end of 2001 the first central bank without banknotes on its liability side. This embarrassing innovation did really hurt the Governing Council of the Eurosystem [ ]. Therefore, on 6 December 2001, the Council came up with a no less surprising remedy. Not only the NCBs [National Central Banks] but also the ECB 'shall issue banknotes' (ECB 2001, 1 [Decisions on the Issue of Euro Banknotes and on the Allocation of Monetary Income, ECB Press Release, December 6, p. 1-2]) without, however, changing anything in substance. What does that mean?

The Council simply stated: 'The ECB will be *allocated* a share of 8% of the total value of the euro banknotes in circulation from the start of 2002, while 92% of the euro banknotes will be issued by the 12 NCBs'. At the same time, however, the Council confirmed that [ ] the twelve NCBs exclusively will continue to 'put into and withdraw from circulation   *all* euro banknotes, *including those issued by the ECB*' (ECB 2001, 1)."[168]

The ECB's balance sheet of 31 December 2002 thus contains an item labelled 'banknotes in circulation'. The corresponding item on the asset side, however, represents not any claims of the ECB on commercial banks but 'Intra-Eurosystem claims related to the allocation of euro banknotes within the Eurosystem', i.e. 8 percent of the NCBs' claims on commercial banks due to their issuance of Euro notes.[169]

Therefore, Spethmann & Steiger conclude that the ECB cannot control the issuance of Euros by the Eurosystem. In addition, the Eurosystem tries to conceal the fact that it is the NCBs, which issue the euro notes: Euro banknotes practically lack any indication of this and rather give the impression that it is the ECB that issues them.[170] This obfuscation of facts is probably due to fears that political or economic crises of Eurosystem members could result in a scenario, in which the euro notes issued by the central bank of the crisis-ridden country are not exchanged at par any more, thus nullifying the advantages of the single currency.

Spethmann & Steiger warn about such de facto re-nationalisation of the euro for another reason: Nonmarketable collateral issued by the public sector. These titles normally do not represent "adequate collateral" as their liquidity is limited and a classification as eligible with Eurosystem member central banks implies the potential for a violation of one of the Eurosystem's principles: "[A] counterparty may not submit as underlying assets any debt instruments issued or guaranteed by that counterparty, or by any other entity with which the counterparty

---

168 See Spethmann & Steiger (2005) p. 8f; all emphases in their original.

169 Cf. Spethmann & Steiger (2005).

170 Cf. Spethmann & Steiger (2005) p. 11. The obfuscation is incomplete as the first letter of the serial number printed on each euro banknote indicates the issuing national central bank: Z for Belgium, Y for Greece, X for Germany, V for Spain, U for France, T for Ireland, S for Italy, R for Luxembourg, P for the Netherlands, N for Austria, M for Portugal, and L for Finland.

has close links."[171] This sound principle, however, does not apply to nonmarketable collateral issued by the public sector as state-owned banks that are naturally closely linked to public authorities are exempt from the above principle, which opens the door to financing the government's deficit via its central bank. This argument becomes even stronger given that each NCB controls itself in this respect and that all collateral is eligible for cross-border use.[172]

Furthermore, Spethmann & Steiger criticise the Eurosystem's institutional design for the lack of a LOLR, "[ ] the very rationale of a central bank".[173] Therefore, it has to be concluded that any institution responsible for the financial stability of the Eurosystem as a whole is missing as the Eurosystem possesses no banking supervision authority either and given that all responsibilities concerning financial stability rest with the national institutions, which do not have common guidelines.

Overall findings of the literature on central banks' raison d'être can be summarised as follows: A broad consensus exists on LOLR representing a necessary condition for a banking system's capability to withstand financial crises and thus representing a central banks' primary raison d'être.[174] This consensus, however, is not yet accounted for in an international context: Despite increasing internationalisation in the banking sector there is neither an international LOLR nor does the Eurosystem possess a Eurozone wide LOLR. The issuance of currency and with it monetary policy has nowadays become the defining characteristic of a modern central bank but does not – at least in this strand of literature – represent its raison d'être. This view is reinforced by those authors who prefer monetary laissez faire.[175]

Collateral enters considerations only insofar as it is understood that all central bank credit – including LOLR credits – must be collateralised. Begg et al. argue for a loosening of requirements for LOLR credit regarding eligible collateral, while Goodhart prefers sticking to the rules laid down by Bagehot in the 19th century. According to these only *good collateral* should be accepted.[176] This represents, however, only a marginal difference of opinion. Goodhart and Begg et al. agree that potential central bank losses due to its role as LOLR must be covered by government if the central bank's equity is at risk.[177] Thus, emphasis is put on the claim that a strong central bank must be backed by a strong treasury. Potential consequences of central bank losses if these are not covered by government are, however, not an issue. Similarly, the notion of good collateral is

---

171 See ECB (2005) p. 39 and 42. See also Spethmann & Steiger (2005) p 17ff.
172 Cf. Spethmann & Steiger (2005).
173 See Spethmann & Steiger (2005) p 20.
174 For an exemplary statement of this thesis see Buiter (2004) p. 42 f.
175 On theories of monetary laissez faire see also the discussion in section 2.5.
176 Cf. Bagehot (1873), Begg et al. (1998) and Goodhart (1999).
177 See Freixas et al. (2002) for an overview on the LOLR-literature.

generally not discussed with regard to the qualities good collateral must possess to be regarded as such.[178] Last but not least, it remains debatable to what extent the discussion on central banks' raison d'être delivers insights that transcend those of Bagehot – at least after this short review.

2.3 Effects of and remedies for central bank losses

The number of papers concerned with central bank balance sheets is rather small and the majority of these was published during the last decade by central bank and IMF officials.[179] Most papers on issues like central bank losses or central bank capital mention a widespread ignorance regarding potential problems due to central bank losses. One statement of this ignorance stems from Peter Stella:

> "[U]nlike the situation for commercial banks, there is no reason why a central bank cannot continually make losses and have a persistently negative net worth. Therefore, unlike other public sector entities, central bank losses need not be 'funded'."[180]

Since then, a lot of case studies and data collected by Leone demonstrated the existence and persistence of central bank losses as well as episodes of negative central bank capital.[181] Leone reports that central bank losses in Latin America during the 1980s have sometimes reached magnitudes best expressed as single digit percentages of GDP. Data collected in this survey confirm that central bank losses are a current issue: Almost half of the sample's central banks recorded losses at least in one year between 1990 and 2003.[182] Of course, not all central bank losses cause serious problems. In fact, central bank losses often represent not more than a minor nuisance in the conduct of monetary policy. Yet, in 2006 central bank losses are estimated to have reached 75% of GDP in Zimbabwe and the financing of these losses is said to have been the major force causing inflation to jump to 1,594 percent as of January 2007.[183] This very recent example of the potentially disastrous effects of central bank losses reveals that there remains some work to be done before proposed remedies for central bank losses will have a similar impact on monetary policy as the literature on central bank independence has had in recent years.

---

178 Exceptions are the papers by Begg *et al.* (1998) and Spethmann & Steiger (2005).
179 Cf. Jeanne & Svensson (2004) for a similar appraisal of this strand of literature.
180 See Stella (1987) p. 8. This quotation is the only citeable quotation the author came across. Ironically, it originates from today's most prominent scholar on central bank losses, Peter Stella.
181 Cf. Leone (1993) and Dalton & Dziobek (2005).
182 See chapter 4 and appendix A for further details on this survey's results.
183 Cf. Muñoz (2007).

2.3.1 Quasi-fiscal activities as root cause of central bank losses

In one of the first papers considering central bank losses as potentially danger-
ous Vaez-Zadeh analyses repercussions of and remedies for central bank
losses.[184] He notes that central banks – as monopoly suppliers of an essential
commodity like currency – should normally make profits, but frequently record
losses due to so called quasi-fiscal activities conducted on behalf of the government. Such quasi-fiscal activities encompass everything not being counted
among usually accepted central bank responsibilities: Activities, such as the
provision of subsidised (below market rates) credits to special sectors, the take-
over of nonperforming loans from troubled banks, and exchange rate guarantees
to promote exports are regarded as central bank quasi-fiscal activities since these
are considered by government to be in the public's interest and could be provided by other government agencies. But, not only quasi-fiscal activities can
cause central bank losses: Already a sharp monetary contraction might entail
central bank losses via its effects on central bank income and expenditure.[185]
Central bank income would drop in response to lower interest earnings due to a
reduction in central bank credits while expenditures would rise as interest payments for central bank debt – issued to absorb liquidity – increase.[186]

Vaez-Zadeh goes on to analyse macroeconomic effects of central bank
losses: As central bank losses represent an injection of liquidity, a central bank
might have to sterilise, i.e. neutralise, their impact to meet monetary policy
goals. The absorption of the extra liquidity in the system due to central bank
losses could entail further losses as the central bank would have to issue debt
titles, for which it would have to pay interest. Such sterilisation thus involves the
risk of exponentially growing losses. Moreover, as a central bank continues to
sterilise the monetary impact of its losses by issuing debt titles, pressures grow
to reduce losses via an expansionary policy, which represents nothing less than
an inflationary bias. Consequently, Vaez-Zadeh defines a central bank as insolvent "[ ] if it can only continue to service its debt through accelerating inflation or decelerating growth."[187] He concludes his analysis of central bank losses
by noting that these usually represent a substitute for larger fiscal deficits and
that their macroeconomic impact is identical to a monetisation of the government deficit. Accordingly, large central bank losses would have to be covered by
the government to avoid their detrimental consequences. Vaez-Zadeh criticises

---

184 Cf. Vaez-Zadeh (1991).
185 Such a monetary contraction could be due to, for instance, a monetary expansion that
turned out *ex post* to have been too pronounced.
186 Cf. Vaez-Zadeh (1991). Beckerman (1997) notes that increased interest payments on
central bank debt could be avoided if the central bank possesses sufficient liquid assets,
such as government debt titles, which it could sell instead.
187 See Vaez-Zadeh (1991) p. 77 footnote 17.

that arrangements regulating the financing of central bank losses – in case these occur – are often missing or are ignored until the sheer size of the problem renders ignoring it impossible.[188]

Fry embarks on an analysis of what he terms the fiscal abuse of central banks.[189] He asserts that central banks' independence and, more importantly, monetary stability is threatened where central banks are burdened with a wide selection of fiscal activities as in many developing countries. These fiscal expenditures reduce central bank profits and could eventually result in losses. Fry classifies fiscal activities into five categories: i) The collection of seigniorage; ii) the implementation of financial restrictions; iii) the provision of subsidised credits to special sectors, which usually implies not only below market interest rates but also a higher risk of default; iv) the granting of foreign exchange guarantees; and v) the provision of deposit insurance as well as the bailing out of insolvent commercial banks, which already lead to central bank losses exceeding 10 percent of GDP. In case such losses are not covered by the government, the central bank ultimately has to increase its money issuance jeopardising any notion of monetary stability:

> "Since their invention, central banks have served as a source of government revenue. Indeed, the central bank is the goose that lays the golden eggs. The free-range goose, conducting conservative monetary policy with a fair degree of independence, produces golden eggs worth less than 1 percent of GNP [gross national product] (most OECD [Organisation for Economic Cooperation and Development] countries). The battery-farm goose, bred specially for intensive egg-laying, can produce golden eggs in the form of an inflation tax yielding 5 to 10 percent of GNP (Mexico, Peru, and Yugoslavia in the 1980s). The force-fed goose can produce revenue of up to 25 percent of GNP for a limited period before the inevitable demise of the goose and collapse of the economy (Chile in the early 1970s). All three forms of central bank geese have been sighted since the 1920s."[190]

Central banks cannot miraculously produce wealth. Thus, the central bank either transfers recorded profits directly to government or the latter imposes fiscal activities on the central bank. "They [i.e. the government] cannot, however, have their cake and eat it."[191]

Stella assesses whether central banks need capital and analyses conditions that would require a recapitalisation of a central bank.[192] He sets out to analyse central banks' capital and net worth by a comparison with commercial banks' and defines commercial banks' capital as shareholders' investment plus accrued

---

188 Cf. Vaez-Zadeh (1991).
189 Cf. Fry (1993).
190 See Fry (1993) p. 23.
191 See Fry (1993) p. iii.
192 Cf. Stella (1997).

profits and minus losses, whereas provisions made for unanticipated losses are not recorded as capital. Net worth is defined as the selling price for a bank, which a fully informed risk neutral investor would be willing to pay under normal market conditions. Stella uses the concepts of capital and net worth to assess a central bank's financial strength as these could differ dramatically. One reason for such a gap could be that negative hidden reserves, i.e. unrecognised losses, often due to inappropriate accounting standards should be regarded as reducing capital. Another reason is that generally accepted accounting principles (GAAP) do not include assets such as the 'franchise value' of the monopoly right to issue currency or 'name recognition' in the balance sheet while an investor might take these into consideration. Quasi-fiscal activities – comprising subsidised credits to certain borrowers, bail-out of troubled banks and exchange rate guarantees – usually have a detrimental effect on central bank earnings. Their present discounted value, however, is not considered in the balance sheet but clearly affects net worth.[193]

Commercial banks hold capital as a cushion against losses and are very interested in a reliable access to liquidity. Commercial bank capital helps to safeguard this access to liquidity as it reassures potential creditors of the bank's creditworthiness. By contrast central banks surely have to worry about many things but liquidity. One major concern of central banks is monetary stability and this is where an effective capital cushion against losses is crucial as financing losses by printing money jeopardises any goals of price stability.[194] A continuous sterilisation of the financing of central bank losses without a repression of the financial system is prone to fail as the central bank neither possesses an infinite number of valuable liquid assets nor can the central bank issue its own debt titles without building up an unsustainable debt burden. The only alternative to central bank capital would be for the treasury to cover losses in a timely manner. Stella, however, doubts that the treasury could be able to do so due to its complex budget procedures and the fact that many central bank losses only came about because government did not meet its obligations vis-à-vis the central bank, i.e. delegated fiscal activities to the central bank. Therefore, central banks need sufficient capital if monetary stability is to be preserved without repression of the financial system and if a financial dependence on the government is to be avoided. In case of persistent central bank losses a recapitalisation – involving the transfer of real resources, i.e. a transfer of interest-bearing, marketable assets – is thus inescapable as central bank independence would otherwise become ineffective.[195]

---

193 Cf. Stella (1997).
194 Cf. Stella (1997). If losses remain 'unrealised' they affect expectations about future inflation as shown by Sargent & Wallace (1981).
195 Cf. Stella (1997).

Providing numerous illustrating examples from the world of central banking, Stella observes that central banks with high and stable profits hold very little capital while central banks with high volatility concerning their earnings hold relatively large capital cushions. In some cases government achieved a smoothing of transfers from the central bank by using moving averages. Stella notes, however, that profits based on, for instance, accrued interest on uncollateralised loans to troubled banks should not be transferred to government. Instead provisions should be made to cover potential losses due to these loans. This strongly indicates a general requirement for transparent central bank accounting.[196]

Data on central bank losses for a group of fourteen Latin American countries between 1987 and 1992 are provided by Leone.[197] Examining his data he finds that central bank losses have reached considerable magnitudes in all of the covered countries as losses lend themselves to be expressed as percentages of GDP. Some countries even report fiscal deficits smaller than their central banks' losses. Leone estimates that monetary financing of these central bank losses would result in further acceleration of money growth and provides a comprehensive list of quasi-fiscal activities explaining how these might result in losses for a central bank.[198]

Leone also notes that central bank profits and losses can be measured in three different but complementary ways: i) As net cash-flow capturing short term effects on monetary policy; ii) as change in the net worth capturing changes in the overall financial position of a central bank and thus long term effects; and iii) as difference between income and expenses accrued which represents a mix of the previous two. In reality, he observes, there might be large differences between these three measures. The best measure, however, is of no use if central bank accounting offers only a distorted picture of reality: Many central banks that suffer losses due to quasi-fiscal activities officially report large profits and even transfer these to government.[199]

The cure for a central bank, Leone postulates, whose monetary policy goals have already been adversely affected by losses due to quasi-fiscal activities can only begin with a complete elimination of quasi-fiscal activities, i.e. these need to be taken over by some other government agency or have to be abandoned altogether. His proposal thus differs from Stella's who demands only a sufficient capital base.[200] Furthermore, central bank functions need to be restructured and the balance sheet has to be freed from nonperforming assets as well as accrued

---

196 Cf. Stella (1997) who notes that transparency in accounting might only be confined by the need to protect commercial banks receiving emergency assistance in order to preserve financial stability.
197 Cf. Leone (1993).
198 Cf. Leone (1993).
199 Cf. Leone (1993).
200 Cf. Leone (1993) and Stella (1997).

losses. Finally, such central bank needs to be recapitalised. Leone describes this central bank reform as a 'zero-sum' game as the proposed reform boils down to transfers inside the public sector, i.e. losses, debts and costs have to be allocated to government and assets to the central bank. He is, unlike Stella, not concerned about the level of central bank capital as some arrangement should guarantee that central bank profits minus appropriate transfers to reserves are transferred to government while losses would have to be covered by the government. Yet, Leone is aware that such reform will take time to work its magic as it requires changes of central bank legislation as well as a completely different mindset regarding a central bank's raison d'être.[201]

Beckerman analyses central bank decapitalisation in developing countries.[202] The term decapitalisation refers to the effects of what others have called quasi-fiscal activities and indeed the argumentation of Beckerman breathes the same spirit as can be found in earlier papers by Fry, Leone and Vaez-Zadeh.[203] Beckerman emphasises the role of exchange rate guarantees as catalyst for central bank losses. Such losses come about if the domestic currency devalues after the central bank provided exchange rate guarantees since the foreign exchange denominated liabilities suddenly exceed the corresponding assets by far. Beckerman furthermore stresses that a central bank needs a strong capital position not so much to meet its obligations – a central bank can virtually never be illiquid, but it paradoxically can be insolvent, at the same time[204] – but rather to safeguard the funds necessary to maintain monetary stability. Since a central bank's capital position represents its capacity to absorb excess liquidity and thus to sustain price stability.[205]

Thus, Beckerman is concerned about the backing of a central bank's money issue by central bank assets. He notes that these assets should be marketable and highly liquid and that a central bank should opt for reserves of foreign exchange in case domestic government debt titles, as the usual backing of the money issue, are perceived to be dubious. Beckerman regards quasi-fiscal activities generally as decapitalising, i.e. inflicting losses, and thus advises central banks to limit such activities. He argues that Argentina's hyperinflation of 1989 was largely due to its central bank's quasi-fiscal activities and the losses caused by the latter. More important, however, would be to guarantee that a central bank's capital position allows for the realisation of monetary stability. This, in turn, raises the question of how much capital a central bank needs.[206]

---

201 Cf. Leone (1993).
202 Cf. Beckerman (1997).
203 Cf. Beckerman (1997). See also the discussion above of the contributions by Fry (1993), Leone (1993) and Vaez-Zadeh (1991).
204 Cf. Beckerman (1997) p. 171 and note 15, p. 176.
205 Cf. Beckerman (1997).
206 Cf. Beckerman (1997).

An attempt to answer the question of how much capital a central bank requires is made by Ernhagen *et al.* based on the case of the Swedish Riksbank.[207] Their analysis rests on the conclusion that central banks need as much capital as is sufficient to safeguard its financial independence. Ernhagen *et al.* identify four risks for a central bank's solvency, two minor ones: Interest risk and credit risk; and two major ones linked to the management of foreign reserves and the consequences of LOLR credits with potentially inadequate collateral. Note that quasi-fiscal activities are not mentioned as there are usually none on developed countries' central bank balance sheets. Ernhagen *et al.* are aware of the Riksbank's seigniorage income, which could in principal substitute for capital. They do not include it in their calculations though, as this seigniorage income is uncertain like any future profits. For a similar reason, unrealised profits should not be available for distribution to government. Furthermore, enormous difficulties are pointed out associated with calculating the potential costs of, for instance, a banking crisis with LOLR assistance. Ernhagen *et al.* conclude that if financial stability and credibility of a central bank and thus ultimately monetary stability are regarded as desirable, central banks should be provided with a "generous" amount of capital.[208] Too much capital, however, could only be unfavourable if the 'invested' capital delivers a yield lower than the interest government has to pay for the corresponding debt.[209]

Blejer & Schumacher develop a methodological approach to examine determinants of central banks' solvency.[210] Their paper is based on the idea that an insolvent central bank might be unable to sustain monetary stability. They use the concept of Value-at-Risk, i.e. the expected maximum loss of an item, to develop a framework encompassing the total financial position – including contingent liabilities such as deposit insurance – of a central bank since ratios like reserves to currency would not allow for a proper assessment of central bank solvency.[211] The resulting model renders possible the estimation of policy variables' and exogenous prices' influence on central bank solvency. Such an exercise would enable economic agents to assess a central bank's financial strength and thus allow for a well-founded conclusion regarding the central bank's ability to sustain monetary stability.[212] Blejer & Schumacher note that "[i]n general, the value of the central bank portfolios, when properly accounted for the economic value of assets and liabilities, is negative and, as a rule, it becomes more negative as contingent liabilities are added to the portfolio."[213] Therefore, they argue,

---

207 Cf. Ernhagen *et al.* (2002).
208 Cf. Ernhagen *et al.* (2002) p. 17.
209 Cf. Ernhagen *et al.* (2002).
210 Cf. Blejer & Schumacher (1998).
211 Cf. Blejer & Schumacher (1998) p. 7 ff.
212 Cf. Blejer & Schumacher (1998).
213 See Blejer & Schumacher (2003) p. 324.

a central bank with negative capital is rather likely, since the standard approach to central bank accounting ignores contingent liabilities and overrates central bank capital.

Sullivan discusses the evolution of measurement and accounting of central bank profits and their consequences for central bank capital.[214] He observes that central banks' financial statements followed numerous different accounting frameworks and that these were not concerned with a transparent supply of information but rather with secrecy, which was regarded as necessary for an effective monetary policy. Only when more and more central banks gained independence, the issue of accountability came up and so the need for transparent central bank accounting oriented towards international standards. Stella notes, however, that intransparent central bank accounting and lack of external audits are still quite widespread making surveillance by, for instance, the IMF very difficult.[215]

Regarding arrangements regulating the distribution of profits, Sullivan notes that these should guarantee a central bank capital sufficient to cover any losses as well as restricting distributable profits to realised profits. Moreover, profits should not be transferred before realised and unrealised losses have been charged against income. As international accounting standards (IAS) permit merely the recognition of realised losses central banks should diverge from these standards as it is crucial for central banks to build up appropriate reserves out of realised profits for future unquantifiable losses since such losses can be sudden and very high.[216] Sullivan regards potential losses due to exchange rate movements of unhedged items and costs of financial system crises as main threats to central bank solvency.

Sullivan concludes that central banks should hold sufficient capital to cover any losses. Given that excess central bank capital is inefficient from a fiscal point of view, since it could be used to reduce government borrowing costs, central banks would need a capital adequacy framework considering all potential risks to be able to estimate and justify the sufficient level of central bank capital.[217] Therefore, each central bank should have its own dynamic capital adequacy framework since risks are dynamic. However, building such framework seems very difficult as no central bank possesses one so far.

---

214 Cf. Sullivan (2002).
215 Cf. Stella (2005). Stella reports that two thirds of 49 central banks assessed by the IMF in 2002 had no or inadequate external audit while 40% still did not publish annual reports timely and almost 90% had inadequate accounting standards.
216 Cf. Sullivan (2002). See also Stella (2002) for numerous examples of central banks' profit distribution rules.
217 Cf. Sullivan (2002). See also Stella (2002) who argues that excess central bank capital might threaten central bank independence due to government pressures to make use of this excess capital.

Referring to the example of the Bank of Japan Pringle argues that in practice central banks need capital for reasons of credibility but that a common approach to assess sufficient central bank capital is unlikely to be found.[218] He states that rules governing the distribution of central bank profits are most important for central bank financial strength as it is not evident that central bank capital will be a sufficient cushion against all possible losses. A regulation concerning the distribution of profits and the coverage of losses, which leaves no scope for interventions, would be a characteristic of the optimal rule as this would preserve central bank independence and guarantee that the government is always responsible for the central bank's financial strength.[219]

A model to assess under which conditions central banks need capital is developed by Bindseil *et al.*[220] Reviewing the recent literature on central bank capital they find that sufficient capital is regarded as crucial prerequisite for a central bank's ability to achieve monetary stability. Bindseil *et al.* criticise, however, that evidence is rather anecdotal and that analyses lack the exactness of the usual economic models. Furthermore, they observe that the connection between insufficient central bank capital and inflation seems to rest on the assumption that a central bank can become illiquid. Since there is technically no limit on the amount of debt certificates a central bank could issue to absorb excess liquidity in order to safeguard monetary stability. Central bank losses and negative capital are regarded as irrelevant as a "[   ] central bank does not need to 'finance itself' [   ]".[221] Unsurprisingly, Bindseil *et al.*'s analysis shows that, if − by assumption − the central bank never loses the monopoly right to issue legal tender and economic agents' expectations play no role, then negative capital poses no problem; neither for the central bank nor for monetary stability. Monte Carlo simulations furthermore reveal that central banks always return to profitability in the long run − meaning more than a century. In view of the fact that these results contradict the evidence brought forward in the literature on central bank losses Bindseil *et al.* conclude that the problem must lie outside their model: As there is always a positive probability of the central bank losing its right to issue legal tender, central bank capital matters. Central banks can thus only restore a positive capital − given that government refuses to recapitalise − by issuing money in a fashion inconsistent with monetary stability. Finally, Bindseil *et al.* note that an automatic rule to have central bank losses covered by government is theoretically equivalent to central bank capital but in practice very difficult − if at all − to implement. Therefore, "[   ] positive capital seems

---

218 Cf. Pringle (2003).
219 Cf. Pringle (2003).
220 Cf. Bindseil *et al.* (2004).
221 Cf. Bindseil *et al.* (2004) p. 11.

to remain a key tool to ensure that independent central bankers always concentrate on price stability in their monetary policy decisions."[222]

Finally, Ize argues that central bank recapitalisations call for an extensive policy debate.[223] He develops a simple framework to assess central bank capital adequacy and, using capital structure data for a broad sample of central banks, shows that adequate capital "[ ] is likely to be substantially positive in many low- and middle-income countries."[224] Ize argues that such capitalisations necessarily involve a broad discussion among the central bank, the treasury and the legislature on how much monetary and financial stability are allowed to cost as only such a debate can deliver a socially optimal outcome.

2.3.2 Central bank financial independence

The above literature frequently mentions that central bank losses and resulting negative capital could have adverse effects on central bank independence. In the literature on central banks' raison d'être (see section 2.2) it has been argued that in case of LOLR operations it is the government that has to cover potential losses. An extreme position on this issue is taken by Buiter who argues that "[c]entral Bank independence, whatever it means, must be consistent with complete financial dependence of the Central Bank on the Treasury."[225] The following literature, however, does not quite agree to Buiter's statement as this literature is concerned with the notion of central bank financial independence and the effect of central bank losses on central bank independence.

Sims analyses fiscal aspects of central bank independence distinguishing two different types of central banks – one resembling the Fed (type F), the other the ECB (type E).[226] He asserts that a type F central bank has – under certain conditions – to rely on its treasury for cooperation and financial assistance in order to guarantee monetary stability. As long as it can rely on its treasury, however, the type F bank should be very independent. The type E central bank in contrast possesses a higher probability of facing losses and negative capital, which would – contrary to the type F bank – seriously hamper its ability to control inflation. In particular the ECB, due to its construction and the missing single treasury to back it in cases of negative capital, is regarded as likely to develop a large capital cushion against potential losses. This capital cushion might undermine the ECB's independence when the cushion attracts politicians' interest. Sims thus demands the development of strong fiscal institutions at the European level.[227]

---

222 Cf. Bindseil et al. (2004) p. 32.
223 Cf. Ize (2005).
224 See Ize (2005) p. 290.
225 See Buiter (2004) p. 45.
226 Cf. Sims (2001).
227 Cf. Sims (2001).

Jácome summarises the IMF's agenda in the course of its technical assistance provided during the 1990s to reform central bank charters.[228] Most parts of this agenda were related to central bank independence, the establishment of clear rules for the treatment of central bank losses and profits and the publication of independently audited annual reports based on generally accepted accounting principles. He reports that progress in the area of central bank independence has been significant. But Latin American central banks still lacked financial independence, in particular with regard to recapitalisation by government,[229] transparent annual reports, including audited financial statements, and effective limits on LOLR credits, which often result in serious losses:

> "If there is no limit on the assistance that central banks can provide to troubled financial institutions, as in most Latin American countries, this could ultimately derail monetary policy and divert it from the objective of preserving price stability."[230]

Jácome reports on Latin American central banks' regulations regarding the treatment of central bank capital and potential losses.[231] Most Latin American central banks' capital integrity is not guaranteed by their respective governments, i.e. government is not obliged to assure the soundness of central bank's capital.[232] Furthermore, central bank losses that would wipe out central bank capital are not properly recorded as such in order to avoid reporting negative capital in official financial statements.[233]

Guatemala – as reported in Jácome – provides an example of a fundamentally mistaken view of central banking: Banguat, the central bank of Guatemala, served as LOLR for some minor commercial banks.[234] These banks are to be liquidated and Banguat will have to absorb the resulting losses as Banguat neither received any collateral for its emergency credits nor can it hope to receive help from government as the government is not legally obliged to cover central bank losses. Moreover, Banguat itself has made no provisions to cover such losses. The lax treatment of LOLR credits and the high frequency of banking crisis, especially in Latin America, expose central banks and ultimately monetary policy to the greatest risks. Jácome cites the case of Ecuador as an extreme

---

228 Cf. Jácome (2001).
229 Dalton & Dziobek (2005) report that, in case of negative central bank capital, the IMF recommends that government recapitalises the central bank by transferring interest bearing marketable government securities.
230 Cf. Jácome (2001) p. 11.
231 Cf. Jácome (2001) p. 34-39.
232 Cf. Jácome (2001) p. 11.
233 Cf. Jácome (2001). See also Dalton & Dziobek (2005) who note that central bank losses should not show up as an asset on the balance sheet – despite certain central banks' practices – as such 'accounting' does not conform to any accepted standards.
234 Cf. Jácome (2001) p. 15.

example: "[T]he systemic banking crisis in Ecuador and the huge monetization associated with the crisis, ended up with the adoption of the dollar as a legal tender, given that the market lost total confidence in the stability of the domestic currency."[235]

Stella introduces the notion of central bank financial strength characterising central banks that possess sufficient financial resources to meet their policy target(s).[236] He argues that the concept of financial independence has not been considered sufficiently in surveys dealing with central bank independence as the usual measures work only for developed countries. Stella's simple argument in favour of central bank financial strength is that a lack of financial strength provokes central bank losses, which in turn either lead to a repression of the financial sector or to high inflation. He argues that a financially weak central bank needs to be recapitalised by government in a timely manner as this is distinctly more efficient than a government promising a future recapitalisation. The reasoning for the latter thesis is that the two options have exactly the same impact on government budget implying that a deferred recapitalisation is incredible. This is especially so as times in which central bank finances are in need often correspond to episodes of fiscal distress rendering financial support by government very improbable.[237]

Furthermore, Stella investigates the effect of central bank financial strength on inflation.[238] He uses the ratio of the sum of capital and other items net to total assets, as a proxy for central bank financial strength.[239] Stella argues that if other items net are very large relative to total assets these are either dubious or should not be on a central bank's balance sheet in the first place. In a sample of 157 central banks for 2002 he finds that high (low) central bank financial strength is significantly associated with low (high) inflation, which he interprets as consistent with his hypothesis. Stella furthermore presents evidence on net foreign assets as a percentage of central bank capital. For some central banks this percentage represents a multiple of its capital showing that small appreciations of their currencies could wipe out capital. Therefore, there is no one size fits all level of central bank financial strength, rather the adequate level of central bank financial strength depends on a central bank's policy targets, its degree of independence and the risks it faces.[240]

---

235 See. Jácome (2001) p. 16, footnote 18. Similarly, Hawkins (2004) cites the Philippines as an extreme example of central bank recapitalisation: In 1992 a new central bank was founded to replace the old one, which had incurred large amounts of bad debts.

236 Cf. Stella (2002).

237 Cf. Stella (2002). See also Stella (2005).

238 Cf. Stella (2003).

239 Other items net are a residual representing those assets that do not fit under any of the usual accounting standards.

240 Cf. Stella (2003). See also Ize (2005).

Financial aspects of central bank independence are analysed by Martínez-Resano.[241] He rejects the common view of central banks as optimising some objective function. Rather, Martínez-Resano argues that monetary policy affects a central bank's balance sheet and vice versa. He asserts that a central bank needs assets that can be used to take money out of circulation if some absorption of liquidity is required to safeguard monetary stability. Martínez-Resano observes that the amounts necessary in banking crises often exceed central banks' funds, which entails that central banks might – in case of a banking crisis – give up monetary policy goals in favour of financing operations for bank recoveries. Explicit deposit insurance could serve as a buffer on the costs of such rescue operations. Martínez-Resano furthermore lists several other causes of central bank losses, which might undermine central bank financial strength necessary to pursue a policy of monetary stability. In case, however, central bank capital is insufficient there are two options for the central bank: Either government is asked to recapitalise the central bank, which could violate the latter's independence, or the central bank tries to avoid situations of insufficient capital at the cost of abandoning monetary stability. Thus, adequate central bank capital or – as a second best solution – some contingent arrangement with the government, anchored in the respective legal framework, to cover central bank losses are paramount for effective central bank independence and ultimately monetary stability. Fry et al. regard the case of Chile as the only exception to this rule.[242] The central bank was recording losses due to past quasi-fiscal activities but also due to monetary policy as it constantly had to absorb excess liquidity by issuing central bank debt certificates. This absorption of liquidity was necessary because the government was recording surpluses, which reduced outstanding government debt and thus increased liquidity making the central bank essentially the only issuer of public debt in Chile.[243] Thus, because government pursued a very prudent fiscal policy Chile was able to sustain monetary stability despite its central bank recording losses.

Gros investigates the effects of a central bank's quasi-fiscal activities on its inflation performance and its independence vis-à-vis the government.[244] He constructs a clean balance sheet indicator measuring the degree to which a central bank's balance sheet is burdened with items unrelated to a central bank's major task, i.e. the issuance of currency. Gros finds a statistically significant correlation between average inflation and his clean balance sheet indicator for a sample of Eurosystem members for the period 1967 to 1990. The better a central bank could concentrate on fighting inflation, i.e. the lower the amount of quasi-fiscal activities it had to perform, the better its inflation performance. This reflects,

---

241 Cf. Martínez-Resano (2004).
242 Cf. Fry et al. (1996).
243 Cf. Fry et al. (1996). See also Stella (2005).
244 Cf. Gros (2004).

according to Gros, the low degree of central bank independence during that time and might still pose problems as balance sheet structures of Eurosystem members remained largely unchanged. Similarly to Martínez-Resano he argues that the conduct of monetary policy directly affects the central bank's balance sheet and that avoiding losses is essential to preserving independence. Gros further notes that whether or not high inflation rates permit the central bank to gain high profits depends on its balance sheet structure.[245] The papers by Gros and Stella thus seem to represent the first empirical studies to link inflation performance to some measure of central bank financial independence.[246]

A rather auxiliary but nevertheless important issue with respect to central bank losses is central bank accounting. After all, any discussion of central bank capital, losses, and negative capital ultimately has to rely on empirical evidence and thus on financial statements published by central banks. Kurtzig & Mander report the results of a survey on central bank accounting practices based on a questionnaire answered by 44 central banks.[247] Their main result is that accounting standards among the more than 160 central banks in the world have recently converged. The reason behind this development seems to be the IMF's safeguards assessment policy. Kurtzig & Mander observe that there are diverging views among central banks and governments about the best arrangements for the distribution of profits. Surveyed central banks distributed between 0% and more than 60% of their profits to government. Moreover, Kurtzig & Mander report a disturbing trend: More and more central banks have their distributable profits predetermined at the beginning of an accounting year in order to smooth government revenues. This practice, however, opens the door to government 'determining' central bank profits for the purpose of meeting fiscal targets and thus might entail central banks reporting negative capital. Kurtzig & Mander also cover arrangements concerning central bank capital in their survey. They report that many of the 44 central banks examined have been recapitalised and that two of them currently operate with negative capital. Furthermore, Kurtzig & Mander report that there is only little agreement among countries regarding central bank recapitalisation and that two out of three central banks reported to possess no arrangements governing central bank recapitalisation. Finally, they report a significant increase in central bank transparency, despite the fact that in 2002 only 12% of central banks were audited by one of the big auditing firms.[248]

---

245 Cf. Gros (2004).

246 Hawkins (2004) observes that none of the major studies on the effect of central bank independence on inflation uses balance sheet data to assess financial independence. See also Gros (2004) and Stella (2003).

247 Cf. Kurtzig (2003).

248 Cf. Kurtzig (2003). The big auditing firms comprise PricewaterhouseCoopers, KPMG, Ernst & Young, and Deloitte & Touche.

Kurtzig discusses central bank transparency with regard to accounting standards originally designed for commercial banks.[249] In particular the treatment of profits and losses on foreign exchange and the evaluation of assets issued by government in traditional central bank accounting are in conflict with IAS. Kurtzig worries that recording unrealised profits as part of distributable ones will have inflationary effects as government will spend such revenue. He thus prefers central banks reporting in compliance with IAS but limiting distributable profits to realised ones. Another problem for central banks is that IAS demand fair value accounting. Fair values, however, can be difficult to ascertain as a market for government bonds is often missing. As IAS prescribes a value of zero in such cases, many central banks might become technically insolvent. Kurtzig considers it as evidence for his argumentation that central banks increasingly try to obtain proper debt titles from government, i.e. debt titles carrying market related rates.[250]

Finally, the notion of central bank capital is being discussed with regard to the recent crises in Japan. Jeanne & Svensson propose a mechanism that relies on a central bank's concern for its capital to escape from a liquidity trap.[251] The optimal way to escape from a liquidity trap is to raise expectations of higher future inflation through depreciation of the currency as well as a commitment to maintain a weaker currency in the future. Establishing a credible commitment to such monetary policy represents a problem, however, given most central banks commitment to price stability. Jeanne & Svensson argue that central banks' often have been more concerned about their balance sheet and capital than about inflation and output – probably for reasons of sustaining central bank independence.[252] A commitment based on central banks' balance sheet concerns in such a situation is credible since a future currency appreciation to undo the current depreciation would remain incomplete, i.e. future inflation would be higher. The currency depreciation would not be undone completely as this would cause losses on foreign exchange reserves of the central bank threatening its capital. Therefore, Jeanne & Svensson conclude that "[ ] there are situations [ ] where central bankers' balance sheet concerns might matter in a nontrivial way for monetary policy-making."[253]

The Bank of Japan's concerns for its capital adequacy are challenged by Cargill.[254] It has been argued that the Bank of Japan's monetary policy was not

---

249 Cf. Kurtzig (2003).
250 Cf. Kurtzig (2003).
251 Cf. Jeanne & Svensson (2004).
252 A negative central bank capital would entail a recapitalisation by the government, which the central bank tries to avoid by maintaining a certain positive minimum capital as financial help from the government is perceived to weaken central bank independence.
253 See Jeanne & Svensson (2004) p. 31.
254 Cf. Cargill (2005).

sufficiently expansionary after 1994 and that the Bank should buy more Japanese government bonds (JGB). By contrast, the Bank of Japan argued, inter alia, that increased purchases of JGBs would threaten to wipe out its capital as an expected recovery of the economy would lead to higher interest rates, in turn causing losses due to lower JGB values. This would impair the Bank of Japan's credibility as such losses would inhibit any attempts to absorb potential excess liquidity. Furthermore, the Bank of Japan argued that its capital is exposed to credit risk as counterparties suffered from a large nonperforming loan problem. Cargill acknowledges that central banks need capital to cover potential future losses. However, the Bank of Japan should generally disregard concerns about capital adequacy when deciding monetary policy. In case of large central bank losses Cargill assumes that Japan's ministry of finance will find a way to safeguard the Bank of Japan's capital without interfering with its independence.[255]

Stella observes that a central banks' financial capability to pursue its policy targets has rarely, been questioned by researchers.[256] He argues that this is due to the fact that most central banks in developed countries have been very profitable for many decades. Another reason seems to be a theoretical argument along the following lines: i) Operation of a commercial bank requires liquid capital to guarantee that it can always meet its obligations; ii) Central banks can always meet their obligations as they can create liquidity (currency); iii) Therefore, central banks need no capital. Stella argues that central banks nonetheless need capital as "[c]entral banks cannot both attain a nominal policy objective and create an unlimited amount of fiat money."[257] Thus, central banks need sufficient financial strength to credibly commit to any nominal policy target. Sullivan summarises the typical consequences of central bank losses and negative capital for central banks:

> "Negative capital not only limits central bank independence, it represents a de facto, non transparent, interest free, credit to government. While the inflationary effect of old stocks of negative equity have already passed through into the economy, any increase will have an expansionary effect on the money supply with a deleterious effect on the efficacy of central bank monetary or exchange rate policy. By maintaining a matching fiscal surplus the government can offset this, but history is not replete with examples of governments moving to redress the capital deficiencies when fiscal positions weaken."[258]

There remains little to be added to Stella and Sullivan's conclusions. Central bank losses have to be regarded as a rather widespread phenomenon given the

---

255 Cf. Cargill (2005).
256 Cf. Stella (2005).
257 See Stella (2005) p. 337.
258 Cf. Sullivan (2002) p. 2 f.

evidence provided in the literature.[259] The analysis of central bank losses is a fairly recent phenomenon in the literature on monetary policy and such losses generally seem to pose difficulties when a theoretically driven analysis is needed as most papers rely on anecdotal evidence.

The discussed literature identifies so called quasi-fiscal activities as the root cause of central bank losses. Quasi-fiscal activities include among others the purchase of overvalued assets from troubled banks and the granting of exchange rate guarantees. Furthermore, many authors agree with Vaez-Zadeh who claims that "[ ] in most cases, the persistence of central bank losses are due to non-compliance of the government with its financial obligations to the central bank." [260] To avoid the negative consequences for monetary stability associated with negative central bank capital and central bank losses the following remedies are proposed:

i) A first essential requirement is that central banks should publish financial statements, which are independently audited and that comply with internationally accepted accounting standards. Otherwise a proper assessment of a central bank's financial strength is almost impossible to achieve.

ii) Quasi-fiscal activities performed by the central bank should be abandoned or at least strictly limited. In the latter case government should endow the central bank with sufficient capital to be able to absorb potential losses.

iii) The central bank balance sheet needs to be freed from nonperforming assets and accrued losses and the central bank needs to be recapitalised by government. The assets provided to the central bank for this end must be remunerated at market-related rates to guarantee their liquidity.

iv) Central bank capital should be well above zero. However, the exact level of central bank capital needed to preserve monetary stability is difficult to assess and depends on a number of different factors: "The appropriate level of central bank financial strength is that sufficient to ensure that in a proportion of future states of the world determined by society, the bank will be able to meet its policy goals and preserve its financial independence."[261]

v) Finally, some arrangement between government and central bank needs to be found governing the distribution of central bank profits and losses in a way safeguarding that central bank financial strength will remain sufficient. This implies that government should cover losses that significantly endanger central bank capital and that only realised profits are considered for distribution to government.

There are several papers in the literature on central bank capital that include the value of a central bank's monopoly on the issuance of currency in the

---

259 Cf. for instance Stella (2005). See also section 4.2 for a description of data collected in this survey.

260 See Vaez-Zadeh (1991) p. 81 footnote 19.

261 See Stella (2005) p. 361.

evaluation of a central bank's financial strength.[262] The 'value' of the right to issue the sole legal tender is usually estimated to be quite enormous, which implies that actually reported central bank capital and reserves would be rather insignificant and thus negligible. This view is problematic for two reasons:

First, the value of the monopoly right to issue legal tender is impossible to assess. Central bank balance sheets must follow some generally accepted central bank accounting guidelines. These prescribe that unrealised potential profits and valuation gains must not show up as part of assets, especially if market evaluations are missing.[263] Accordingly, the value of the monopoly right on the issuance of currency does not form part of central banks' balance sheets. Correspondingly a 'franchise value' of the monopoly right to issue currency shall form part of central bank net worth, i.e. some kind of hidden reserve. This franchise value will always be notional, i.e. without market price, since a state will never privatise its currency issue. If one is to assume that some state would sell its monopoly right to issue legal tender, the resulting private central bank would have to be profit maximising to justify the investment.[264] Such private central bank would thus create all those inconsistencies which caused the nationalisation of central banks in the first place.[265] Moreover, not a single instance of a state selling or privatising its monopoly right to issue currency has been observed. Even when central banks were nationalised in the past, the actually paid compensations – if any – were far from being close to the franchise values calculated by Fry and others.[266] Thus, the probability of the monopoly right to issue currency being sold is zero and therefore some notional franchise value of this right must not be considered when assessing a central bank's financial strength.

The second reason why counting on some notional franchise value of the monopoly right to issue legal tender is problematic is that this value relies entirely on expectations about the future. Stella and others generally assume a stream of future central bank profits just like commercial bank managers expect that their bank will generate profits. It must be kept in mind, however, that central banks do not have a profit objective. Additionally, the uncertainty of future revenues is one reason why central banks and commercial banks usually possess capital as a cushion against unforeseen future losses. Such a cushion cannot be provided by some potential hidden reserve as this reserve, as argued above, would not be sold and hence cannot provide liquidity. Therefore, central bank

---

262 See for instance Cargill (2005), Fry (1993), Hawkins (2004), Ize (2005), Pringle (2003) and Stella (1997; 2002; 2005).

263 See for example Sullivan (2002) who claims that unrealised profits should never form part of transfers to government.

264 The lack of a profit objective constitutes one of the main characteristics of a central bank. Cf. Sullivan (2002).

265 Cf. Goodhart (1985) and the discussion in section 2.2 above.

266 See footnote 262 above.

capital is the only item that matters in case of losses and is usually rather too low than too high as Blejer & Schumacher note: "In general, the value of the central bank portfolios, when properly accounted for the economic value of assets and liabilities, is negative and, as a rule, it becomes more negative as contingent liabilities are added to the portfolio."[267]

2.4 Collateral in the economic literature

Stadermann & Steiger discuss what prominent economists have to say on property, money and collateral.[268] They observe that only a few economists – among these are Sir James Steuart, Jean-Baptiste Say, David Ricardo, Henry Thornton, Knut Wicksell, Alfred Marshall, Walter Bagehot, Ralph Hawtrey and Joseph Schumpeter – discussed collateral.[269] Yet, no economist of the last 250 years comes even close to Steuart's analysis.[270] In his analysis Steuart anticipates in large part the theory of property economics. One of the first and undoubtedly the most prominent economic analysis since Steuart that assigns collateral an important role in economic analysis stems from Stiglitz & Weiss.[271] Hubbard describes information and incentive problems in capital markets as the heading under which collateral is discussed in the literature following Stiglitz & Weiss.[272] The macroeconomic strand of this literature searches an explanation for the magnitude of changes in investment due to business cycle movements. The keywords here are financial accelerator as well as balance sheet and bank lending channel. The microeconomic approach is concerned with informational imperfections in credit markets and tries to explain the higher costs of external finance – relative to internal finance, i.e. investments financed with funds internal to the firm – with recourse to asymmetric information between borrowers and lender. Adverse selection and moral hazard represent the keywords here.[273] The following subsection gives an account of the macroeconomic literature that considers collateral. Subsection 2.4.2 reviews the microeconomic literature that refers to Stiglitz & Weiss.

---

267 See Blejer & Schumacher (2003) p. 324.
268 Cf. Stadermann & Steiger (2001).
269 Cf. in detail Stadermann & Steiger (2001) concerning the first six economists p. 54-66, 146-151, 157-162, 179-184, 266-270, 274-277, as well as Heinsohn & Steiger (2007a) for a more detailed account on Hawtrey and Schumpeter.
270 Cf. Steuart (1767) volume 2 p. 97-216 and 311-424 as well as Stadermann & Steiger (2001) p. 45-86.
271 Cf. Stiglitz & Weiss (1981).
272 Cf. Hubbard (1998).
273 Cf. Hubbard (1998).

2.4.1 The role of collateral in macroeconomic analyses

The importance of the so called *credit channel* for monetary policy's transmission mechanism has been pointed out by Bernanke & Blinder.[274] They show that the federal funds rate, i.e. the Fed's key interest rate, represents a good indicator of the Fed's monetary policy. An increase in the federal funds rate negatively affects commercial banks' granting of loans, which significantly influences private sector investment. Thus, Bernanke & Blinder show that monetary policy possesses a strong effect on the so called real economy.[275] The literature on the credit channel differentiates between a *balance sheet channel* and a *bank lending channel*. The balance sheet channel is based on the thesis that the costs of an external financing of investments depend on the financial position of the potential borrower. More precisely, the higher the value of liquid assets and marketable collateral in a borrower's portfolio, the lower should be his costs for external financing.[276] The reason lies in the lower risk of default and the thus lower risk premium: A credit sufficiently collateralised with good securities or a firm with an immaculate creditworthiness should – at least in a country with an efficient legal system – always minimise the default risk since the bank can enforce into the debtor's property in case of default.[277] Bernanke *et al.* argue in a similar vein: For completely collateralised credits the costs of external financing should be concordant with internal financing, i.e. investments financed with in-house funds. Otherwise, external financing should exhibit higher costs than internal financing.[278] A restrictive monetary policy directly affects asset values and thus collateral values since rising interest rates reduce the former. Bernanke & Gertler regard this mechanism as one of the most eminent causes of the Japanese recession at the beginning of the 1990s.[279] Especially small firms and those short of capital are affected by higher interest rates and thus lower demand as the costs of external finance for these firms rise, for instance, due to costs of increased stocks, forcing them to cut back production.[280]

The bank lending channel is based on the balance sheet channel and additionally on the thesis that the costs of external finance depend on commercial banks' supply of credit.[281] The balance sheet channel is assumed to hold true not only for firms but also for banks. In the event of a credit crunch higher interest rates generally imply a lower valuation of assets, which impairs assets held by

---

274 Cf. Bernanke & Blinder (1992).
275 Cf. Bernanke & Blinder (1992).
276 Cf. Bernanke & Gertler (1995) p. 35.
277 Cf. Heinsohn & Steiger (2000b) p. 3 f.
278 Cf. Bernanke *et al.* (1996) p. 2.
279 Cf. Bernanke & Gertler (1995) p. 36.
280 Cf. Bernanke & Gertler (1995) p. 38 ff.
281 Cf. Bernanke *et al.* (1996).

firms and commercial banks. The latter thus reduce their credit volume also due to increased defaults and this in turn hits small low net-worth firms the hardest as these cannot substitute bank credits easily.[282] Affected firms face higher costs for external finance in such a case and are thus often forced to cut back production. This is due to banks shortening their credit supply to less solvent firms in favour of credits to markedly solvent firms.[283] Bernanke et al. describe this phenomenon as flight to quality.[284] Their results are supported by the survey of Berger & Udell.[285]

The credit channel's effect unfolds typically at the beginning of a restrictive phase of monetary policy. Bernanke & Gertler describe the stylized facts following the beginning of such phase: i) Interest rates rise for a short time but return relatively fast to their original level. The effects of a restrictive monetary policy on real GDP and inflation have to be regarded as rather long-lasting. ii) Consumer demand drops quite fast after an increase in interest rates and production follows demand causing an increase in stocks. iii) The drop in demand is largely due to a relatively strong decline of investments in real estate. iv) Finally, investments in equipment drop too, however, only with a substantial delay to all other variables.[286] These stylized facts can be explained by the concept of the credit channel and the latter can thus be regarded as supported by empirical findings.[287]

The idea of the *financial accelerator* is described in a general fashion by Bernanke et al.: Changes in debtor's assets value due to changes in interest rates possess a considerable effect on debtor's business activity.[288] Similarly, Mishkin regards changes in value of firms' and banks' assets as one determinant of business activity.[289] He believes this to be one of the major reasons for recessions that follow currency depreciations as happened in Mexico and South-east Asia in 1994 and 1997-98 respectively. Gelos & Werner provide the first survey on the role of landed property as collateral based on microeconomic data.[290] Their results suggest that investment is significantly linked to the value of collateral. This result is consistent with the thesis of the financial accelerator. This indicates, moreover, that financial liberalisation in Mexico lead to an increase in the

282 Cf. Bernanke et al. (1996) p. 5. See also Holmström & Tirole (1997).
283 Cf. Bernanke & Gertler (1995) p. 40-42.
284 Cf. Bernanke et al. (1996) p. 5-7.
285 Cf. Berger & Udell (1990) p. 21-26. See also Kim (1999) who finds evidence of the bank lending channel for South Korea.
286 Cf. Bernanke & Gertler (1995) p. 29-33.
287 Cf. Bernanke et al. (1996) p. 7-13 and Kashyap & Stein (1995).
288 Cf. Bernanke et al. (1996) p. 2 ff.
289 Cf. Mishkin (1999) p. 585.
290 Cf. Gelos & Werner (2002).

number of agents eligible for credit and in the importance of real estate for this end.[291]

Kiyotaki & Moore develop a model to show how credit constraints can amplify the effects of comparatively small shocks to the economy on output and asset values:[292] A shock causes a decline in the value of some asset that serves as collateral. The lower value of collateral aggravates problems of asymmetric information, which entails greater difficulties in attaining external finance and has a negative effect on output and thus depresses asset values even more. Kiyotaki & Moore regard this dynamic interaction between asset values and credit constraints as a very forceful mechanism aggravating the effects of small shocks to an economy.[293] Similarly, Córdoba & Ripoll assess the size of collateral constraints' effect on output in case of exogenous shocks.[294] Employing standard assumptions they find, however, that collateral constraints typically create merely a small amplification of output whereas large effects obtain only under rather unrealistic assumptions. Thus, Córdoba & Ripoll conclude that credit constraints alone cannot account for the large fluctuation in output found in the data.[295]

A model in which financial imperfections might possess stabilising effects is developed by Elul.[296] The literature following Kiyotaki & Moore so far focused on the notion of a financial accelerator. Elul shows in his model that borrowers might strategically default to secure more wealth for the current period, if values of assets serving as collateral are already low. Such behaviour would stabilise collateral values – the financial decelerator.[297] Tse & Leung argue that financial development increases growth by providing access to foreign capital but also renders such an economy more susceptible to suffer from small changes on the international capital market.[298] These small changes could affect collateral values like in the Kiyotaki & Moore model and thus amplify interest rate shocks.

Another strand of literature discussing collateral in a macroeconomic context analyses the recent Japanese crisis. Caballero et al. analyse the consequences of misallocation of credit in the Japanese economy during the 1990s.[299] They state that stock prices and commercial land prices fell by 80% and 60% respectively from their peak in the early 1990s until 2003. These shocks, Caballero et al. argue, had such a strong effect on collateral values that significant problems for

---

291 Cf. Gelos & Werner (2002).
292 Cf. Kiyotaki & Moore (1997).
293 Cf. Kiyotaki & Moore (1997).
294 Cf. Córdoba & Ripoll (2002).
295 Cf. Córdoba & Ripoll (2002).
296 Cf. Elul (2005).
297 Cf. Elul (2005).
298 Cf. Tse & Leung (2002).
299 Cf. Caballero et al. (2006).

the banking system were inevitable. The response of Japanese authorities, however, is said to have been completely inadequate: Necessary reforms were delayed as well as the restructuring of banks. Nonetheless, banks were forced to comply with the Basle capital standards. As a result banks continued to lend to insolvent borrowers due to fears of not meeting capital standards anymore since nonperforming loans – when properly provisioned for – possess a negative effect on commercial bank capital.[300] Thus, many of these loans were not recognised as nonperforming and insolvent firms were allowed to continue operations. These firms are found to have distorted competition in the whole Japanese economy. As a consequence job creation was depressed and investment and employment growth of solvent firms fell further the higher the percentage of insolvent but alive firms in their industry – Caballero *et al.* term these firms zombies. Therefore, Caballero *et al.* show that commercial banks possess incentives to continue lending to insolvent borrowers if capital constraints are binding. More importantly, however, they show that a sharp decline in collateral values in combination with capital standards has a significant effect on the real economy unless banking supervision acts more strictly but potentially at the cost of a breakdown of the financial system.[301]

Kocherlakota & Shim set out to answer which is the optimal response of banking supervision to a banking crisis due to a collateral shock; liquidating a failing bank immediately or allowing the bank to continue operations.[302] The former is called prompt corrective action while the latter is referred to as forbearance lending. Kocherlakota & Shim find that prompt corrective action represents not always the best solution despite the fact that forbearance lending implies that taxpayers' funds will be employed. The adequate response of the regulator rather depends on the a priori probability of collateral shocks: If this probability is low forbearance is the optimal solution whereas prompt corrective action is superior in case of a high probability of a fall in collateral values.[303]

Observing that central bankers and banking supervision often pursue different goals, Cecchetti & Li argue that central banks ought to act in response to the state of their counterparties' balance sheets as capital adequacy requirements, like Basle II, are procyclical.[304] This procyclical effect of prudential regulation, however, could be offset by lowering (raising) interest rates more strongly in case the banking system is capital constrained and the economy is in a slump (upswing). Cecchetti & Li present evidence showing that the Fed was adhering

---

300 Cf. Caballero *et al.* (2006).
301 Cf. Caballero *et al.* (2006).
302 Cf. Kocherlakota & Shim (2005).
303 Cf. Kocherlakota & Shim (2005).
304 Cf. Cecchetti & Li (2005).

to this principle when taking monetary policy decisions while the Bundesbank and the Bank of Japan did not.[305]

Whether banks exercise forbearance lending, i.e. the rolling over of nonperforming loans, is analysed by Chen *et al.*[306] Hypotheses are tested using firm-level data of Taiwan for the period 1991 to 2001. Their results suggest that forbearance lending is likely to occur during economic downturns that have a significant effect on property prices. Asset values might drop in such a way that auctioning off borrowers' collateral becomes less attractive for banks than continued lending to defaulting borrowers. They explain this by the fact that bank loans are usually backed by real estate or land and that a decline in real estate prices will thus have not only an effect on collateral values but should also affect banks lending behaviour. Auctioning off collateral would have reduced property prices even more, which would have been detrimental for banks trying to recover their losses. However, as property prices fell even more during the Asian crisis (1997-2001) forbearance lending was no longer present and remaining collateral values were liquidated.[307] Inaba *et al.* discuss the increase in nonperforming loans in the Japanese banking sector and its effect on output since the 1990s.[308] They find that the sharp decline in real estate values is responsible for the deterioration in firms' balance sheets, which in turn lead to an increase of nonperforming loans. Thus, firms cut investment and banks limited lending in response to the collapse of the asset bubble, which fits the story that output was affected by a credit crunch. Moreover, forbearance lending is found to have taken place, which further weakened the performance of the Japanese economy.[309]

Dekle & Kletzer develop a model of a banking crisis, which ensues as banks renegotiate loans to insolvent borrowers.[310] Their model is supposed to fit the Japanese story: Due to an adverse shock to the economy commercial banks face high nonperforming loan ratios as collateral values collapsed, which caused a decline in bank lending and aggravated Japan's recent recession. Dekle & Kletzer note that the magnitude of nonperforming loans on Japanese banks' balance sheets rose sharply from 2% of GDP at the beginning of the 1990s to 7% in the year 2000, which provoked government to provide funds of 9% of GDP to recapitalise weakened banks. Dekle & Kletzer thus conclude that banking

---

305 Cf. Cecchetti & Li (2005).

306 Cf. Chen *et al.* (2006). Rising interest rates have a negative effect on asset values – implying that the value of commercial banks' capital diminishes while risks rise – banking supervision will demand commercial banks to adjust their capital base. This has the effect of limiting bank lending and thus further lowers economic activity that relies on bank lending.

307 Chen *et al.* (2006).

308 Cf. Inaba *et al.* (2005).

309 Cf. Inaba *et al.* (2005). See also Sekine *et al.* (2003).

310 Cf. Dekle & Kletzer (2002).

supervision should define certain minimum standards for banks and strictly close those that do not meet these standards.[311]

Koo argues that the Japanese economy suffers from a balance sheet recession.[312] The fall in asset and real estate prices is said to have been worth two years of Japanese GDP. Koo argues that firms and households had financed these assets with borrowed money, which lead to firm balance sheets featuring negative capital. Thus, firms and households were predominantly concerned about their balance sheets, which caused a sharp fall in demand and investment as agents priority changed "[ ] from maximizing profits to minimizing debt."[313] Koo regards this change in behaviour also as the cause of the ensuing deflation since household sector savings were not borrowed and subsequently spend by firms resulting in a huge gap in aggregate demand. This gap, he argues, was filled by increased government spending accompanied by rising government deficits. This policy, however, is said to have been the only reasonable response as otherwise a deflationary vicious circle would have been unavoidable. Moreover, Koo argues, that monetary policy lost its effectiveness in influencing investment by changing interest rates due to firms priority for minimising debt.[314]

Furthermore, Koo argues that commercial banks' nonperforming loans represent only a minor issue as even without these problem loans banks would not be able to increase lending. One reason is again firms concerns for their balance sheets, which implies that firms try to reduce their borrowing instead of increasing it. The other reason is that the creditworthiness of potential borrowers and especially their collateral values are at very low levels given a decade of economic recession. Thus, there are hardly any potential borrowers left that comply with the standards demanded by supervision authorities.[315]

A review of the macroeconomic literature referring to Stiglitz & Weiss is offered by Reichlin.[316] This literature regards collateral as a key factor in explaining the business cycle. Moreover, commercial banks are considered to face essentially the same problems as non-financial firms with respect to changes in values of banks' and firms' assets. In these analyses, however, the central bank represents merely the exogenous source of interest rate shocks triggering the transmission mechanism. An analysis of central banks with regard to changes in collateral values is thus lacking. The literature that analyses the recent Japanese crisis in this context highlights the role of collateral in aggravating the crisis. Sharp decreases in asset prices also depressed collateral values, which in turn

---

311 Cf. Dekle & Kletzer (2002).
312 Cf. Koo (2001).
313 See Koo (2001) p. 16.
314 Cf. Koo (2001).
315 Cf. Koo (2001).
316 Cf. Reichlin (2004).

lead to a rising problem of nonperforming loans on commercial banks' balance sheets. The response of supervisory authorities to the nonperforming loan problem is discussed and most papers advise a stricter policy. Especially the paper by Koo, however, casts doubt on the thesis that collateral played a significant role in the recent Japanese recession rather than the general state of balance sheets. Therefore, the macroeconomic literature on collateral fails to deliver insights concerning different qualities of collateral or central banking – apart from minor supervisory issues.

2.4.2 Collateral in the microeconomic literature

In light of the fact that roughly three out of four credits in developed nations are secured by collateral and given that the use of collateral in developed economies is not a recent phenomenon, economic research on collateral is quite young.[317] This is especially true because the microeconomic literature on collateral does not consider older economic analyses of collateral.[318] Since Stiglitz & Weiss' seminal paper the credit market cannot be regarded as just another market anymore.[319] Interest is not a price able to equilibrate the supply of and the demand for credit. Rather, the 'price', i.e. the interest rate, affects the debtor's ability to repay or – equivalently – the debtor's probability of default. A high rate of interest increases the probability of default and thus lowers the credit's expected return. Therefore, an investor asking a profit-maximising bank for a credit might be refused by the bank even if he were willing to pay a higher interest. At Stiglitz & Weiss' equilibrium interest rate an excess demand is likely, in which case credits are rationed. If the equilibrium interest rate in a credit market implies an excess demand, potential debtors have to be chosen by a different criterion: collateral.[320] The idea of credit rationing thus established the notion of collateral in the microeconomic discussion.[321]

Rudolph discusses why collateral is pledged despite the fact that creditors can always enforce their claims against all assets of a debtor firm.[322] The first reason proposed in the literature is that creditor risk is reallocated from the more risk averse creditors to the less risk averse creditors if a credit is collateralised.[323] The second reason why collateral is pledged is that this way priority

---

317 Cf. Bigus *et al.* (2004). See also Berger & Udell (1990) p. 21 for evidence on the United States and Hanser (2001) p. 154 for evidence on Germany.
318 See above section 2.4.
319 Cf. Stiglitz & Weiss (1981).
320 Cf. Stiglitz & Weiss (1981).
321 Cf. Kanatas (1992).
322 Cf. Rudolph (1982).
323 This argument becomes invalid if the debtor has only one creditor. See Rudolph (1984).

claims of, for instance, the tax authorities can be outstripped in the sense that collateralised claims have the highest priority and are satisfied first.[324]

The evidence presented in Boot *et al.* shows that collateral is used extensively and to an increasing degree.[325] To explain this they design a model, in which borrowers possess unrestricted access to collateral. Their model is part of an exercise to find optimal contracts for 'bad' (risky) and 'good' (less risky) borrowers with moral hazard and private information. This illustrates the point that the pledging of collateral is analysed as a signalling option of the borrower instead of as a necessary condition to have access to credit, which is ultimately decided by the bank.[326] Boot *et al.* note that in reality banks will often face various difficulties when liquidating the collateral of defaulting borrowers; for instance transaction costs and the possibility that pledged assets yield prices far below those that can usually be expected. Therefore, they argue, the bank will usually appraise assets pledged as collateral as being worth less than what the borrower and asset owner would assume.[327]

Manove & Padilla argue that the pledging of collateral tempts banks to offer credit irrespective of potential borrowers' riskiness because collateral is a substitute for screening potential borrowers.[328] This causes overinvestment and ultimately welfare losses as collateral lowers the costs of external finance. In fact, Manove & Padilla show that collateral – contrary to most of the literature following Stiglitz & Weiss – might reduce the efficiency of credit markets but cannot raise it. This result is due to the assumption that potential borrowers will not reveal their riskiness: The more risky borrowers are characterised – in line with empirically established human behaviour – as optimists who believe to be realists with a low probability of default when in fact the opposite is true. Banks, however, are assumed to lend to any borrower regardless of his riskiness as long as the credit is sufficiently collateralised as this renders unnecessary the costly screening of credit applications.[329]

An interesting argument is brought forward by Faig & Gagnon who analyse potential remedies for inefficiencies that arise due to scarceness of collateral.[330] They note that most loans are collateralised – typically with mortgages on real estate – while unsecured loans are not uncommon either, especially in connection with credit cards. Uncollateralised loans, however, pay higher interest as the probability of default is greater and monitoring costs as well as costs of en-

---

324 Cf. Rudolph (1982).
325 Cf. Boot *et al.* (1991) p. 458.
326 Cf. Boot *et al.* (1991).
327 Cf. Boot *et al.* (1991) p. 461.
328 Cf. Manove & Padilla (1999).
329 Cf. Manove & Padilla (1999). Jiménez *et al.* (2004) and Jiménez & Saurina (2004) provide evidence supporting this thesis.
330 Cf. Faig & Gagnon (2002).

forcement need to be covered. These higher costs associated with unsecured loans, Faig & Gagnon argue, has to be interpreted as evidence of a scarceness of collateral as 'unsecured' borrowers would otherwise avoid paying higher interest on such loans.[331] Maiangwa et al. review alternatives to the use of collateral in credit contracts.[332] They note that access to the formal credit market is often limited due to a lack of collateral. Maiangwa et al. highlight that it is not the land, houses or machines that are missing but rather legally enforceable titles to these, which impedes access to formal credit. Among the alternatives to collateralised lending presented are third party guarantees, group lending, incremental and repayment dependent lending as well as the existence of an efficient legal system for contract enforcement.[333] Nkurunziza shows that the existence of a credit market is independent from the use of collateral if reputation effects can be exploited.[334] In his model debtors receive a new loan as long as the previous loan has been repaid and are cut off from access to credit in case of default. This punishment, however, is only credible if longer time horizons are considered. Nkurunziza argues that even formal credit markets in Africa rely on such reputation effects as legal institutions usually fail to establish collateral as an instrument of contract enforcement.[335]

A review of the theoretical literature on the collateralisation of credit is offered by Bigus et al.[336] They note that the existence of collateral in credit contracts is due to a lack of information on the part of creditors since collateral is irrelevant in a perfect neoclassical world.[337] There are two main reasons identified in the literature why collateral is beneficial for creditors and debtors: The first is based on the assumption that creditors cannot identify the riskiness of a potential borrower. This forces a creditor to demand a high rate of interest in order to remain profitable as demanding 'average' interest would result in losses since such average interest would be too high for less risky debtors and attract only more risky debtors. The high rate of interest thus entails *adverse selection* as it suits the more risky borrowers. If there is adverse selection, profitable projects of the low risk borrowers are not realised, which implies welfare losses. The pledging of collateral by the potential debtor, however, should resolve the problem of asymmetric information, i.e. the bank cannot know the riskiness of a potential debtor. Since collateralisation increases the costs of default for the

---

331 Cf. Faig & Gagnon (2002).
332 Cf. Maiangwa et al. (2004).
333 See for instance Kritikos & Vigenina (2005) on group lending as well as Nkurunziza (2005) on repayment dependent lending.
334 Cf. Nkurunziza (2005).
335 Cf. Nkurunziza (2005).
336 Cf. Bigus et al. (2005).
337 See also Rudolph (1982).

risky debtor, who might loose the asset pledged as collateral to the bank in case of default, the risky debtor would not pledge collateral. The 'safe' debtor, in contrast, can reasonably expect not to default and thus offers to pledge collateral. Therefore, the asymmetric information is overcome since the risky debtors reveal themselves as risky by not pledging collateral. This gives rise to different credit contracts: One for relatively safe borrowers featuring a low interest rate as well as collateral and another contract for risky debtors featuring no collateralisation but high interest.[338]

The second reason identified in the literature, why collateral is beneficial for creditors and debtors, is based on the idea that borrowers might default strategically, i.e. deliberately. At the end of the credit contract a rational borrower defaults if the project financed by the credit has positive revenue. If the bank demands collateral, however, the borrower 'pays' in case of default with the collateral.[339] Therefore, collateral represents an incentive to repay the loan and limits *moral hazard* on the part of the borrower. Risky borrowers, i.e those with an unfavourable credit history, should thus pledge collateral.[340] Summarising the predictions of theoretical models Bigus *et al.* note that to avoid adverse selection it should be the safer borrowers pledging collateral whereas to avoid moral hazard on the part of borrowers the more risky borrowers should pledge collateral. If adverse selection and moral hazard problems are analysed combined in one model the results are less clear. The answer to the question of whether to collateralise or not moreover depends heavily on models' specifications.

Furthermore, Bigus *et al.* highlight a rather neglected issue in the literature on collateral: Most papers do not differentiate between internal and external collateral.[341] Internal collateral represents assets of the firm, which – if the credit defaults – the creditor can sell in any case to satisfy his claims irrespective of whether assets have been pledged as collateral or not. Contrary to internal collateral, the pledging of external collateral implies an incentive on the part of the debtor to repay since external collateral represents claims on the debtor's private assets. This differentiation is crucial since theoretical models are predominantly concerned with the effects of external collateral without, however, mentioning this explicitly.[342] Internal collateral is correspondingly regarded as rather useless except for those cases where a defaulting debtor has several creditors. In such a case and given that the firm's assets are insufficient to satisfy all claims internal

---

338 Cf. Bigus *et al.* (2005).
339 See, for instance, Barro (1976).
340 Cf. Bigus *et al.* (2005).
341 An exception is the paper by Manove & Padilla (1999). See also the empirical survey by Pozzolo (2004).
342 Rudolph (1982) for instance regards Stiglitz & Weiss (1981) paper as dealing with external collateral.

collateral might serve to rank claims in the sense that collateralised claims are satisfied before uncollateralised ones are considered.[343]

Coco reviews the microeconomic literature on collateral.[344] The initial research following Stiglitz & Weiss focused on the interrelation of collateral and credit risk.[345] Two different theses were pursued: The so called *sorting-by-private-information* and the *sorting-by-observed-risk* thesis. According to the latter thesis that corresponds to conventional wisdom in the banking industry, potential debtors facing a high probability of default are more likely to pledge collateral.[346] According to the sorting-by-private-information thesis the debtor possesses private information concerning his default risk. This implies that debtors facing a lower probability of default are more likely to pledge collateral. Another strand of literature tries to answer whether collateralised credits exhibit a higher risk of default or not. The empirical evidence suggests that the probability to enter into a collateralised credit contract rises with risky debtors, risky banks and higher risk of default, implying that bankers are – fortunately for them – ahead of theoretical models in this respect.[347] More recently the literature investigated the effects of creditor-debtor relationships on the pledging of collateral.[348]

Bigus et al. review the empirical literature on the collateralisation of credit.[349] Their findings can be summarised as follows: The probability of collateral being pledged is higher the smaller and younger potential debtor firms are, the longer the credit period and the larger credit volumes are, the weaker the competition among banks is and the worse overall economic conditions are.[350] Berger et al. find that small firms tend to receive credit from small domestic banks rather than from large or foreign-owned banks.[351] Several surveys show that collateralised credit contracts feature higher interest rates than uncollateralised credits, which is taken as evidence in support of the thesis that collateral helps to reduce moral hazard.[352] However, main banks seem to hold more

---

343 Cf. Bigus et al. (2005).
344 Cf. Coco (2000).
345 Cf. Coco (2000) and Berger & Udell (1990) p. 21-26.
346 Cf., for instance, Igawa & Kanatas (1990) who conjecture that debtor's might not take actions necessary to avoid losses in the value of pledged assets as the right to physically use assets pledged as collateral stays with the debtor during a credit contract.
347 Cf. Berger & Udell (1990) p. 21-26.
348 Cf. Coco (2000). See also Elsas & Krahnen (1999) on so called relationship-lending, i.e. firms that have the majority of their credits with just one main bank.
349 Cf. Bigus et al. (2004).
350 See for instance Jiménez et al. (2004) who provide evidence for the Spanish credit market.
351 Cf. Berger et al. (2001). See also Berger et al. (2003).
352 Jiménez & Saurina (2004) and Gonas et al. (2004) provide additional evidence supporting the thesis that risky borrowers are more likely to pledge collateral to reduce

collateral than other creditors, which represents contradictory evidence regarding moral hazard since main banks typically have long relationships with their borrowers. In general evidence on relationship lending is inconsistent like the theoretical literature.[353] Gonas *et al.* find that commercial banks with a strong capital base are less likely to demand collateral.[354] Pledged collateral seems to consist much more frequently in firm assets than in external private assets.[355] This somewhat challenges the results of older empirical studies on collateral as these did not differentiate between internal and external collateral.[356]

Overall, the results of empirical studies do not support the thesis that collateral helps to identify 'good' and 'bad' debtors – the sorting-by-private-information thesis.[357] Somewhat little empirical support receives the thesis that collateral limits moral hazard, which, however, seems to apply rather to collateral consisting in private assets. The thesis that creditors demand collateral consisting in firm assets if they expect conflicts of interest with other creditors receives the broadest empirical support.[358] Finally, 70% to 90% of all credits are found to be collateralised establishing the importance of collateral for credit markets.[359]

Pozzolo analyses the role of personal guarantees in bank lending.[360] He argues that personal guarantees always represent external collateral and finds that these are – unlike internal collateral – employed to mitigate the problems associated with moral hazard in credit contracts.[361] Pozzolo also finds evidence – contrary to previous empirical works – suggesting that collateralised credits feature lower interest rates, which implies that collateralised credits are less risky. These results deserve special attention as Pozzolo's data allow for testing the different effects of securing credits with internal and external collateral.[362]

---

moral hazard. Jiménez & Saurina's (2004) measure of riskiness is based on the *ex post* probability of default while Gonas *et al.* (2004) use borrowers' ratings and find that non-investment grade borrowers virtually always have to pledge collateral.

353 See for instance Elsas & Krahnen (1999), Gonas *et al.* (2004), Jiménez *et al.* (2004) and Ono & Uesugi (2005).

354 Cf. Gonas *et al.* (2004).

355 Cf. Bigus *et al.* (2004).

356 Cf. Pozzolo (2004). Jiménez *et al.* (2004) claim to measure only the effects of external collateral. They do this, however, simply by assumption: "[ ] the precise nature of the collateral is not known and the possibility that collateral is, in some cases, internal [ ] can not be totally ruled out." See footnote 1, page 9.

357 Cf. Bigus *et al.* (2004).

358 Cf. Bigus *et al.* (2004). See also Gonas *et al.* (2004), Ono & Uesugi (2005) and Pozzolo (2004).

359 Cf. Bigus *et al.* (2004).

360 Cf. Pozzolo (2004).

361 Cf. Pozzolo (2004). See also Ono & Uesugi (2005) who also interpret personal guarantees as external collateral.

362 Cf. Pozzolo (2004).

Bankruptcy laws in eastern European countries lacked effectiveness in the early 1990s.[363] Dittus argues that if banks cannot employ bankruptcy law to secure their claims completely, they are likely to make use of a combination of the following options: i) to offer loans only to the most creditworthy borrowers – explaining why credit is so difficult to get; ii) to demand immense collateral – described as excessive collateral requirements by western experts; and iii) to simply raise risk premia. All of these options do a disservice to the efficiency of financial intermediation and could be remedied with appropriate enforcement laws.[364]

Cossin & Hricko develop a methodology for the determination of haircuts on risky collateral.[365] They note that the size and complexity of the issue of credit risk have grown immensely in recent years due to the liberalisation of financial markets. Though collateralisation has become the most preferred means to handle credit risk haircut determination has so far largely been left to rules of thumb. Cossin & Hricko regard collateralisation as an elegant solution to the challenge of pricing credit risk as collateralisation transforms credit risk into market risk. Haircuts are used since, in principal, many different kinds of assets, which entail differing risks, can be used for collateralisation purposes. Thus, haircuts specify the percentage of the collateral's nominal value that is needed to secure a credit depending on the type of assets used: The greater the haircut the higher the assets perceived riskiness.[366]

Employing marking-to-market, i.e. regularly controlling assets' current market prices, can be regarded as a substitute to collateralisation with regard to credit risk. Since, if the frequency of marking-to-market is sufficiently high, credit risk should not reach extreme levels.[367] Therefore, a bank can choose the optimal mix of the two instruments, marking-to-market and collateralisation, given costs and regulations. However, it should be kept in mind that marking-to-market represents a substitute for collateralisation only if assets are sufficiently liquid to enable the monitoring of price developments at least on a day to day basis. In other words, if assets are not sufficiently liquid collateralisation cannot be substituted by marking-to-market. Moreover, doubts of a general nature arise concerning the substitutability of collateralisation and marking-to-market in a central banking context. The literature on LOLR operations (see section 2.2) assumes that an evaluation of commercial banks' asset portfolios might be impossible in the short term, i.e. in a matter of hours – or at least likely to turn out rather unsound *ex post*. In light of these considerations marking-to-market

---

363 Cf. Dittus (1996).
364 Cf. Dittus (1996).
365 Cf. Cossin & Hricko (2003).
366 Cf. Cossin & Hricko (2003).
367 Cf. Cossin & Hricko (2003).

appears to be a somewhat risky means for minimising credit risk – at least for central banks.

Overall, the microeconomic literature on collateral has to be regarded as rather inconsistent. Lacker shows, for instance, that collateral can be part of an optimal credit contract while Hudson challenges collateral's raison d'être and Coco points out collateral's economic relevance.[368] Thus, it can be stated that the microeconomic literature on collateral finds it rather difficult to establish a consensus on its logic and especially so in consideration of the widespread use of collateral. The literature focuses on the effects of external collateral but fails in most empirical surveys to differentiate between internal and external collateral. This somewhat invalidates many empirical findings as internal collateral is found to be used considerably more frequently than external collateral. Moreover, collateral is neither discussed in connection with central banks' monetary policy – the paper by Cossin & Hricko represents a notable exception – nor has it any role in the general equilibrium model.[369]

2.5 The emergence, present, and future of money in neoclassical economics

Since Adam Smith's Wealth of Nations man's propensity to barter represents one of classical and neoclassical economics' dogmas.[370] Barter, however, is the exchange of goods against goods without money whereas today goods are exchanged against money thus making an explanation of the very existence of money inescapable. Jones builds a model around the neoclassical explanation of the emergence of money: Growing specialisation and division of labour in connection with man's universal propensity to barter render it possible to leave behind the stage of subsistence economy.[371] The expanding barter trade, however, faces rising transaction costs due to an increasing number of goods entering the markets and the thus increasing number of relative prices, e.g. the relative price of a pound of butter to a dozen of eggs. These relative prices imply another problem: For every barter intended a partner needs to be found who has an exactly reciprocal want. Given that an individual wants to exchange butter for eggs, she needs to find someone who is willing to offer eggs and needs butter. In this situation the use of money offers two advantages: The number of relevant prices is fixed to the number of different goods, which greatly reduces the number of prices economic agents need to know implying that each good has only one price. Money's second advantage is that it represents an elegant solution to

---

368 Cf. Lacker (2001), Hudson (1995) and Coco (2000) respectively.
369 Cf. Kanatas (1992) p. 382 and Coco (2000).
370 Cf. Smith (1776) volume 1, p. 25 f. as well as Hart (1998).
371 Cf. Jones (1976).

the problem of the *double coincidence of wants*.[372] The emergence of money in neoclassical economics is thus due to a transaction cost motive.[373]

In Jones' model one good might turn into a medium of exchange solely for reasons of economic agents' self-interest.[374] The community in his model engages initially in barter and ultimately either switches over to a partial or complete use of money or not. To what extent money is used depends on the level of search costs of finding a matching partner – the double coincidence of wants – relative to expected cost savings due to the use of money. The expected cost savings in turn depend upon individuals' expectation of the probability that other market participants want to use the same good as money as chosen by themselves.[375] Money is thus regarded as a good, which is appreciated frequently and by many due to its physical utility. For instance, Jones mentions rice, tobacco and butter as potential currencies while the Bundesbank's money museum exhibits stuffed cattle among other things as examples of former monies.[376]

Ritter tackles the problem of why intrinsically worthless paper money can be exchanged for goods of value.[377] He develops a model to explain – always remaining on an equilibrium path – the transition from barter to today's use of money. Ritter claims this to be essential as irredeemable money, fiat money, cannot emerge solely due to individuals' self-interest like the commodity money in Jones' model as it is intrinsically worthless, i.e. no one would want to exchange it for goods in Jones' model. Ritter identifies a credible limit on money issue on the part of government as condition for the circulation of paper money. To meet this condition, market participants must form a coalition sufficient in size that issues standardised money and is sufficiently patient with respect to seigniorage earnings.[378] Irredeemable paper money can thus circulate only if government, which is what Ritter promptly calls his coalition of market participants, credibly promises not to engage unduly in printing money.[379]

A critical review of the literature that recommends alternative payment systems is offered by White who also investigates the interrelation of a unit of

---

372 This expression is due to William Stanley Jevons, one of the founders of neoclassical economics. See Jones (1976) p. 757.
373 Cf. White (1984) p. 703 f.
374 Cf. Jones (1976).
375 Cf. Jones (1976).
376 Cf. Jones (1976) p. 775, footnote 16. See also Stadermann (1994b) p. 23 f. for a critical appraisal of these commodity moneys.
377 Cf. Ritter (1995).
378 For common definitions of seigniorage see Bofinger *et al.* (1996) p. 47 ff., Black (1998) and Beckerman (1997) note 21, p. 177. According to Bofinger *et al.* (1996) seigniorage earnings correspond to the difference between the nominal value of issued money and its costs of production (paper, ink and printing).
379 Cf. Ritter (1995) p. 146.

account and a medium of exchange.[380] White's arguments are based on historic banking systems like free banking in Scotland, which had no central bank. Money emerges – as in Jones' model – due to a transaction cost motive. Media of exchange are said to have always been units of *outside money* or *inside money*. The latter representing claims on the former and outside money being defined as irredeemable. The examination of alternative payment systems leads White to the conclusion that the unit of outside money always corresponds to the unit of account. Currently the unit of account is represented by an irredeemable *fiat currency* and in former times it had been represented by gold and silver.[381] Paper money as fiat currency was able to assume the role of medium of exchange because it had previously been able to gain the public's trust as inside money. Finally, the unit of account will remain tied to outside money even in case of complete deregulation of the money market as other units of account would cause additional conversion costs.[382]

Friedman & Schwartz hold the view that today's monetary systems with their "inconvertible paper money" differ fundamentally from systems like free banking or the gold standard.[383] In the currently widespread monetary system banknotes issued by a central bank are regarded as inconvertible, i.e. not redeemable in anything else than itself. Correspondingly Friedman & Schwartz declare the fact that central banks still hold a considerable part of their reserves in gold as unnecessary.[384] In previous monetary systems, however, banknotes were redeemable into precious metals, which are said to have represented the real money. The unit of account is said to have been tied to a good, i.e. some precious metal, while today's unit of account is said to be utterly abstract and not tied to anything. Friedman & Schwartz would like to get back to a monetary system à la free banking without any government intervention as these are regarded as inherently inflationary. They assume, however, that only a severe crisis of today's monetary system could offer an opportunity for change. Friedman & Schwartz are moreover sceptical about the chances for survival of a new free banking system that features neither public banking supervision nor an ultimately public LOLR.[385]

A review of the literature on theories of monetary laissez faire, i.e. monetary systems without any public regulation is provided by Selgin & White.[386] Historical research is said to have found evidence suggesting that financial sector crises

---

380 Cf. White (1984).
381 Cf. White (1984).
382 Cf. White (1984).
383 Cf. Friedman & Schwartz (1986).
384 Cf. Friedman & Schwartz (1986) p. 60. See also the discussion of their paper in section 2.2.
385 Cf. Friedman & Schwartz (1986).
386 Cf. Selgin & White (1994).

would be less frequent under laissez faire since LOLR institutions had encouraged risk taking by providing some kind of insurance to troubled banks. This has naturally raised the question of why central banks have been established and laissez faire removed in the first place.[387] In an envisaged free banking system the base money should not be some fiat money as the value of the unit of account would swiftly tend to zero.[388] Fiat money would be of no value due to, on the one hand only monetary demand for fiat currency and, on the other hand, fiat money's inherent profitability of issuing more of it – at least as long as it still possesses some positive value. Therefore, modern advocates of free banking believe that such a system would feature banks issuing banknotes redeemable in a common base money, which would serve as unit of account. This base money could consist of gold or silver but could also represent some fiat money in strictly regulated supply.[389]

Another vision of the future of money is one of payments entirely based on an "accounting system of exchange"[390], i.e. without any money. Such a system would make use of the concept of a numeraire and a Walrasian auctioneer, none of which, however, exists or is likely to operate in the real world. Therefore, Selgin & White doubt whether such system could attain a stable equilibrium.[391]

Selgin & White challenge the consensus that in order to avoid exchange-rate crises a country should either officially dollarise or abandon any restrictions on the exchange rate.[392] Instead, they argue, the credibility problem as described by Kydland & Prescott should be solved by allowing commercial banks to issue banknotes redeemable in some foreign currency – as currently practiced in Scotland and Northern Ireland. Commercial banks would not endanger their solvency and reputation by issuing more banknotes than they can redeem whereas central banks are said to gain from devaluations of their respective currencies because fiat currency "[ ] buys more than the cost of printing it, and does not pay interest."[393] Selgin & White claim that during the era of free banking systems of commercial banks were responsible for sustaining the gold standard and that the establishment of central banks made note issue a matter of public policy establishing nominalism. "Nominalism awards to public monetary authorities the right to redefine a nation's unit of account at any time. The unit and obligations expressed in it bear no enforceable relationship to any scarce commodity

---

387 Cf. Selgin & White (1994). See also the discussion above in section 2.2 on a central bank's raison d'être.
388 Cf. Selgin & White (1994).
389 Cf. Selgin & White (1994).
390 Cf. Selgin & White (1994) p. 1737.
391 Cf. Selgin & White (1994).
392 Cf. Selgin & White (2005).
393 See Selgin & White (2005) p. 72.

or external money."[394] In what follows the presented literature on the emergence, present, and future of money in neoclassical economics will be summarised.

The desire for monetary systems without any public regulation obviously stems from a deep distrust against current state-regulated monetary systems that are viewed as being permanently on the brink of near complete devaluation of currency. The present money is described as inconvertible, i.e. not redeemable in anything else than itself, and today's unit of account is regarded as utterly abstract and not tied to anything. In contrast to current monetary systems, previous monetary systems are said to have been unregulated – as in the era of free banking in Scotland. Paper currencies in these former systems are said to have been redeemable into gold and silver, which also represented the 'real' money or outside money. Government control of the currency is seen as the root cause of current monetary systems' shortcomings and visions of future monetary systems are thus often rather modelled on the idea of free banking, which is said to have been more stable and less crisis-ridden. Overall, this short review of the literature on present and future monetary systems thus reveals a certain revisionist tendency and seems to disregard the relative stability of monetary systems in most developed countries since the 1980s.

The presented theories on the emergence of money are certainly logical and coherent – from a theoretical point of view. Yet, these theories have to be rejected due to discrepancies with empirical evidence.[395] The rejection of these theories is not due to the fact that collateral plays not even a rudimentary role in the neoclassical tale of the emergence of money. Rather, the neoclassical theory of the emergence of money has to be rejected because barter – the neoclassical dogma and point of origin of the emergence of money – never existed to any significant extent. Gregory, drawing this conclusion, refers to more than half a century of anthropological research.[396] Hart finds signs of contemporary barter but none for the alleged primitive state of barter.[397] In the light of these problems and given that money so far could not be assigned a meaningful place in the general equilibrium model[398] the conclusion regarding the neoclassical theory of money can only be; back at square one. The third chapter shows – employing a narrow definition of money – which new insights Property Economics offers.

---

394 See Selgin & White (2005) p. 75.
395 Cf. Heinsohn & Steiger (1989). This paper represents moreover one of the first formulations of the theory of property economics.
396 Cf. Gregory (1998).
397 Cf. Hart (1998). See also Stadermann (2002) on the role of money in theories since Ricardo and until Keynes.
398 Cf. Ritter (1995) p. 134 f. and Jones (1976) p. 757 f.

3 Hypotheses of the Theory of Property Economics

The following argumentation shows how the quality of assets eligible for the issue of money by a central bank affects the long-term level of inflation. The quality of an eligible asset generally depends on the creditworthiness of its issuer and on the liquidity or marketability of the asset.[399] Three scenarios are developed, in which collateralisation and the quality of eligible assets affects inflation: i) The collateralisation of a central bank's issuance of money as a general protection against an unlimited issuance of money; ii) Eligible assets of a quality sufficient to prevent a financing of public debt by 'printing money'; and iii) A scenario, in which central bank losses accruing from bad debts lead to a reduction of a central bank's room of manoeuvre. These scenarios are based on the Theory of Property Economics by Heinsohn and Steiger.[400] Correspondingly, three hypotheses will be derived, and their validity will be tested empirically. However, prior to explaining the quality of eligible assets' effect on the long-term level of inflation, it seems appropriate to give an introduction to the notion of 'good' money as employed by Heinsohn and Steiger.

3.1 Introduction to Property Economics' theory of money and central banking

To begin with, the meaning of some potentially ambiguous notions needs to be clarified. Heinsohn and Steiger term the right to physically use a good *possession*. This use of the word possession complies inter alia with the German legal definition.[401] New Institutional Economics denotes the right to physically use a good as a *property right*[402] while the notion possession is not utilized.[403] Thus, Heinsohn and Steiger employ the notion of possession to denote the use of, for instance, machines and real estate for the purposes of production whereas Alchian would speak of property rights.[404] Heinsohn & Steiger employ the notion *property* to denote a bundle of rights, comprising the options of buying and

---

399 Cf. Bank of Japan (2003) p. 1-3.
400 Cf. here and in the following Heinsohn & Steiger (2000a) as well as Heinsohn & Steiger (1996; 2005b; 2006; 2007a and 2008) for a more detailed account.
401 Cf. Heinsohn & Steiger (2000a) and, for instance, Bürgerliches Gesetzbuch (2002) book 3. Sachenrecht, section 1. Besitz (possession) and section 3. Eigentum (property).
402 Cf. Alchian (1992).
403 Cf. Steiger (2006a).
404 Cf. Alchian (1992). See also Demsetz (1967 and 1998).

selling, of depositing as collateral in a credit contract (debtor), of burdening one's equity (creditor) and of leasing.[405]

For Heinsohn and Steiger, property's most important feature is its role in the emergence of money.[406] According to Heinsohn and Steiger, good money represents a claim to the property of the issuer of money. Money is created in a credit contract. Such a contract is signed by two proprietors. The creditor issues money by handing out documents to a debtor. Each of these documents (notes) represents a claim to a part of the creditor's property. Therefore, money is backed by the property of the issuer. The debtor receives the issued money if he pledges a part of his property to collateralise the loan. He is furthermore obliged to repay the loan plus interest. Why is money created exactly in this way? First of all, such money represents claims to property, i.e. an asset, even though the money itself, for instance a banknote, might be without any intrinsic value. Secondly, the issuer has to insure herself against the risk that her money could be presented for redemption out of her property if the debtor does not repay the loan. Insurance against this risk is achieved by demanding collateral from the debtor: In case the debtor defaults, the pledged property of the debtor becomes the property of the creditor.[407]

During the contract term both creditor and debtor lose their freedom of disposition over their property, i.e. they lose the opportunities of selling or pledging their burdened property. If the credit contract is to be respected neither the creditor can sell that part of her property, on which she issued claims that might be presented for redemption, nor can the debtor sell property that was pledged as collateral.[408] Heinsohn and Steiger denote the freedom of disposition of a proprietor over his property as *property premium*.[409] Such a freedom of disposition over one's property can only exist if there is a legal system that effectively protects the rights of the individual against violations from powerful groups. If such a legal system does not exist, the individual will only be able to use the physical side of his possession to produce a yield. Legal security, which comes into existence with the emergence of a legal system that does not favour anybody, gives rise to an immaterial yield, the property premium. To enter into a credit contract implies the loss of freedom of disposition over one's property but does not affect the possessory side of a property title. Despite burdening a

---

405 Cf. Heinsohn & Steiger (2000a). In what follows the notion *property* will be used according to Heinsohn and Steiger.

406 Cf. here and in the following Heinsohn & Steiger (2005b), especially chapter III p. 87-153.

407 This is the reason why both parties entering into a credit contract have to be proprietors. If the debtor does not pledge his property explicitly, the creditor usually has the right to execute her claims against the debtor into his property.

408 The same applies to pledging the respective parts of property (again) as collateral.

409 Cf. Heinsohn & Steiger (1996) p. 133-205 and Heinsohn & Steiger (2006).

property title, e.g. to a house, the proprietor can still use the physical side of it, i.e. she can continue to live in her house or rent it.

The loss of property premium, however, has to be compensated. The creditor receives interest payments from the debtor as compensation for her loss of the property premium.[410] For these interest payments the debtor receives Keynes' liquidity premium that accompanies the holding of money.[411] Of course, the debtor, too, has to be compensated for the loss of property premium. This compensation comes in the form of security over the possessory side of his property. That is, the debtor might lose his property at the end of the credit contract if he defaults, but during the contract term his burdened property is save – all else being equal.

At this point of the argumentation it might be asked if it would not be simpler and thus better for the debtor to issue his own money. To answer this question, a simple example will be employed. Assume agent Z owns a firm that produces a certain commodity A with machines of type I. Agent Z's firm yields a small but sufficient profit to pay his family's cost of living. Now technical change takes place and a new machine of type II is available that significantly reduces the costs of production for one unit of commodity A. After this technological revolution agent Z's firm incurs losses since the price on the world market for commodity A has dropped sharply. In this situation agent Z has got several options to react to the new market conditions:

i)   Agent Z could continue to produce with machines of type I and would incur losses. This option is thus virtually impossible.

ii)   Agent Z could sell his firm and use the revenue to buy new machines. The technological change, however, casts the achievement of a 'fair' price for the enterprise and especially the machines into doubt. Hence, it should be impossible to simply replace the old machines with new ones.

iii) Agent Z could issue Z-money and try to buy new machines of type II with this money. The catch, however, would be twofold: Either potential sellers of the new machines might not accept Z-money as medium of exchange because they do not know Z and cannot assess whether Z-money is worth anything. If Z-money is accepted, those who come to own Z-money would present this money to agent Z demanding redemption in agent Z's property. Since self-issued money can be nothing else than a certificate of debt, an 'I owe you' note (IOU). Thus, agent Z might have to redeem his Z-money with the new machines he had bought with it. Therefore, agent Z would have no security over the possessory side of his property if he issued his own money.

iv)   Agent Z could ask for a credit to buy the new machines of type II. This way agent Z would have the chance to keep his firm and to realise profits.

---

410 This represents Property Economics' answer to the question why interest has to be paid.
411 Cf. Heinsohn & Steiger (2000a) and Keynes (1936) chapter 13 in particular p. 167.

Out of those profits, agent Z would have to repay the loan and interest due. However, for the duration of the credit contract, agent Z would be able to produce and realise profits without the risk of claims being presented against his property, i.e. agent Z would have security over the possessory side of his property.

The risk of being forced to redeem one's self-issued money and thus the loss of one's property should keep such a 'debtor' from issuing his own money. Since to issue one's own money would usually be like selling one's property against someone else's property. Our debtor, however, prefers to produce without interference with the possessory, physical, side of his property. If the debtor signs a credit contract, this is exactly what is guaranteed: During the credit contract and as long as the debtor does not default, his property and therefore his possession remain untouched. Whereas the creditor has to assume the risk of losing parts of her property and hence her possession, in case someone demands redemption of money issued by her. When the credit contract expires, the debtor pays back the loan plus interest to the creditor and the latter retracts her money from circulation, i.e this money does not represent claims to the creditor's property anymore. In case the debtor defaults, the pledged property of the debtor passes into the property of the creditor, and the money, representing claims on the creditor's property, remains in circulation. For this reason, the creditor receives the property pledged by the debtor in case of the latter's default. Issuers of money are thus forced not to endanger their property by permitting claims on their property to become reality without adequate collateral.[412] An issuer of money has to face the risk of being forced to redeem issued money and losing property. This is the reason for a creditor's precaution and prudence, when assigning a credit. How to achieve that redeemable money is not presented for redemption will be the subject of the next paragraphs.

Now that terms and concepts of Property Economics have been clarified, it is possible to sketch the theory of money and central banking that is tested in this survey.[413] Nowadays, money is issued in a two-tiered banking system by a central bank that holds a monopoly on the issuance of money. In such a system the central bank is not obliged to redeem its notes vis-à-vis the non-bank public, but only vis-à-vis its counterparties, i.e. the commercial banks.[414] The obligation to redeem can only be satisfied if the central bank permanently holds property respectively equity, immediately available. Commercial banks presenting banknotes for redemption surely represents no everyday occurrence. This, however, does not affect the fact, that the central bank has to be able to absorb surplus

---

412 Cf. Heinsohn & Steiger (1996) p. 284.
413 Cf. here and in the following Heinsohn & Steiger (2005b), especially chapter III p. 117-153.
414 Cf. Steiger (2005). In section 2.5 it was shown that neoclassical economics regards today's currencies as completely irredeemable.

money if it finds that the public or commercial banks hold too much money. The absorption of surplus money is feasible only if the central bank holds assets that can be sold against such surplus money.[415]

Commercial banks can only obtain money if they pledge good securities to the central bank to collateralise the credit and if they promise to repay the loan plus interest.[416] Since every good security represents property, such banking system can only exist in countries where an effective legal system is present that protects property rights. Furthermore, central banks are not permitted to accept assets from counterparties that issued or guaranteed those assets. The same rule applies to counterparties that have close ties with the issuers of assets.[417] It is these rules that constitute the difference between monies that are easily accepted as medium of exchange and others, like Z-money, which represent nothing else than IOU notes, that have to be expected to be presented for redemption. For some banknote to be accepted as money, that is not hastily presented for redemption, two conditions must be met: i) The intrinsically worthless piece of paper has to represent something of value, i.e. the banknote must be backed by assets; and ii) it must be guaranteed that the ratio of the backing asset's value and its representations remains more or less constant. That is, an over-issue of banknotes relative to their property base must be excluded. The mechanisms that guarantee that, for instance, the Swiss franc meets those two conditions will be sketched next.

A central bank's counterparties, i.e. commercial banks, have to assume liability for defaulting collateral. This implies that commercial banks have to cover the losses in case their pledged assets, which are debt instruments of other institutions, default. In this way good money is always backed by the property of at least three proprietors: The central bank's property (creditor to a commercial bank), the commercial bank's property (debtor to the central bank but at the same time creditor to its debtors), and the property of the commercial bank's debtors. In other words, good money is "creditor's money", i.e. it is backed by the property of creditors.[418] Thereby the first condition is satisfied, since an issue of money on the basis of good collateral guarantees that the issued banknotes represent assets. This, however, is only the obvious condition, since everyone issuing an IOU note can likewise claim to have his notes backed triply by prop-

---

415 Cf. Stadermann (1994b) p. 63-80, in particular p. 79.
416 It has to be considered that repo operations, i.e. operations with repurchase agreements, make up the bulk of today's liquidity providing operations. These repo operations are in essence nothing else than collateralised credits. Cf. Bank of Japan (2003) p. 1.
417 In the Guidelines of the Swiss National Bank (SNB) on Monetary Policy Instruments (2004) p. 7 (http://www.snb.ch/d/download/geldpol_instr_e.pdf) this rule reads as follows: "The SNB does not accept counterparties' own securities or those issued by persons or companies that form an economic entity with the counterparty."
418 See Heinsohn & Steiger (2002) p. 5.

erty. The mechanism, ensuring that an over-issue of banknotes relative to their property base is excluded, is elaborated in the following.

The demand for central bank credit is generally limited by the commercial bank's willingness to accept liability with their property vis-à-vis the central bank for debt instruments of the commercial bank's debtors. If this basic principle of creditor liability is disregarded, an arbitrarily growing money base with an inherent tendency towards worthless paper money, i.e. debtor's money, will be the result. A debtor's money becomes reality as soon as the government decides that its own debt instruments will be directly eligible collateral at the central bank. In such a case, the debtor government uses its self-issued assets as collateral to obtain a credit. It is therefore already a matter of bad money if the central bank's debtors do not have to pledge assets as creditors but are permitted to pledge assets issued by themselves, i.e. as debtors, since IOU notes can generally be issued infinitely.[419] This would be nothing else than financing the government's deficit by 'printing money'. If, however, public debt instruments first have to take what seems to be a 'loop way' across the asset market to become proper eligible collateral, this loop way will be the best safeguard against an inflationary currency.[420]

What are the reasons for good collateral having to take the loop way across the asset market? A debtor is only liable for his own debt instruments, while a creditor, as a central bank's debtor, is liable vis-à-vis the central bank for the pledged collateral even if the pledged debt instrument defaults. Accordingly, a creditor will scrutinise the creditworthiness of her debtors to protect her property. Debt instruments that are traded on the asset market are by definition marketable and usually represent eligible collateral. Contrary to marketable debt instruments, nonmarketable debt instruments, especially nonmarketable public debt instruments, are usually not eligible as collateral at a central bank. The marketability of a debt instrument has to be proven on the market, i.e. the combination of risk and price has to be seen as acceptable for purchase by market participants. Thus, it can be stated that the creation of good money, i.e. creditor's money, is influenced by operations on the asset market. An over-issue of money seems impossible under these circumstances, while an avoidance of the asset market will almost inevitably lead to the creation of a worthless debtor's money.[421]

---

419 Cf. Heinsohn & Steiger (2002) p. 5 and Heinsohn & Steiger (2000b) p. 6-12 as well as Heinsohn & Steiger (1996) p. 207-287. Bad money is also referred to as debtor's money, cf. Steiger (2006b).

420 Only the government is treated here as a potential originator of a debtor's money, since only the government is able to enforce the circulation of a money that tends to be worthless. Cf. Steiger (2006b).

421 For the differences of creditor's and debtor's money see Heinsohn & Steiger (2000a; 2005b; 2006; 2007a, and 2008). The postulation that good money always has to be

Some final remarks on Property Economics are in order here. It should be noted that Property Economics as an alternative to the neoclassical theory of a general equilibrium is not limited to the notions presented above. In fact, Property Economics sets out to explain the emergence of markets and other real world phenomena that cannot be explained, for instance, in classical or neoclassical economics as these theories simply postulate their existence. Property Economics is not a theory supposed to be valid for all times and places – like neoclassical economics – but only for those societies that are characterised by an effective legal system protecting property.[422] Moreover, the loss of property premium discussed above represents a novel explanation for the existence of interest that is neither based on some alleged time preference nor on the notion of a liquidity premium.[423] Finally, Property Economics' explanation of the issuance of money in a credit contract resolves, somewhat along the way, the dilemma of creating money out of nothing. Schumpeter who realised that nothing has to be saved to allow for an accumulation of assets took recourse to this explanation of the issuance of money.[424] Indeed, not savings are crucial for the entrepreneur's credit, rather property gives rise to interest, money and markets.[425] In the following hypotheses will be derived from the theory of Property Economics.

3.2 Hypotheses derived from the theory of Property Economics

Among modern economists, it is commonplace that central banks issue money out of nothing and without any limitation, since today's money is said to be irredeemable.[426] In reality, however, most central banks have to comply with legal requirements such as to ensure a stable and noninflationary currency.[427] Moreover, central banks are usually obliged by law to grant credits only if these are sufficiently collateralised.[428] The issuance of money by central banks is

---

creditor's money corresponds widely with the claim that government should not receive any credit directly from the central bank, but has to place its debt instruments on the asset market.

422 Cf. Heinsohn & Steiger (2005b) p. 9-28. Similarly, Bailey (1998) analyses "property rights in aboriginal societies".

423 Cf. Heinsohn & Steiger (2005b).

424 Cf. Schumpeter (1911) third chapter first section in particular p. 164.

425 Cf. Heinsohn & Steiger (2005b).

426 Cf. Friedman & Schwartz (1986) for the thesis of a prevailing irredeemable money, see also Buiter (2004), Heinsohn & Steiger (2005a), White (1984) and Ritter (1995).

427 Cf. Cukierman et al. (1992a) p. 357 on central bank's legal duties.

428 As far as the author's knowledge is concerned there exists no comprehensive study on the arrangements concerning the collateralisation of central banks' credit. Cf. Kopcke (2002), BIS (2001), Blenck et al. (2001) and Borio (2001) for the practices of some industrialised countries. See also the survey conducted by Lehmbecker (2004).

commonly administrated by granting credits to commercial banks.[429] This implies that a central bank's issuance of money is not independent from the demand for credit by commercial banks.[430] In the light of a generally limited stock of assets, which always represents scarce property, a requirement to collateralise central bank credit means that the issuance of money is strictly finite.[431] After all, a good is not scarce because it can be found only in relatively small quantities but because someone is the proprietor of that good. If the free good air had one or several proprietors it would be not a free but scarce good despite its relative abundance.[432]

What happens if the collateralisation of the issuance of money is missing and instead faith is put only in the power of interest due? The experiences of some transition countries feature the best object-lesson. The normal case is runaway and speedily further accelerating inflation.[433] The collateralisation of the issuance of money can therefore be expected to act upon the latter as a restriction, and hence also as a check against inflation. The first hypothesis reads accordingly:

[H1] *The collateralisation of a central bank's issuance of money directly limits inflation through the scarceness of eligible assets.*

Of greater relevance for monetary stability, however, is the principle of creditor's money or rather the principle of creditor's liability. As illustrated above, the banking system's liquidity is strictly limited by the commercial banks' willingness to accept liability vis-à-vis the central bank with their property for debt instruments that serve as collateral. Correspondingly, the government must not borrow directly from the central bank but imperatively has to

---

429 Here, the rule is a two-tiered banking system, in which a central bank holds the monopoly on the issuance of money, while private commercial banks as the public's financial intermediaries are ultimately dependent on the central bank for provision of liquidity. Cf. Bofinger *et al.* (1996) p. 223-237.

430 Martínez-Resano (2004) notes that issuance of banknotes is initiated by commercial banks and that this demand for currency can be quite volatile. The accuracy of this thesis can be substantiated with reference to Japan: Interest rates were at an extremely low level after the crisis of the early 1990s but even so the Bank of Japan was not able to issue money in dimensions that would have freed the economy from fears of deflation. See also Koo (2001).

431 In industrialised countries the availability of eligible collateral represents usually no binding restriction. This, however, does not necessarily hold in exceptional circumstances and possibly even less so in developing countries. Cf. Borio (2001) p. 18.

432 Cf. Heinsohn & Steiger (1996) p. 259. See also Demsetz (1998) p. 151 f.

433 Cf. Ulf Heinsohn cited in Heinsohn & Steiger (1996) p. 278 f. on Vietnamese experiences. The average annual inflation rate in Vietnam for the period 1986-1995 amounted to approximately 100 percent.

borrow on the asset market. The consequence of violating these principles would entail nothing else than financing government deficits by 'printing money'. In essence, the argument boils down to a comparison of different qualities of eligible collateral: Eligible collateral represents debt certificates, mostly government bonds.[434] The crucial feature of 'good' collateral is, however, neither directly linked to the quality of the debt certificate itself nor to the creditworthiness of the issuer. Since claims against oneself can in principle be issued infinitely and debt certificates represent in this regard nothing else than IOUs, the scarceness of debt certificates cannot be secured by the issuers of such titles. Rather, the scarceness of eligible collateral is secured by those who buy these titles on the asset market as this guarantees that titles possess an observable positive price, which – economically speaking – signifies scarceness. Therefore, good collateral must take the scarceness guaranteeing loop way across the asset market or, in other words, good collateral has to be marketable.

The standards for the quality of eligible collateral, however, are still unsatisfied as the marketability of an eligible asset alone is insufficient to guarantee a genuine anchor for the issuance of money.[435] The quality of an eligible asset consists in the buyer's readiness to accept liability for potential losses from an asset, the occurrence of which generally cannot be influenced by the buyer. Good central bank money, creditor's money, is thus based on the property of liable creditors. The crucial point to note is the fixation of the issuance of money to an anchor that is not arbitrarily augmentable and hence scarce, i.e. collateral representing scarce property. It is this anchor that would be eliminated if government had the option to directly pledge self-issued debt instruments to the central bank. Therefore, a second hypothesis reads as follows:

[H2] *Ensuring the preservation of the principle of creditor's liability in the collateralisation of the issuance of money limits in particular government's demand for credit in such a way that a threat to monetary stability can be ruled out.*

The procedure outlined above would nonetheless be readily identifiable. Thus, the principle of creditor's liability was often not abandoned directly and apparently. Rather techniques such as pseudo-bills (Scheinwechsel) and similar methods, capable of giving a debtor's asset the appearance of a creditor's asset,

---

434 Cf. Martínez-Resano (2004) p. 22.
435 It should be emphasized that this anchor for the issuance of money does neither consist in the accidental scarceness of a real good like gold, nor does it consist in the 'scarceness' of an ever so real basket of goods. Rather the anchor consists in the additional scarceness originating from the liability condition of by definition already scarce property.

were used.[436] Unfortunately, the detection of such methods to finance a government deficit via printing money is far from simple. Nonetheless, it should be possible to detect some – if not all – cases, in which government possesses the option of financing its deficit with the help of direct central bank credit. Summarising, hypothesis [H1] demands that issued money be backed by assets while hypothesis [H2] requires that eligible collateral always proves its quality on the asset market.

The following derives the third hypothesis concerning the effect of central bank losses on monetary stability. It should be kept in mind that this hypothesis is not primarily based on the theory of Property Economics by Heinsohn and Steiger but rather takes up the abundant anecdotal evidence provided in the literature on central bank losses (see section 2.3). According to this literature central bank losses can be described as a substitute for larger government deficits.[437] The effect of central bank losses is generally seen as identical to monetising the fiscal deficit: Central bank losses represent an injection of liquidity into the economy. Absorbing this extra liquidity might bring about additional losses. Since the central bank cannot buy liquidity with money but only with assets, it would have to issue interest bearing debt titles – at least when capital is depleted and thus zero. The neutralisation of the effect of central bank losses therefore entails the potential for exponentially growing losses.

To avoid such losses in the first place, a central bank requires a sufficiently large capital position to be able to maintain monetary stability. The problem is thus not one of being unable to meet one's obligations since a central bank can practically never be illiquid. A central bank can, however, be insolvent as its capital position also represents its capacity to absorb excess liquidity and thus ultimately the capacity to defend monetary stability. A loss at the end of an accounting year will ultimately cause the equity to shrink, if shareholders do not provide additional deposits.[438] Empirical evidence shows that if losses are recorded in several subsequent years a negative central bank capital is a rather likely phenomenon, whereas modern economic theory can see no problem arising from insufficient central bank capital: The money issued by a central bank is

---

436 Cf. Stadermann (1994a) p. 115-160 for methods employed before and during the first German republic (1919-1933) with its hyperinflation.

437 Cf., for instance, Vaez-Zadeh (1991) or Sullivan (2002).

438 Central bank losses resulting from the issuance of money can be significant: In 2000 the share of irrecoverable debts to total credits at the Philippine central bank was 11.52 percent. In Mongolia at the beginning of the nineties the ratio of central bank bad debts to credits granted was so high that accountants did not even calculate the exact value. Given equity-to-assets ratios of less than 10 percent for 78 out of 136 countries reported in Ueda (2003), losses of the aforementioned magnitude mean that a total loss of a central bank's equity in a time span of a few years is far from presenting an unrealistic scenario.

always seen as an asset – whether it is backed by property or not.[439] In economic reality, however, capital of near or less than zero means that the central bank has to face severe problems. Repeated central bank losses result in negative capital, which, in turn, forces the central bank to abandon any goal of monetary stability. The evidence in the literature on central bank losses supporting this thesis has been summarised in section 2.3.

Therefore a central bank must have a vital interest in defending its capital to be capable of acting as LOLR. The role of LOLR requires that the central bank, in order to avoid banking crises, always holds sufficient equity.[440] More importantly, however, a central bank has to fear an insufficient capital due to bad debts resulting from a banking crisis. In such a crisis the central bank might not be able to execute into its debtor's property. Additionally, it has been observed that the amounts necessary in banking crises often exceed central banks' funds: If limits on central bank LOLR assistance to troubled commercial banks are missing this could ultimately hinder monetary policy in the sense that the objective of preserving price stability has to be abandoned.[441]

Central bank losses due to the issuance of money imply that an equivalent share of issued notes is not backed by debtor's property. Therefore, some of the money in circulation is not backed by those funds, i.e. collateral, that were intended to serve this function and hence cannot be absorbed with the help of those funds. Given the central bank decided that there was too much liquidity in the market and consequently that this liquidity had to be absorbed, it would have to use its capital and reserves.[442] Even this effort, however, would be in vain if losses exceed the central bank's capital resulting in negative capital. The central bank would have to refrain from absorbing unbacked money since financial assistance from government usually cannot be expected in such a situation.[443] On the contrary, the central bank would be forced to recapitalise itself through greater profits from an increased issuance of money.[444] An increased issuance of money, i.e. an increased granting of credits, offers the chance to increase the central bank's profit and thereby an increased accumulation of reserves via additional returns from interest payments.[445] This kind of exercise has always had

439 See, for instance, Bofinger et al. (1996) p. 459-470, who indirectly point out that if a currency is backed by property or not can generally be seen as of no relevance since money always represents a financial asset. See also the literature reviewed in section 2.3.
440 Cf. Steiger (2005a) and Stella (2002).
441 Cf. Martínez-Resano (2004) and Jácome (2001).
442 Cf. Stadermann (2000) p. 536.
443 See the literature reviewed in section 2.3.
444 See, for instance, Fry et al. (1996) p. 38, Ueda (2003) and Stella (1997).
445 Cf. Stella (1997) p. 8-12 for other possibilities for a central bank to become solvent independently. None of these represents a generally justifiable alternative.

devastating consequences for monetary stability apart from the case of Chile.[446] It has to be kept in mind here that commercial banks, which refinance themselves with the central bank, tend to meet the standards for eligible assets only as far as required.[447] This implies that commercial banks will tend to demand less central bank credit, in case the standards for collateral are raised. Raised standards for eligible assets result in rising opportunity costs of employing these assets as collateral relative to more risky assets that are less liquid.[448] Moreover, higher standards for eligible assets result in a smaller volume of assets eligible as collateral at a central bank. Therefore, higher standards for eligible assets have a negative effect on commercial bank's capacities to pledge collateral at the central bank, and thus tend to decrease commercial bank's demand for central bank credit.

It follows from this argumentation that a central bank, which attempts to increase its issuance of money by granting credits to commercial banks to raise its profits and thereby ultimately its capital, will only succeed if the standards for eligible assets are lowered. It goes without saying that the option of lowering the standards for eligible assets represents the central bank's sole option only if it receives no financial help from the government. Lower standards for eligible assets are, on the one hand, likely to increase a central bank's issuance of money thereby offering the chance to recapitalise independently. An increased issuance of money is, on the other hand, likely to result in inflation, since lowered standards for eligible assets increase the central bank's risk to be inadequately collateralised and to suffer even greater losses. If this option is excluded due to its riskiness, there is only one option left: Recapitalisation by government. Permanent financial backing of a central bank by government, however, appears to be a rather unlikely scenario given chronic public deficits.[449] Therefore, it can be stated that a central bank will be able to escape independently from insolvency

---

446 Cf. Fry *et al.* (1996). They argue that so far only Chile's central bank could avoid such practice because it received substantial financial help from the government. Stella (2002) and Jácome (2001) contain several examples for cases, in which central banks had to suffer monstrous losses (23,5 percent of GDP in 1989 in Argentina) often due to providing LOLR assistance in banking crises (e.g. Uruguay, Venezuela, Nicaragua, Mexico). Moreover, Stella argues that given rational expectations, such losses will result in inflation if the government does not step in immediately to recapitalise the central bank.

447 Put differently, a pledging of better and less risky assets than required by the central bank's standards for eligible collateral usually does not take place. Cf. Kopcke (2002) p. 5.

448 On the opportunity costs of pledging assets as collateral see Begg *et al.* (1998) p. 36.

449 If a central bank should indeed be dependent on financial aid from government this would very likely have negative consequences for central bank's independence. Cf., for instance, Stella (1997).

only in highly unlikely circumstances.[450] The granting of insufficiently collateralised credits tends to cause losses for a central bank, which, at least in the long-term, have to be balanced by an increased issuance of money. This leads to the third hypothesis:

[H3] *A high quality of eligible assets helps to limit excessive central bank losses and thereby safeguards monetary stability.*

Heinsohn and Steiger's concern for the soundness of central bank balance sheets coincides widely with the one of Fry *et al.*[451] In particular financial crises in developing countries often prompt central banks to buy assets at clearly excessive prices from troubled commercial banks to save these from insolvency and to protect the banking system at large.[452] Such LOLR operations with substandard collateral, however, threaten central banks' solvency. A central bank usually generates profits only as long as its capital and reserves is sufficient to cover potential losses. In case of an insufficient or even negative equity, a central bank is usually not able to generate profits – until government decides to recapitalise the central bank: "Even when it comes to the central bank's money monopoly, resources are finite: there is still no such thing as a free lunch."[453] The next chapter describes the data and methodology employed to test the three hypotheses derived in this section.

---

450 Chile is no exception to this rule since it received sizeable financial help from government. Cf. Fry *et al.* (1996). Stella (2002) explains this irregularity with an extremely solid fiscal policy of the Chilean government.

451 Cf. Fry *et al.* (1996).

452 Cf. Leone (1993). See also Jácome (2001).

453 Cf. Fry *et al.* (1996) p. 40. Cf. ibid. p. 37-40 for the remarks.

4 Data on the quality of eligible collateral and central bank losses

Before entering into a discussion of this survey's data and methodology it seems advisable to give a broad overview of how central banks try to influence inflation. In general monetary policy proceeds as follows: A central bank uses its instruments to directly affect its operating target(s), which in turn influence its intermediate target(s) that help to reach the central bank's final target(s) and thus ultimately its goal.[454] This chain of different targets and indicators already gives an idea of the difficulties associated with monetary policy as inflation can be affected only indirectly via many different channels. Nowadays, the operating target of virtually all central banks is represented by short-term interest rates. These rates can be very directly controlled via the central banks instruments such as setting the rates for refinancing and deposit facilities. However, to achieve the ultimate goal of maximised social welfare the final goals of price stability and full employment need to be reached. The centrepiece of this scheme, how operating targets influence final targets, is subsumed under the term transmission mechanism of monetary policy covering a broad area of ongoing research. Thus, to facilitate the otherwise overly complicated conduct of monetary policy certain intermediate targets – also referred to as indicators of monetary policy – have been introduced such as monetary aggregates or the exchange rate.

One such facilitation of monetary policy is monetary targeting: Based on the quantity theory of money actual monetary growth is compared to a target level enabling central bankers to assess whether interest rates are well set or not.[455] Monetary targeting was popular among many central banks after the breakdown of the Bretton-Woods-System in 1973. In particular the German Bundesbank officially followed a strategy of monetary targeting until 1998, whereas all other central banks introduced other policy strategies during the 1980s and 1990s like inflation targeting (see section 2.1). The reason for abandoning monetary targeting is an empirical one. The monetary aggregates used in this procedure can be characterised by their degree of liquidity: The monetary base as the definition of liquidity also represents the narrowest concept since broader monetary aggregates such as M2 or M3 contain in addition less liquid items such as time deposits. Central banks, however, somewhat disliked narrow concepts of money even though the central bank can control these directly. Central bankers preferred monetary aggregates were rather broad ones like M2 or M3 since demand for broad money remained relatively stable while narrow money possesses no

---

454 Cf. Bofinger (2001) part II for the comments in this paragraph.
455 Cf. Bofinger (2001) part II, especially chapter 9 for the comments in this paragraph.

stable relation with the price level and thus cannot serve as an indicator for monetary stability. Financial liberalisation during the 1980s, however, resulted in a breakdown of any stable short-term relationship between monetary aggregates and inflation resulting in monetary targeting being replaced by new policy strategies.

A central bank's institutional framework has to be regarded as the basic requirement safeguarding central bankers' ability to focus on monetary policy as described above. The quality of eligible collateral is seen here as part of such an institutional framework as it does not form part of what is commonly described as monetary policy but rather resembles issues that are treated in central bank laws like limits on credit to government.[456] Therefore, this survey on the quality of eligible collateral and central bank losses forms part of the literature on central banks' institutional frameworks and their effects on inflation (see section 2.1). This literature has proposed and empirically tested several potential determinants of average inflation like central bank independence and transparency. This survey's methodology (presented in chapter 5) thus broadly follows the one employed in the empirical literature on central banks' institutional frameworks and their effects on inflation. Continuing this line of research without changes in methodology guarantees a certain consistency of empirical methods and – more importantly – allows for a test of Property Economics' explanatory power with regard to cross-country differences in average inflation.

4.1 A new dataset on eligible collateral and central bank losses

This chapter presents a new dataset on the quality of eligible collateral and central bank losses. The quality of eligible assets was operationalised, taking into account current guidelines (frameworks) on eligible collateral of the Eurosystem, the Bank of Japan and the Swiss National Bank (SNB).[457] These central banks have been chosen as a kind of benchmark due to their inflation performance and, more importantly, because of the detaildness with which these central banks discuss their collateral frameworks publicly on their homepages. Such qualitative data on standards for eligible collateral from central banks' terms and conditions are the only data available, since virtually no quantitative data on type and volume of pledged assets are published so far.[458] These qualitative data, however, are far better than one might think at first sight, since nobody apart from central banks has any other information than what can be found in central

---

456 See the literature on central banks' institutional frameworks and their effects on inflation in section 2.1.

457 Cf. Bank of Japan (2003), EZB (2005) chapter 6,"Eligible Assets", and SNB (2004).

458 The sole exception is the Bank of Japan that publishes statistics on eligible collateral since 2002.

banks' terms and conditions as well as laws. In addition the words written there cannot be understood in any other way than that these state, what a central bank actually practices in everyday operations or rather what it does not practice, i.e. what kind of assets it will not accept as collateral.

There are different methods of measuring central bank losses.[459] Collecting data on central bank losses that comply with a certain definition of how to measure them is, however, not possible. Central bank losses are always part and result of central banks' balance sheets as well as profit and loss accounts respectively. And even though most central banks today publish their financial statements in their annual reports, one should not assume that figures under similar headings contain directly comparable items.[460] Central banks, as of now, do not follow the same accounting rules and guidelines.[461] Despite these caveats data on central bank losses were collected as it is assumed that the only data readily available, i.e. financial statements in central banks' annual reports represent a reasonable approximation of the actual occurrence of central bank losses albeit not necessarily of their size.

To measure the quality of eligible collateral and the magnitude of central bank losses, a questionnaire was designed. There are four reasons to employ a questionnaire: i) Not all relevant texts are gratuitously available as access to texts is hindered either in terms of public accessibility, i.e texts are not downloadable, or in terms of an efficient use of resources as texts are usually written in the language of the country, which would often necessitate translations. Therefore, this survey represents not only a form of expert interview but offers also the best cost-efficiency. ii) What the relevant texts are, is a priori unknown as it could be laws, terms and conditions or special guidelines; and iii) especially texts for the 1990s and before are difficult to find as out of date terms and conditions are typically not preserved let alone accessible. Moreover, central bank staff working in a central bank for more than twenty years is usually not able to compensate for this documentary shortcoming. Nevertheless, Lehmbecker collected information on central banks' collateral frameworks before 1990.[462] iv) Finally, in order to achieve a satisfactory sample size a questionnaire is superior to a content analysis of central bank laws and guidelines regarding efficiency and viability given the project's time constraints of six months for the actual collection of data.[463]

---

459 See Leone (1993) for a discussion of this issue.

460 See, for instance, Cargill (2005) who notes that cross-country capital adequacy measures are not available.

461 Cf. Stella (2002), Courtis & Mander (2003) and Sullivan (2005) on central bank accounting.

462 Cf. Lehmbecker (2005).

463 Cf. Stier (1996) p. 163 ff. for the pros and cons of content analysis relative to other methods of data collection.

4.2 Questionnaire design

The questionnaire is part of a standardised survey among experts, i.e. central bank officials. The bulk of questions is designed as closed or hybrid questions where the respondent has the possibility to give further information. This facilitates completion of the questionnaire and thus raises the probability of receiving a completed answer without forgoing unforeseen answers. Moreover questions are posed neither suggestive nor hypothetical but strictly neutral.[464] The survey by Fry et al. for the Bank of England from 1999 represents the broadest collection of data on central bank frameworks so far and can be regarded as a benchmark for this strand of literature.[465] Data were collected concerning central bank targets, central bank independence, central bank accountability and central bank transparency and thus covering almost all potential determinants of monetary policy frameworks and their effects on inflation that have been identified in the literature.[466]

The questionnaire employed by Fry et al. was used as draft for this survey's form. It is subdivided into five parts, each part containing two to six questions.[467] If and to what extent the art of questionnaire design[468] was applied can be studied online.[469] In 2004 a pre-test for this survey's questionnaire design was conducted that provided valuable information on how to eliminate potential deficiencies and ambiguities.[470] The questions regarding the quality of eligible collateral referred to the current framework and one possibly close to 1990. This imprecision concerning the year (possibly close to 1990) should be conducive to a higher rate of response for an older framework. Data on central bank losses contained in central banks' financial statements were asked to be provided for the period 1990 to 2003.

The first part of the questionnaire asks [1.1][471] which label would best fit the central bank's monetary policy framework (money targeting, inflation targeting, discretionary, exchange rate targeting, balance of payments targeting or other), in order to shed light on the general orientation of a central bank's monetary

---

464 Cf. Stier (1996) p. 173 ff. on different kinds of how to pose questions.
465 Cf. Fry et al. (2000).
466 For an overview on the literature on central bank frameworks see section 2.1.
467 See Fry et al. (2000) p. 163-181.
468 Cf. Stier (1996) p. 183 ff. and 199 ff.
469 The questionnaire and the survey's homepage is available under http://www.wiwi.uni-bremen.de/empwifo/umfrage/questionnaire.htm. Important considerations in this regard are the communication of respectability and the motivation to participate. A copy of the questionnaire can also be found in appendix A.
470 Cf. Stier (1996) p. 205 ff. on the advantages of pre-tests. See Lehmbecker (2004; 2005) for details on the previous questionnaire.
471 Note: Numbers in brackets correspond to questions in the questionnaire, which can be found in appendix A.

policy. Question [1.2] asks since when the current terms and conditions on eligible collateral are valid to show whether the current collateral framework could already have had an effect on inflation. [1.3] requests information on the number of changes to the guidelines on eligible collateral since 1990 to get an idea of a collateral framework's 'usual' duration.

In the second part of the questionnaire it is asked [2.1] whether liquidity is provided if the receiving institution is not pledging sufficient collateral to secure the credit; and [2.2] if non-collateralised advances to the government are provided. The answers to [2.1] and [2.2] are supposed to clarify whether a central bank always demands collateral or if it provides liquidity without collateralisation in special cases such as LOLR credits. The answers to these questions are of relevance for testing hypotheses [H1] and [H2]. Question [2.3] asks whether issuers of assets have the right to pledge these assets as collateral whereas [2.4] asks whether assets are accepted as collateral from institutions that have close ties with the issuers of those assets. The answers to these questions shall disclose if the money issued is debtor's or creditor's money and are therefore most relevant for hypothesis [H2]. In question [2.5] information on procedure or criteria used to evaluate pledged assets are demanded and [2.6] asks what the minimum percentage is that eligible collateral has to satisfy relative to an amount of credit. [2.5] is supposed to indicate to what extent a central bank follows reasonable and commonly accepted accounting principles.[472] Question [2.6] is directly relevant to hypothesis [H1] and [H2] respectively since it is also revealed whether a collateralisation is mandatory or not.

The third part of the questionnaire enquires [3.1] which minimum degree of creditworthiness issuers of assets eligible as collateral have to satisfy; and [3.2] which minimum degree of creditworthiness eligible counterparties that pledge collateral have to satisfy. These questions define minimum standards of creditworthiness for issuers of acceptable assets and counterparties respectively and give an idea of the risk associated with accepted assets.[473]

The fourth part of the questionnaire deals with central banks' balance sheets. [4.1] requests the amounts of bad debts as percentage of the total amount of credits granted by the central bank for each year between 1990 and 2003; [4.2] asks to provide standardised balance sheet information for the years 1990 to 2003; and [4.3] what was the amount of profits transferred to government in the years 1990 to 2003. The answers to question [4.1] are supposed to measure the effectiveness of a central banks collateral framework in protecting it from losses that stem from money issue. This matter is clearly directly relevant for hypothesis [H3]. [4.2] and [4.3] are expected to provide data on central bank losses and

---

472 See for instance Cossin *et al.* (2003) on whether evaluation haircuts represent a sensible and coherent protection against the risk of losses.

473 On the reliability of the usual ratings of creditworthiness by Standard & Poor's or Moody's see Perraudin & Taylor (2004).

related issues such as central bank capital and transfers of central bank profits to the government.

Finally, the fifth part of the questionnaire provides some auxiliary information. [5.1] asks which publication, act or law contains relevant guidelines on eligible collateral; [5.2] to provide the central bank's official title; and [5.3] to provide an email address if the respondent should be interested in the results of the survey. This helps to verify given information on the basis of official central bank laws and guidelines and to improve the validity and reliability of the data entries.

4.3 Description of data on collateral frameworks and central bank losses

The data collection for the survey was conducted over six months between end of January 2006 and July 2006. During this time central banks were contacted via email and asked to complete the online questionnaire. To get an idea of the population size of money issuing central banks it is worth to take a look at the 192 member countries of the United Nations (as at 2007) that encompass almost every recognized independent state. Only two of these states (Liechtenstein and Monaco) do not possess an own central bank. There exist, however, at least five central banks whose home countries are not part of the United Nations (Aruba, Hong Kong, Netherlands Antilles, Taiwan and Trans-Dniester). Furthermore, twenty United Nations member states are part of a currency union with single money issuing central bank (Bank of Central African States, Central Bank of West African States and Eastern Caribbean Central Bank (ECCB)[474]). Thus, there are at least 178 central banks in the world today that issue currency.[475] The homepage of the Bank for International Settlements (BIS) contains a list of 148 central banks (as of November 2006) that possess an Internet representation.[476] These 148 central banks are taken as this survey's population.

---

474 The eight members of the ECCB are Anguilla, Antigua & Barbuda, Dominica, Grenada, Montserrat, St. Kitts & Nevis, St. Lucia, and St. Vincent & the Grenadines.
475 The European Central Bank is not listed here because it does not issue currency. Cf. Spethmann & Steiger (2005) and the discussion in section 2.2.
476 The list can be found under http://www.bis.org/cbanks.htm.

Table 1: Compositions of main samples

Period		1998 to 2003			1995 to 1999			1990 to 1997		
Sample		all	LI	HI	all	LI	HI	all	LI	HI
Country	Sample size	62	36	26	46	25	21	56	39	17
Australia		X		X	X		X	X		X
Austria*		X		X	X		X			
Bahamas		X		X	X		X	X		X
Belgium		X		X	X		X	X		X
Bolivia		X	X					X	X	
Botswana		X	X		X	X		X	X	
Brazil		X	X					X	X	
Canada		X		X	X		X	X		X
Cape Verde		X	X					X	X	
Chile		X	X		X	X		X	X	
China		X	X		X	X		X	X	
Colombia		X	X					X	X	
Croatia		X	X		X	X		X	X	
Czech Republic		X	X		X	X		X	X	
Denmark		X		X				X		X
ECCB		X	X		X	X		X	X	
Estonia		X	X		X	X		X	X	
Finland		X		X	X		X	X		X
France		X		X	X		X	X		X
Germany		X		X	X		X	X		X
Greece		X		X	X	X		X	X	
Guatemala		X	X					X	X	
Honduras		X	X					X	X	
Hungary		X	X		X	X		X	X	
Iceland		X		X	X		X	X		X
Iran		X	X					X	X	
Ireland		X		X	X		X	X		X
Italy*		X		X	X		X			
Japan		X		X	X		X	X		X
Jordan		X	X		X	X		X	X	
Kazakhstan		X	X		X	X		X	X	
Latvia		X	X		X	X		X	X	
Luxembourg*		X		X						
Macedonia		X	X		X	X		X	X	
Malta		X		X	X	X		X	X	
Mauritius		X	X		X	X		X	X	
Mexico		X	X		X	X		X	X	
Mongolia		X	X		X	X		X	X	
Mozambique		X	X		X	X		X	X	
Netherlands		X		X	X		X	X		X

Note: LI, HI and 'all' indicate samples of low income, high income and all countries respectively.

Table 1 (continued): Compositions of main samples

Period		1998 to 2003			1995 to 1999			1990 to 1997		
Sample		all	LI	HI	all	LI	HI	all	LI	HI
Country	Sample size	62	36	26	46	25	21	56	39	17
New Zealand		X		X	X		X	X		X
Nicaragua		X	X					X	X	
Norway		X		X	X		X	X		X
Oman		X	X					X	X	
Paraguay		X	X					X	X	
Peru		X	X		X	X		X	X	
Philippines		X	X					X	X	
Portugal*		X		X	X		X			
Romania		X	X		X	X		X	X	
Saudi Arabia		X	X					X	X	
Slovenia		X		X	X	X		X	X	
South Africa		X	X		X	X		X	X	
Spain*		X		X	X		X			
Sweden		X		X	X		X	X		X
Switzerland		X		X	X		X			
Tajikistan		X	X					X	X	
Thailand		X	X		X	X		X	X	
Trinidad & Tobago		X	X					X	X	
Turkey		X	X		X	X		X	X	
United Kingdom		X		X	X		X	X		X
United States		X		X	X		X	X		X
Uruguay		X	X		X	X		X	X	

Note: LI, HI and 'all' indicate samples of low income, high income and all countries respectively.

Table 1: Compositions of main samples

Table 1 lists the 62 central banks that constitute this surveys main sample. 51 completed questionnaires were received. Another eleven completed question- naires are taken from the pre-test survey by Lehmbecker (Austria, Brazil, Can- ada, Italy, Luxembourg, Mongolia, Nicaragua, Portugal, Spain, Trinidad & To- bago and United States).[477] The survey's response rate reached 35 percent, which is an average value in written surveys.[478] Developed countries are well represented in this sample (26). The same holds true for western and eastern European countries (19 and 9 respectively) as well as for North America (3), South America (10), the Caribbean (10)[479] and the Middle East (4) while only seven Asian, two from the Pacific region and five African countries are repre-

---

477 See Lehmbecker (2005).
478 Cf. Stier (1996) p. 199 ff.
479 This includes the eight members of the ECCB.

sented in this sample. No answers were received from those five countries in table 1, which are marked by an asterisk. Their 'answers' correspond to the answers of other Eurosystem members. This approach is applicable here due to the Eurosystem's unitary collateral framework.[480]

In what follows this survey's data are illustrated by means of convenient diagrams, which can be found in appendix A. The samples underlying the period 1990 to 1997 and for a previous framework as well as for the period 1998 to 2003 and for the current framework are depicted in table 1 and comprise 56 and 62 central banks respectively. Statistics for the two periods display averages over the respective periods. Figures 28 and 29 give an idea of the distribution and evolution of monetary policy frameworks since 1990. While today one third of central banks employs inflation targeting their percentage was much smaller at the beginning of the 1990s when almost 40% practiced exchange rate targeting. The decline of exchange rate targeting and the rise of frameworks with more than one major targeted variable in this sample are mainly due to Euro zone member central banks, which were mostly exchange rate targeters during the convergence period and whose monetary policy framework presently cannot be summarised as targeting one variable.

In the following comparisons with previously collected data on similar issues are impossible since – apart from minor exceptions and the author's previous work – no data on characteristics of central banks' collateral frameworks and balance sheets have been collected so far.[481] Figure 30 shows since when the current collateral frameworks are valid while figure 31 depicts the number of changes in these frameworks since 1990. Nearly 20% of today's collateral frameworks in this sample are in place for already 16 years and three out of five are at least valid since 2000. Figure 31 also shows that seven out of ten collateral frameworks have been changed at most twice since 1990. Only 13% have seen more frequent changes. But these cases consisted of minor alterations, e.g. changes of evaluation haircuts. Given the immense effort necessary to replace an existing collateral framework with a new one it seems improbable that frequent framework changes bring about significant alterations.[482] Thus, we can assume that collateral frameworks are usually valid for many years. Consequently, a collateral framework has generally the potential to influence the level of inflation. This is true even though the number of new frameworks introduced during the 1990s is likely to be rather high and thus exaggerating the normal number of framework changes due to transformations taking place in former communist states that had to develop proper monetary systems. Furthermore this data

---

480 Country specific differences exist only with respect to nonmarketable tier-two collateral. Cf. ECB (2001) and ECB (2006).
481 Cf. Lehmbecker (2005). Previously collected data on certain issues presented here are discussed where required.
482 See ECB (2004) on the revision of the Eurosystem's collateral framework.

structure warrants a separation of the survey's investigated period (1990 to 2006) into two periods of eight years: 1990 to 1997 and 1998 to 2005. The latter period, however, is shortened to six years (1998 to 2003) due to unavailability of macroeconomic data, especially for small countries included in this sample.

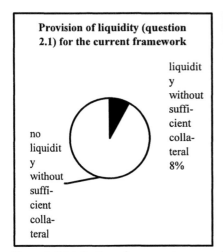
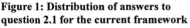

Provision of liquidity (question 2.1) for the current framework

liquidity without sufficient collateral 8%

no liquidity without sufficient collateral

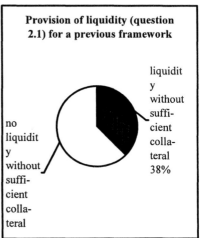

Provision of liquidity (question 2.1) for a previous framework

liquidity without sufficient collateral 38%

no liquidity without sufficient collateral

Figure 1: Distribution of answers to question 2.1 for the current framework

Figure 2: Distribution of answers to question 2.1 for a previous framework

The answers to question 2.1, depicted in figures 1 and 2, draw a clear picture: 92% and 63% of the central banks in the samples of 2003 and 1990 respectively do not provide liquidity – even in emergency situations, i.e. acting as LOLR – unless the counterparty pledges sufficient collateral. The figures also display a strong tendency on the part of central banks to granting less and less uncollateralised loans. An even stronger trend can be said to exist with regard to the provision of uncollateralised advances to government shown in figures 32 and 33. While in 1990 only one third of central banks refuses uncollateralised advances to government, some 15 years later a mere fourth still provides uncollateralised advances to government. This pronounced change in central banks monetary policy frameworks is probably a result of the continuing popularity of the central bank independence paradigm, which recommends the discontinuation of central banks' financing of government deficits.[483] For this reason the answers to question 2.2 are not – unlike the answers to question 2.1 – considered for the construction of the index of the quality of eligible collateral. As including these answers would hamper a theoretical distinction between the concept of central

---

483 Cf. Alesina & Summers (1993) especially p. 153.

bank independence on the one hand and of the quality of eligible collateral on the other.

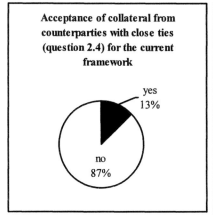

Acceptance of collateral from counterparties with close ties (question 2.4) for the current framework

yes 13%

no 87%

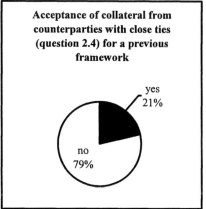

Acceptance of collateral from counterparties with close ties (question 2.4) for a previous framework

yes 21%

no 79%

Figure 3: Distribution of answers to question 2.4 for the current framework

Figure 4: Distribution of answers to question 2.4 for a previous framework

The predominant part of central banks does and did not accept assets as collateral from institutions that are the issuers of those assets. As can be seen from figures 34 and 35 only 11% and 20% of central banks accept counterparties' self-issued collateral under the current and a previous framework respectively. Virtually the same distribution of answers appears in figures 3 and 4 with 13% and 21% under the current and a previous framework respectively. Again the predominant part of central banks does and did not accept assets as collateral from counterparties that have close ties with the issuers of these assets. Furthermore, there exists a distinct tendency not to issue currency against titles that are at least theoretically in unrestricted supply, since the number of central banks in this sample accepting such assets has halved in the last 15 years. The answers to both of these questions are clearly most relevant to the construction of the index of the quality of eligible collateral. However, to evade the problem of multicollinearity and in light of their almost identical distributions of answers only one item is considered for the construction of the index of the quality of eligible collateral. In this regard question 2.4 dominates question 2.3 as the concept of question 2.4 is broader in the sense that central banks that answer question 2.3 in the affirmative have no reason not to do the same regarding question 2.4. The opposite is not necessarily true, i.e. central banks might not accept self-issued assets without at the same time being aware that close links between counterparties and issuers of assets eligible as collateral could have the same effect.

Thus, the informational content of question 2.4 is judged to be better suited for the construction of an index of the quality of eligible collateral.

Figure 36 depicts the distribution of collateral evaluation procedures currently in place. Roughly one fifth of central banks applies strict market value methods to evaluate accepted collateral while another fifth applies other procedures not primarily based on an assets market value probably due to a lack of corresponding markets.[484] The majority (55%) of central banks, however, employs market value methods and applies additional evaluation haircuts according to asset category. Evaluation procedures based on market values are today employed by three out of four central banks and hence represent the dominant evaluation procedure. Figure 37 shows a very similar picture for the previous frameworks, however, a non-response rate of more than 40% concerning this item renders vain any attempts of interpretation of these results. The answers to question 2.5 are therefore not considered for the construction of the index of the quality of eligible collateral.

Today almost all central banks issue currency only against collateral: The minimum percentage eligible collateral has to satisfy relative to an amount of credit, i.e. the minimum sufficient cover, is currently and for more than nine out of ten central banks at least 100%. Less than 10% of central banks are demanding a minimum sufficient cover of less than 100% (figure 5). While, as figure 6 shows, 15 years ago one out of four central banks was demanding a minimum sufficient cover of less than 100% or even no collateralization at all. As the answers to question 2.6 provide information on – among other things – whether the pledging of collateral on the part of counterparties represents a necessary condition for the granting of central bank loans or not, these answers are thus clearly relevant for the construction of an index of the quality of eligible collateral.

Figure 7 illustrates the distribution of answers to question 3.1 concerning the current framework. The minimum creditworthiness of issuers of assets acceptable as collateral corresponds for two out of three central banks to rating agencies' assessments. If issuer's minimum creditworthiness can be expressed as such a rating, more than three out of four central banks demand an issuer's creditworthiness that can be said to be essentially risk free (ratings Aaa to A). To define issuer's minimum creditworthiness in terms of commonly used ratings seems to be a rather recent phenomenon. This view is supported by the fact that the Eurosystem currently employs certain minimum ratings without, however, publishing them.

---

484 On the problem of a missing bond market see for instance Sonakul (2000) and generally Levine (1997).

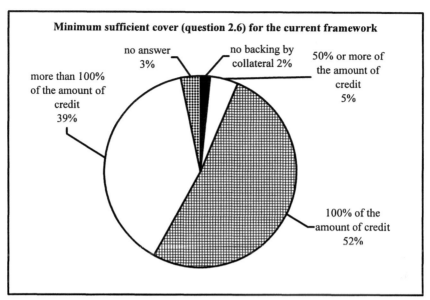

Figure 5: Distribution of answers to question 2.6 for the current framework

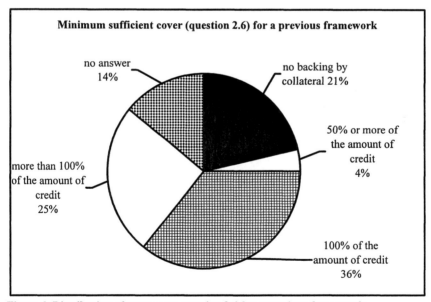

Figure 6: Distribution of answers to question 2.6 for a previous framework

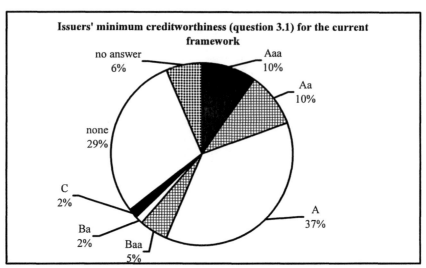

Figure 7: Distribution of answers to question 3.1 for the current framework

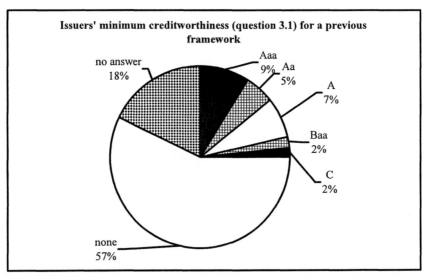

Figure 8: Distribution of answers to question 3.1 for a previous framework

Moreover, as figure 8 shows almost 60% of central banks did not employ such ratings some 15 years ago. The distribution of ratings – in cases of official ratings – was already the same in the sense that more than three out of four central banks demanded an issuer's creditworthiness that can be said to be essentially risk free (ratings Aaa to A). The answers to question 3.1 are thus, unlike the answers to question 3.2, considered for the construction of an index of the quality of eligible collateral. The variance in the answers to question 3.2 is – as depicted in figures 38 and 39 – too small. Merely 9% of central banks are using rating agencies assessments to define minimum creditworthiness for central banks' counterparties. Apparently the creditworthiness of central banks' counterparties depends – at least for central banks themselves – more on an assessment of a commercial bank's creditworthiness by the banking supervision, which is often part of a central bank's mandate.

The effectiveness of central banks' collateral frameworks with regard to the avoidance of bad debts and ultimately central bank losses is the subject matter of question 4.1. Figure 9 and 10 show – apart from a high non-response rate of roughly one third – that 50% of both samples' central banks did not record any bad debts during the last 15 years. Those central banks, however, that recorded bad debts mostly did so in several years of the respective periods. An interpretation of these statistics in the sense that there is a tendency to suffer newly recorded bad debts each year is nonetheless invalid. Bad debts seem to be rather a one-off that stays in a central bank balance sheet as a potential threat to central bank's capital until a settlement has been reached.

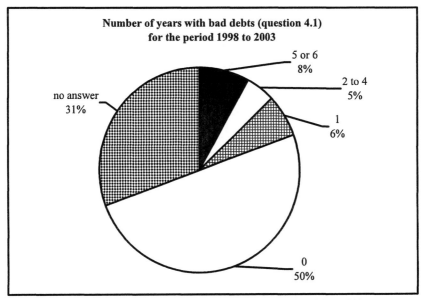

Figure 9: Distribution of answers to question 4.1 for the period 1998 to 2003

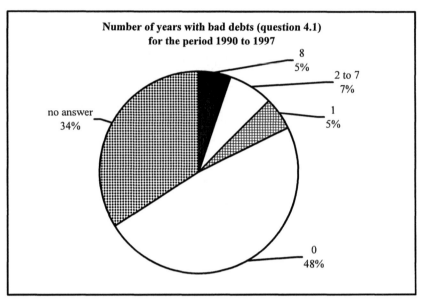

Figure 10: Distribution of answers to question 4.1 for the period 1990 to 1997

To illustrate the magnitude of the problem central banks' bad debts are depicted as the sum of their percentages over the two periods covered in this survey (figures 40 and 41). These diagrams effectively show the same picture. Again there is practically no trend visible from comparing the two period's statistics. What figures 40 and 41 do show, however, is that the magnitude of bad debts – in case these are recorded – can only be neglected by less than a third of the concerned central banks. For another third of these central banks the level of bad debts is well in the range of two digit percentages of total credits granted. Such a magnitude of bad debts is even higher than that, which commercial banks usually have to expect. Despite the high non-response rate the answers to question 4.1 are clearly too important for the construction of an index of the quality of eligible collateral to be omitted.

The answers to question 4.2 give an idea of the level of central banks' balance sheets elements such as currency in circulation, profits and losses as well as capital and reserves. The ratio of currency to total liabilities is depicted in figures 11 and 12. In the following total liabilities generally equal total assets, i.e. total liabilities include capital and reserves. For most central banks the percentage of currency remained below 30% during the whole period covered by this survey. The distribution did not change significantly over time and extreme percentages are rather an exception: Only slightly more than 10% of central banks have or had a balance sheet burdened with such an amount of other activities items that the percentage of currency fell below 10% of total liabilities. To put this in perspective the Federal Reserve System's combined balance sheet displays a percentage of currency of about 90% of total liabilities. Of course the question needs to be asked whether central bank balance sheets that display less than 10% currency as percentage of total liabilities contain only items, which represent genuine central bank activities. A similar measure labelled *clean balance sheet indicator* has been employed by Gros who shows that some correlation exists between average inflation and his indicator.[485] The size of the sample used and the data collected by Gros, however, are rather small and limited and generally rather taken as corroboration of his argument that an overblown central bank balance sheet might represent a threat for central bank independence.[486] This approach is nevertheless useful for the analysis and therefore statistics concerning currency as percentage of total liabilities are considered as a measure of the degree of central banks' quasi-fiscal activities for the construction of an index of the quality of eligible collateral.

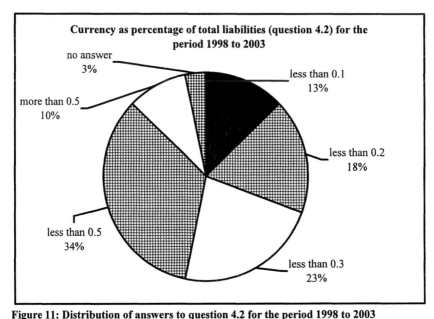

Figure 11: Distribution of answers to question 4.2 for the period 1998 to 2003

---

485 Cf. Gros (2004).
486 For more details on this issue see above subsection 2.1.2.

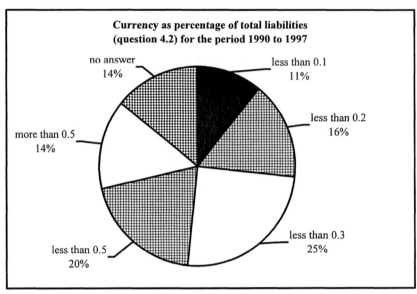

Currency as percentage of total liabilities (question 4.2) for the period 1990 to 1997

no answer 14%

less than 0.1 11%

less than 0.2 16%

more than 0.5 14%

less than 0.3 25%

less than 0.5 20%

Figure 12: Distribution of answers to question 4.2 for the period 1990 to 1997

Figures 42 and 43 illustrate capital and reserves' percentage of currency in circulation. Currency is covered by less than 10% by capital and reserves for one out of three central banks. Every twentieth central bank even exhibits a negative ratio indicating an on average negative capital. For almost 70% of central banks currency is covered by less than 50% by their capital and reserves. Every tenth central bank's currency, however, is more than entirely backed by its capital and reserves. The distribution of answers in the two diagrams is nearly constant over time. Obviously there exists no consensus among central banks regarding the appropriate level of capital and reserves as a cushion against potential central bank losses.[487] This claim is further substantiated by figures 44 and 45 that show central banks' capital and reserves as percentage of total liabilities. Approximately every fourth central bank features a capital of less than 2% of total liabilities. Although it has to be noted that certain central banks' accounting rules lead to an understatement of central banks' true level of reserves, which constrains the validity of further conclusions on this issue. Roughly two thirds of central banks have capital to total liabilities ratios of less than 10%. While capital ratios of more than 25% are a rather recent phenomenon representing 10% of today's central banks. Data on central banks' capital ratios are, therefore, not considered for the construction of an index of the quality of eligible collateral since it is not clear which criteria could define sufficient levels of capital as per-

---

487 See Ueda (2004) for a very similar view on the levels of central bank capital.

centage of total liabilities. Furthermore a very high capital to total liabilities ratio might indicate rather a high-risk environment than over-prudent central banks.

To compare the levels of central banks' profits and losses they are depicted as percentages of capital and reserves as well as total assets. Averages of profits as percentage of capital and reserves are shown in figures 46 and 47. It has to be noted that neither average profits nor average losses are averaged over profits and losses but only over profits and losses respectively as losses are usually charged against capital while profits are usually transferred to government. The return on capital is less than 0.5 for two thirds of central banks. A return on capital of more than 1, i.e. annual profits are higher than capital and reserves, is realised by 13% of central banks. In the first half of the 1990s almost every fifth central bank had realised such a high rate of return on capital. Similarly almost every tenth central bank had no profits at all or an on average negative capital. Today, however, the same holds true for merely every twentieth central bank. Figures 48 and 49 show a similar picture depicting profits as percentage of total assets. Nearly two thirds of central banks display profits of less than 2% of their balance sheet total. Only 15% of central banks record profits of more than 3% of total assets. At the beginning of the 1990s central banks' profitability was slightly higher: less than every second central bank had profits of less than 2% of total assets and almost one out of four central banks had profits of more than 3% of total assets. At the same time, however, there were more central banks with zero profits than there are today with 5% and 3% respectively. These statistics show that central banks' profitability is currently rather low but reliable. Whether the decrease in profitability during the last 15 years is due to the general decline of inflation rates or if other factors play a major role cannot be discussed here even though there are plenty of reasons to support the former assertion.

Central bank losses – as illustrated in figures 50 to 53 – have been identified as potential causes of inflation predominantly by researchers of the IMF.[488] Roughly every second central bank does and did not suffer any losses. One out of four central banks has suffered minor losses in the period since 1998 while in the previous period it had been only every eighth central bank. Losses of a magnitude that could seriously impair central bank capital and reserves have and had been recorded by every tenth central bank. Some of these central banks even displayed losses exceeding capital and reserves. Thus, central bank losses are a rather frequent phenomenon and deserve as such attention from economists specialised in monetary economics. This attention is unfortunately well-earned as is further substantiated by the fact that in this survey's sample every fourth central bank of those suffering losses in the last 15 years recorded losses of a magnitude

---

488 See Vaez-Zadeh (1991), Leone (1993), Dalton & Dziobek (2005) and Stella (2005).

that could seriously impair or even wipe out the respective central bank's capital and reserves. The potential result of recurring losses, negative capital and reserves, is accordingly far from being nonexistent. As figures 54 and 55 show, episodes of negative capital and reserves have been experienced by 8% of central banks in the last 15 years. Figures 56 and 57 illustrate once more the pervasiveness of central bank losses. While roughly three out of five central banks experienced losses at most once during the periods of 8 and 6 years, 13% of central bank recorded losses at least 3 times during the last period of six years. Leone published data on central bank losses as early as 1993.[489] Nonetheless his data are only of limited use for this survey, since he studied merely Latin American central banks, while Dalton & Dziobek who have recently investigated the issue present only case studies.[490] The still popular belief among economists that central banks can in principle issue money without limits and should thus be immune to losses or even negative capital is herewith repeatedly refuted.[491] The data on central bank losses provided by this survey proof not only their often disputed existence but enable us to test the hypothesis regarding the effect of central bank losses on inflation.

Finally, the survey's question concerning the magnitude of transferred profits has to be considered. Figures 58 to 61 depict profits transferred to government as percentages of capital and reserves as well as total assets. Only 8% and 7% of central banks do and did not transfer any profits to their governments in the period 1998 to 2003 and 1990 to 1997 respectively. Similarly 3% and 5% of central banks on average even received transfers from their governments. An interesting point to note here is that many central banks' transfers do not correlate with profits or losses recorded in the same year or the previous year.[492] Obviously many central banks follow a strategy of transfer smoothing, i.e. trying to level transfers, to provide the treasury with more predictable claims and lessen at the same time pressures to transfer profits while often having to negotiate for transfers from government in case of losses.[493] This practice, however, leads sometimes to the unfortunate constellation of transfers to government being remitted while the central bank is in fact recording losses. A refinement of the transfer smoothing rules might thus be advisable in the sense that no transfers to government take place as least as long as losses are recorded.

---

489 See Leone (1993).
490 See Dalton & Dziobek (2005).
491 See the discussion on this issue in section 2.3.
492 A statistic depicting transferred profits as percentage of profits is omitted here because of too many divisions by zero, i.e. zero profit or losses.
493 See Sullivan (2002) for a discussion of this issue.

4.4 Description of cross-country inflation since 1990

The description of data employed in regression analyses is concluded by a look at this survey's dependent variable: cross-country inflation. The basic concept of monetary stability is measured as 'long term' inflation. The negative correlation stated in the hypotheses does not claim to predict annual inflation. Rather the hypotheses are to be understood as predicting that high (low) inflation tends to prevail if the quality of eligible collateral is low (high) during the term of an eligible collateral framework. The degree of monetary stability is measured by the average of annual inflation rates over several following years. The independent variable is thus operationalised in an analogous manner to Cukierman et al., Chortareas et al. and Romer.[494] Inflation is measured by changes in the consumer price index (CPI). Bofinger et al. suggest to measure monetary stability either by the gross domestic product (GDP) deflator, i.e. inflation is measured by changes in the GDPdeflator, or by the CPI.[495] The differences between these two measures of inflation can under normal circumstances be described as negligible. To be sure, however, it is controlled whether the choice of CPI as inflation measure affects the validity of test results.

The sample's 62 countries are arranged into 6 groups according to their rank of average inflation for the period 1990 to 2003 to facilitate the illustration of descriptive statistics on inflation.[496] Group 1 contains those eleven countries with the lowest average inflation; group 2 contains those eleven countries with the second lowest inflation and so on until group 6, which consists of the seven countries with the highest average inflation in this survey's sample. Figures 62 to 67 depict average consumer price inflation for the periods 1990 to 2003, 1990 to 1997 and 1998 to 2003 for all 62 countries. For only four out of the 62 countries in the sample average inflation rates were not significantly higher during the eight years between 1990 and 1997 than they were between 1998 and 2003. As can be seen in figure 13 showing a summary of the six previous diagrams, the fight against inflation has been very successful in recent years. Only four out of 29 countries that recorded two to three digit average inflation between 1990 and 1997 did not succeed yet to bring inflation down to less than 10% per year. Furthermore arranging countries into groups according to average inflation of sub-periods would not have resulted in a significantly different composition of groups. In fact only a few countries went up or down by more than 5 ranks in this sample's ranking order of average inflation. This is most evident from figures 62 and 63 where differences of inflation between the periods 1990 to 1997 and 1998 to 2003 are in the range of 1.5 percentage points.

---

494 Cf. Cukierman et al. (1992a), Chortareas et al. (2002b) and Romer (1993).
495 Cf. Bofinger et al. (1996) p. 12 f.
496 The period covered here was shortened accordingly for those countries that did not exist yet at the beginning of the 1990s.

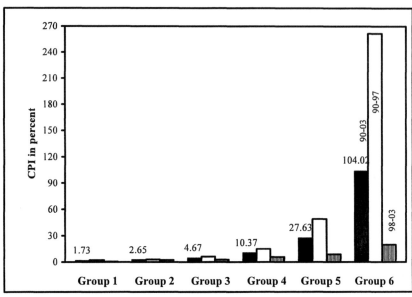

Figure 13: Groups of countries ordered according to level of average inflation during 1990 to 2003

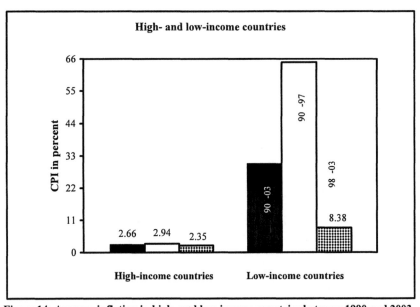

Figure 14: Average inflation in high- and low-income countries between 1990 and 2003

Another striking feature of these statistics on average inflation is the homogeneity of low and high inflation countries with respect to degree of development. Virtually all countries with inflation rates below 10% per year between 1990 and 1997 were high income countries at that time and vice versa, i.e. nearly all countries with inflation rates above 10% per year between 1990 and 1997 were low income countries at that time. This picture is reinforced by figure 14 in which the sample is divided in high-income and developing countries according to World Bank data.[497]

Figure 14 also shows that average inflation among high-income countries has been significantly lower than that of developing countries during all the three periods covered. The differences in average inflation between these two groups of countries, however, have almost disappeared. While average inflation in high-income countries was always between 2% and 3% during the period 1990 to 2003, average inflation in developing countries decreased from 65% during the first period between 1990 and 1997 to merely 8% during the years between 1998 and 2003. Thus, according to these figures it seems obvious that a country's income level affects average inflation in this sample. In addition the variance of country's inflation was evidently much greater between 1990 and 1997 than it was between 1998 and 2003. This might pose problems for some variables, which are considered to explain cross-country differences in average inflation, since a few of these variables, e.g. turnover of central bank governors, cannot explain inflation among high-income countries possibly due to the small variance of cross-country inflation in this group.

4.5 Construction of an index of the quality of eligible collateral

The approach adopted here to construct an index of the quality of eligible collateral (QEC-index) at central banks resembles the procedures applied to construct the indices in Cukierman et al. and Das et al.[498] Das et al. construct indices of regulatory governance and financial system stability to assess whether the former possesses any influence on the latter.[499]

The creation of a QEC-index is aspired for two reasons. Firstly, to avoid the problem of multicollinearity since, due to possibly close interrelations among framework elements, a high correlation between answers to different questions has to be assumed. Chortareas et al. argue in a similar fashion on why to use an

---

497 Cf. World Bank (2007).
498 Cf. Cukierman et al. (1992a) p. 356-369 and Das et al. (2004) p. 28-33.
499 Cf. Das et al. (2004). The stability of the financial system is measured by the capital adequacy ratio and the ratio of nonperforming loans. Das et al. find that regulatory governance matters for financial system stability and that this effect is more pronounced the better is public sector governance.

index or a scale instead of single variables.[500] Secondly, to obtain a high validity in operationalising the independent variable (QEC-index), since the interaction of several indicators in one index usually raises the validity of an operationalisation relative to the case in which only one indicator is employed.[501]

In a first step periods have to be defined for which index values can be generated. As was already discussed above, answers regarding the framework in place in 2006 are applicable for the period 1998 to 2003 and answers for a previous framework correspondingly for the period 1990 to 1997. This separation of the investigated years between 1990 and 2003 is feasible since – similar to the lawful definition of the relationship between central bank and government – frameworks rarely undergo significant changes for the worse and complete replacements of collateral frameworks are even more uncommon.[502] Moreover, nearly all collateral frameworks in this survey's sample have seen an improvement or rest unchanged as is evident from figure 15. This figure shows a scatter plot of QEC-90-1 against QEC-03-1. These variables – in anticipation of the QEC-index, see below – are formed out of the answers to questions 2.1, 2.4, 2.6 and 3.1 using equal weights. Figures depicting single questions make little sense here as half of the answers are binary. The diagonal from the origin depicts the line of no change: All points on this line represent collateral frameworks that have not been changed according to the characteristics controlled by the four questions 2.1, 2.4, 2.6 and 3.1 between 1990 and 2003. All points below this line indicate an improvement in terms of index values, i.e. by the standards of eligible collateral proposed here. Evidently the bulk of central bank collateral frameworks (59%) has been changed – a few even dramatically – for the better while only one framework has somewhat worsened (Trinidad & Tobago). Another four collateral frameworks have worsened but arguably to only a negligible extent as the respective index values represent rather top-class standards while every third framework rests unchanged. The claim that frameworks rarely undergo significant changes for the worse is therefore and once more corroborated.

500 Cf. Chortareas et al. (2002b).
501 See Stier (1996).
502 See Cukierman et. al. (1992a) p. 360 and Alesina & Summers (1993) p. 153 concerning central bank frameworks' frequency of change.

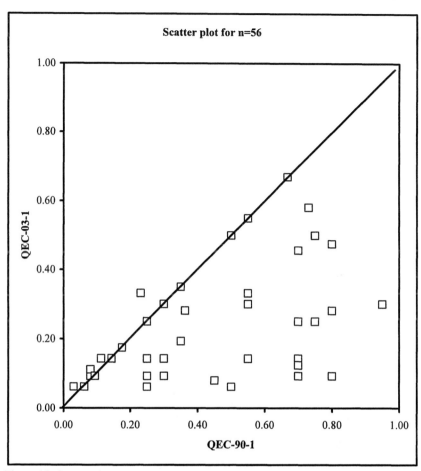

Figure 15: Changes in characteristics of collateral frameworks between 1990 and 2003

A second step is to examine the usability of answers to questions from the questionnaire. The usability depends on whether a question's response rate is sufficiently high and if answers to a question provide an informational content that is significantly different from other questions. The issue whether a question is to be included in the QEC-index has already been tackled in section 4.2 for reasons of convenience. The questions considered for the construction of such an index are listed in table 2. In a third step answers are somewhat arbitrarily assigned to certain numeric values, which are also shown in table 2. With two possible answers the respective values are 0 and 1, with three possible answers the respective values are 1, 2 and 3 and so forth. These answers correspond to all a priori possible answers and, thus, open in principle the door to manipulations of distances between different answers/values. Of course no manipulation has taken place in this survey. This claim can be verified by comparing actually recorded answers and a priori expected ones in figures 1 to 8 and table 2 respectively. Merely the answer 'minimum sufficient cover of less than 50 percent' to question 2.6 (figures 5 and 6) and answer 'B' to question 3.1 (figures 7 and 8) have not been recorded. Missing answers are replaced with the mode of corresponding answers or – where this is not possible, i.e. for most quantitative answers – with the arithmetic average. This approach renders possible the inclusion of countries into the sample that feature a few unanswered questions. Still this approach turns out to be conservative since the mode in this survey typically corresponds to the answer that reflects the highest quality of eligible collateral. Therefore, index values can in case of missing answers not be artificially exaggerated and rather overstate the true quality of eligible collateral.

According to the hypotheses and due to a preference for positive correlations, a high (low) value in the index should correlate with high (low) inflation. This is realised with values assigned to questions 2.1 and 2.6 since an obligation to pledge collateral for every central bank credit should have a negative effect on inflation. Similarly, the higher the creditworthiness of issuers of eligible collateral (question 3.1) the lower inflation should be. Care needs to be taken nonetheless that assigned values do not cause accidental dominance of one question over another. For this reason the answers to question 3.1 as well as those to question 2.6 need to be scaled in the construction of the index, i.e. the formulas for the index contain scale factors for questions 2.6 and 3.1 (see table 3). In this context it should be noted that answers have not been standardised to achieve a standard normal distribution. Such standardisation might have resulted in a reduction of the variance of answers since it is usually only a few observations that account for the bulk of variance in the data. It is, however, this variance and the information behind it that is most interesting in this survey.

Table 2: Questions, answers and assigned numerical values

Question	Answers	Assigned values
2.1	Does your central bank provide liquidity if the receiving institution is not pledging sufficient collateral to secure the credit, e.g. for short-term liquidity shortages?	
	No, collateral is never dispensed with.	0
	Yes, collateral is exceptionally dispensed with.	1
2.4	Does your central bank accept assets as collateral from institutions that have close ties with the issuers of those assets?	
	No, assets issued by linked institutions can not be pledged.	0
	Yes, such assets are accepted as collateral.	1

Table 2 (continued): Questions, answers and assigned numerical values

Question	Answer	Assigned values
2.6	What is the minimum percentage eligible collateral has to satisfy relative to an amount of credit? That is, what is the minimum sufficient cover?	
	minimum sufficient cover of more than 100 percent	1
	minimum sufficient cover of 100 percent	2
	minimum sufficient cover of 50 percent or more	3
	minimum sufficient cover of less than 50 percent	4
	no backing by collateral needed	5
3.1	Which is the minimum degree of creditworthiness that issuers of assets eligible as collateral at your central bank have to satisfy?	
	Aaa (most creditworthy)	1
	Aa (highly creditworthy)	2
	A (creditworthy)	3
	Baa (less creditworthy but investment-grade)	4
	Ba (low-risk speculative)	5
	B (moderate-risk speculative)	6
	C (high-risk speculative)	7
	None	8
4.1	What was the amount of bad debts as percentage of the total amount of credits granted by your central bank in each year?	
	no classification/quantitative variable	
4.2	Please complete the following balance sheets for your central bank. (What was the amount of banknotes in circulation as percentage of total assets in each year?)	
	no classification/quantitative variable	

Table 1: Questions, answers and assigned numerical value

Table 3: Employed weightings and formulas

QEC #	Q2.1	Q2.4	Q2.6	Q3.1	Q4.1 (bad debts)	Q4.2 (currency)
1	0.250	0.250	0.250	0.250	0.000	0.000
2	0.200	0.200	0.200	0.200	0.200	0.000
3	0.175	0.175	0.175	0.175	0.000	0.300
4	0.150	0.150	0.150	0.150	0.200	0.200

QEC #	Formula
1	0.25*(Q2.1+Q2.4+0.2*Q2.6+(1/8)*Q3.1)
2	0.8*0.25*(Q2.1+Q2.4+0.2*Q2.6+(1/8)*Q3.1)+0.2*Q4.1
3	0.7*0.25*(Q2.1+Q2.4+0.2*Q2.6+(1/8)*Q3.1)+0.3*(1-Q4.2)
4	0.6*0.25*(Q2.1+Q2.4+0.2*Q2.6+(1/8)*Q3.1)+0.2*Q4.1+0.2*(1-Q4.2)

Index of bad debts: BadDebtsX		
Number of bad debts per period	**Sum of bad debts per period**	**average of bad debts per year**

Weight	0.333	0.333	0.333
Period	Formula		
90-97	(1/3)*((1/8)* # bad debts/period + Σ bad debts/period + average bad debts/year)		
98-03	(1/3)*((1/6)* # bad debts/period + Σ bad debts/period + average bad debts/year)		

Table 2: Employed formulas for the construction of the QEC-Index

The possibility to issue debtor's money (question 2.4), i.e. money that is effectively only backed by a central bank's capital, should have a positive effect on inflation. The same holds true for currency as percentage of total assets (question 4.2) as a balance sheet burdened with quasi-fiscal activities should go along with higher inflation as well as low percentages of currency. However, to incorporate this interrelation properly into the QEC-index the algebraic sign (see table 3) needs to be reversed. To operationalise the occurrence and magnitude of bad debts (question 4.1) the numbers of years per period, in which bad debts have been recorded, are included in an additional index together with the sums of bad debts as percentage of total credits granted and the average percentage of bad debts per year. This way the concept of central bank bad debts is thought to be measured more accurately and unbiased than it would be the case with any of the single measures. These single measures frequently deliver potentially biased results due to missing data. The formula of this extra index of bad debts is summarised in the second part of table 3 and contains the number of years per period, i.e. six or eight years, in which bad debts have been recorded, the sum of percentages of bad debts relative to total credits granted and the average percentage of bad debts per year. This index of bad debts allows to capture all potential factors leading to a problem of bad debts: Bad debts being recorded in most of the years, large percentages of bad debts (to recognise also those cases where data have only been provided for a few years) and the average percentage of bad debts per year as the potentially best measure, which, however, contains only very little variance – often due to missing data. Finally, the index of bad debts is adjusted for the number of years per period, in which bad debts have been recorded, by division with the maximum value, i.e. the number of years in the period.

All of the above leads – in a fourth and final step – to the formulas for the calculation of QEC-index values presented in table 3. The weighting vectors are chosen as to confine possible QEC-index values between 0 and 1 with 0 representing the highest standard for the quality of eligible collateral. Evidently the weights assigned in different weightings are rather unsophisticated and generally not far from equal weights – if not identical altogether. These weights are chosen to evade the accusation that potential correlations depend unduly on weights chosen for the construction of the QEC-index.

Finally, central bank losses are operationalised as the number of years per period in which losses are recorded by the central bank. To measure losses as percentage of capital and reserves would undoubtedly have been more relevant to hypothesis [H3], however, due to the huge variance of capital and reserves as percentage of total assets such a measurement would have been highly biased. A construction of more than those two variables out of the answers to question 4.2 is impossible since so far there exists neither a theoretical nor an empirically validated central bank balance sheet structure that could be taken as a benchmark.[503]

---

503 The only exception might be currency as percentage of total assets. See Gros (2004).

5 Methodology and results of data analysis

In this chapter cross-country data are used to test the prediction of property economics that inflation will be higher in countries whose central banks do not issue currency in compliance with the principle of creditor's money. The hypotheses are tested using ordinary least squares (OLS) regressions. The employed sample's size of 62 central banks and its composition was largely determined by the willingness of central banks to answer this survey's questionnaire. The time span chosen for testing the hypotheses is given by the fourteen years between 1990 and 2003 and is divided into three sub periods 1998 to 2003, 1990 to 1997 and 1995 to 1999. The robustness of the results obtained is controlled employing other variables that might also have an impact on inflation and which have been proposed as determinants of monetary stability in the empirical literature on central bank independence and transparency. As this literature attempts to explain average inflation with the help of institutional characteristics it is reasonable to consider this literature's modus operandi as a blue print for the analysis of the survey at hand.[504] More importantly, however, doing so allows for comparing the explanatory power of determinants proposed by Property Economics with those suggested in the literature on central bank independence and transparency.

To check the validity of test results, six different robustness-tests are employed.

i)   The independent or explanatory variable's robustness is controlled to find out, whether a result holds true regardless of the weights used for the QEC-index' elements or if a result depends on a certain vector of weights being used. Berger et al. discuss different methods of aggregating elements of indices.[505]

ii)   The dependent variable's robustness is controlled to find out, if monetary stability has been operationalised in a way that corresponds to this paper's research questions and whether different ways of operationalising the dependent variable give rise to the same or different results.[506] To control for the dependent variable's robustness, three additional variables are considered for each sub period: the GDP deflator, the log of the CPI and the log

---

504 Cf. Cukierman et al. (1992a; 1992b), Loungani & Sheets (1997), Berger et al. (2001) and Arnone et al. (2006a) regarding exemplary surveys on central banks' independence and Chortareas et al. (2002a) and Fry et al. (2000) for a survey on central banks' transparency.

505 Cf. Berger et al. (2001) p. 16-23.

506 Posen argues that the dependent variable used in Chortareas et al. (2002a) was improperly operationalised. See subsection 2.1.1 above.

of the GDP deflator.[507] Using the average of the log of inflation as a measure for monetary stability is a well-established procedure in the empirical literature on central bank independence. It is argued that this procedure lessens the potentially distorting influence of outliers with extreme inflation rates.[508]

iii) The results are tested for sub-sample robustness, i.e. whether results are only valid for the main sample or if they are also valid in subsamples of high income and developing countries respectively. Such a test for sub-sample validity is a common exercise in the literature on monetary policy frameworks.[509] Cukierman et al. separate their sample because their legal central bank independence index is merely significant for high income countries while an alternative central bank independence index, central bank governor turnover rate, is only significant among developing countries.[510]

iv) The robustness of results is controlled for small changes of the samples to find out if a result depends unduly on a few influential observations – the outlier problem.[511]

v) The results' robustness is controlled by employing additional explanatory variables, i.e. control variables. The incorporation of other independent variables is supposed to reveal the explanatory power of a certain variable relative to other potentially relevant independent variables.[512] In total eleven additional explanatory variables are included in the different regression analyses. The use of these variables often necessitates a reduction of sample size due to imperfection of data, i.e. data are not available for all countries in the sample.

vi) Finally, the robustness of results is controlled for variations of examined periods, since statistical correlations might exist only in certain periods, which would raise the issue of additional important factors not yet accounted for in the survey at hand.[513]

Summaries of OLS regression results are shown in appendix B, tables 5 to 7. The data employed in these regressions can be found on the survey's home-

---

507 Detailed descriptions and sources of these variables can be found in table 4.
508 Cf. Romer (1993) p. 875 and Cukierman et al. (1992a).
509 See Cukierman et al. (1992a) and Chortareas et al. (2002a).
510 Cf. Cukierman et al. (1992a).
511 Cf. Berger et al. (2001) p. 27 and Stier (1996) p. 253.
512 Cf. Berger et al. (2001) p. 26 for an overview on control variables used in the empirical literature on central banking theory. See also Campillo & Miron (1997).
513 Cf. Berger et al. (2001) p. 25 f. A check on the possibility of inverse causation is not performed, since no reason has yet been proposed why the standards for eligible collateral should be raised systematically in countries, which had achieved a low level of inflation before.

page.[514] To confine the number of regression models represented in tables 5 to 7, only models with a minimum statistical significance level of P = 0.1 are listed. Furthermore, the method of stepwise selection – available in the standard statistics software SPSS – is employed together with the standard approach of simply entering the explanatory variables of each model to avoid showing all possible compositions of independent variables.[515] In the stepwise selection procedure employed, the first variable to enter the model as explanatory variable is the most significant. A prerequisite for including this variable into the model as explanatory variable is that the considered variable is statistically significant at the 5% level. Other explanatory variables are only added if they contribute significantly to the explanatory power of the model, i.e. if they are statistically significant given the precursory model. An already accepted explanatory variable is eliminated from the model if it is not significant at the 10% level, i.e. if it is statistically insignificant. This stepwise selection routine helps to circumvent the problem of 'arbitrary' results in multivariate regressions as it provides small and readily interpretable models by incorporating the statistically most important explanatory variables.[516] The problem of 'arbitrary' results is due to potentially strong reactions of explanatory variables' significance levels to changes in the model, depending on which group of independent variables is employed.[517] The stepwise selection routine, however, should not be used to define the 'best' model as it relies only on significance levels.[518] It goes without saying that this procedure does not immunise the QEC-index from becoming insignificant. Each model is moreover controlled for heteroskedasticity, i.e. unequal variance in the regression errors, using the White test.[519] In case of statistically significant test results regarding heteroskedasticity, regression results shown in tables 5 to 7 are based on heteroskedasticity consistent standard errors according to White.[520] The following sections will illustrate this survey's results and robustness thereof.

514 Data are available in Excel-format. See http://www.wiwi.uni-bremen.de/empwifo/ forschung/survey.html.
515 Cf. Stier (1996) p. 248 f. for a discussion of advantages and disadvantages of the stepwise selection routine. The stepwise selection routine is available in the standard statistics software SPSS.
516 Cf. Stier (1996).
517 Cf. Campillo & Miron (1997) for an example of this effect concerning the variable GDP per capita.
518 Cf. Stier (1996).
519 Cf. White (1980).
520 Cf. White (1980). Unfortunately standardised coefficients are missing for these models.

5.1 Results of regression analyses for the period 1998 to 2003

The regression results for the period 1998 to 2003 are shown in table 5 and are based on the sample of 62 countries (see table 1). The results of a regression analysis with average inflation (CPI-98-03)[521] as dependent variable and the QEC-index' six constituent parts as independent variables are shown in model 1 of table 5. All variables apart from 3.1Creditworth-03 have the sign that could be expected given hypotheses [H1], [H2] and [H3], though none of these explanatory variables in model 1 is statistically significant. What is more important, however, is that there are several significant correlations among the six constituent parts of the QEC-index. These correlations are presented in table 8 and render the use of these six variables as separate explanatory variables rather improper. Thus, the construction of an index of the quality of eligible collateral to evade the problems associated with multicollinearity is well-founded.

5.1.1 Results for the complete sample

Models 2 to 5 (see table 5) show results of regressions with CPI-98-03 as dependent and QEC-indices each representing a different weighting of its constituent parts as independent variable. All four QEC-indices possess a positive correlation with average inflation. These results correspond to the predictions made in chapter 3, namely that a low (high) standard of eligible collateral – equivalent to a high (low) value of the QEC-index – tends to go with high (low) average inflation. A positive correlation between average inflation and the QEC-index thus implies a negative correlation between average inflation and the quality of eligible collateral. According to the results presented in models 2 to 5 the QEC-index including all six components, QEC-03-4, is best in explaining average inflation followed by QEC-03-2 where CurrencyTA-98-03 is not part of the index as can be seen in table 3. All QEC-indices are, however, statistically significant, which entails that this result is fairly robust to changes of weightings of the QEC-index.

Models 6a and 6b comprise the dependent variable CPI-98-03 as a measure of average inflation, the independent variable QEC-03-4 as a measure of the quality of eligible collateral as well as seven other explanatory variables generally expected to possess an effect on average inflation. The variable PolStab-98-03 is supposed to measure the degree of political stability or rather political violence in a country.[522] Index averages are based on annual data collected by Kaufmann et al. and were commissioned by the World Bank.[523] According to

---

521 See table 4 in appendix B for detailed descriptions and sources of all employed variables.
522 See table 4 in appendix B for descriptions and sources of all variables employed in these analyses.
523 Cf. Kaufmann et al. (2006).

Cukierman *et al.* political stability possesses a negative influence on inflation, i.e. leads to lower inflation.[524] The variables RuloLaw-98-03, RegQuality-98-03 and GovEffect-98-03 are supposed to measure respectively the degree of the rule of law, the degree of regulatory quality and the degree of government effectiveness prevalent in a country. Index averages are based as well on annual data collected by Kaufmann *et al.*[525] These three variables suggest themselves to possess a negative influence on inflation and are considered here, to find out whether the QEC-index actually measures the quality of eligible collateral or if it represents merely a good instrument to detect different degrees of these three variables, i.e. the rule of law, the degree of regulatory quality and the degree of government effectiveness.[526] The variables LogGDPpc-98-03, GDPpc-98-03 and Status-98-03 are each supposed to represent an overall measure of a country's stage of development. More precisely, GDPpc-98-03 measures average GDP per capita and LogGDPpc-98-03 is the average of the log of GDP per capita. GDP per capita was introduced by Campillo & Miron as a control variable to assess the explanatory power of central bank independence indices and is expected to possess a negative influence on inflation.[527] The log of GDP per capita represents a frequently employed transformation to lessen the influence of extreme values.[528]

The variable Status-98-03 represents a dummy variable with value one for developing countries and zero for high income countries respectively. The variables expected influence on inflation is accordingly positive. The variable Status-98-03 is employed as the most basic measure of a country's stage of development and serves also to subdivide the sample into developing and developed countries. Using the stepwise selection routine to reduce the number of potential explanatory variables, QEC-03-4 and PolStab-98-03 emerge as the sole independent variables to form the model. Their coefficients reveal the expected relationships and are statistically significant while none of the other potential explanatory variables can significantly contribute to explain average inflation over and above that, which is 'explained' by QEC-03-4 and PolStab-98-03.

The models 7a and 7b resemble models 6a and 6b respectively except for the dependent variable: GDPdeflator-98-03 replaces CPI-98-03, i.e. average inflation is measured with the GDP deflator instead of CPI. The results remain virtually unchanged. Average inflation is best explained by the quality of eligible collateral and the degree of political stability. The coefficients significance,

---

524 Cf. Cukierman *et al.* (1992b).
525 Cf. Kaufmann *et al.* (2006). More detailed descriptions of these variables can be found in appendix B, table 4.
526 For the idea for this robustness test the author is indebted to participants of the Brown-Bag-Seminar in the Department of Economics at the University of Kiel in June 2005.
527 Cf. Campillo & Miron (1997).
528 See for example Berger *et al.* (2001) and Campillo & Miron (1997).

however, is very weak due to heteroskedasticity in connection with PolStab-98-03. Models 8a and 8b as well as 9a and 9b replicate the previous four except for the dependent variable: In models 8a and 8b average inflation is measured by the log of the GDP deflator (LogGDPdeflator-98-03) and the log of CPI (Log-CPI-98-03) in models 9a and 9b. The log transformation has often been used in studies on the effect of central bank independence on average inflation and is supposed to lessen the potentially distorting influence of outliers.[529] The results, however, remain again almost unchanged apart from the coefficients' sizes, which are much smaller due to the log transformation. The quality of eligible collateral and the degree of political stability each possess a statistically significant negative effect on average inflation irrespective of the latter's operationalisation. The effect of the QEC-index on average inflation is thus robust to variations in the dependent variable.

Models 10 to 13 all contain CPI-98-03 as dependent variable and QEC-03-4 and LogGDPpc-98-03 as explanatory variables. Furthermore in each of the four models one of the following variables is included: PolStab-98-03, RuloLaw-98-03, RegQuality-98-03 and GovEffect-98-03. These models give an idea of the explanatory power of the QEC-index relative to each of these four variables and GDP per capita without inflating the number of independent variables. A large number of independent variables might raise the probability to encounter undesired side effects like over- or underestimated standard errors and the above mentioned problem of 'arbitrary' results. Model 10 confirms the results of models 6a to 9b, namely that the QEC-index and the degree of political stability both possess a significant negative effect on average inflation while GDP per capita is not significant in this model. The results of models 11 to 13 reconfirm those of models 6a to 10, i.e. QEC-03-4 possesses a statistically significant correlation with average inflation while measures of a country's stage of development (LogGDPpc-98-03), its degree of the rule of law (RuloLaw-98-03), its degree of regulatory quality (RegQuality-98-03) and its degree of government effectiveness (GovEffect-98-03) all cannot significantly contribute to explain average inflation.

The potential effect of central bank losses on average inflation is assessed in model 14. The number of years in which a central bank recorded losses is taken as independent variable while CPI as dependent variable measures average inflation. The result is in favour of chapter three's prediction: In this model central bank losses (#LossespP-98-03) possess a statistically significant positive effect on average inflation. Furthermore, model 15 shows that the quality of eligible collateral correlates significantly with central bank losses. A high quality of eligible collateral thus seems to help in avoiding central bank losses.

529 Cf. Cukierman et al. (1992a).

Models 16a and 16b correspond to models 6a to 9b, i.e. CPI-98-03 is the dependent variable and QEC-03-4 forms part of potential independent variables. With Openness-98-03 one additional control variable is included, which necessitates the exclusion of Bahamas from the sample due to missing data. Openness-98-03 is supposed to measure the degree of a country's openness to trade and represents annual averages of imports of goods and services as percentage of GDP. According to Romer this variable possesses a negative influence on inflation.[530] Again the stepwise selection routine is employed to reduce the number of explanatory variables. The results of models 16a and 16b confirm the previous results: A country's openness to trade does not possess explanatory power regarding average inflation if indices of political stability and the quality of eligible collateral form part of the model. Similarly, model 17 directly shows the nonexistent explanatory power of Openness-98-03 if QEC-03-4 and LogGDPpc-98-03 form part of the model. Thus, the QEC-index' statistical significance is robust to the inclusion of control variables.

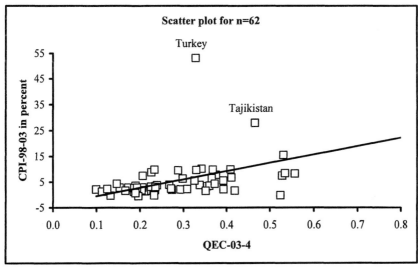

Figure 16: Scatter plot for QEC-03-4 versus CPI-98-03 (n=62)

Figure 16 depicts the scatter plot of QEC-03-4 versus CPI-98-03 for the complete sample. The sample includes three high-inflation countries – Romania, Tajikistan and Turkey feature pronounced above average inflation – that might possess an inadmissibly strong effect on the results presented so far. These three outliers are therefore excluded from the sample. Models 18a and 18b contain

---

530 Cf. Romer (1993).

CPI-98-03 as dependent and QEC-03-4, PolStab-98-03 and GDPpc-98-03 as independent variables to assess the explanatory power of the QEC-index after the exclusion of outliers and in the presence of its strongest explanatory variable rivals. For this task the stepwise selection routine is employed as exercised above. The estimated equations confirm the general result that the quality of eligible collateral and political stability both possess a statistically significant effect on average inflation. The size of coefficients, however, decreases distinctly as the maximum average inflation in the sample drops from more than 50% per year to roughly 15% as is also evident in figure 17. Model 19 reveals that, if the same three variables as before all enter the model, only QEC-03-4 remains weakly significant. If LogGDPpc-98-03 is entered into the model instead of GDPpc-98-03 – as can be seen in model 20 – this renders the QEC-index insignificant. Obviously the three variables are strongly correlated among each other as simple correlation analyses reveal (not shown here).

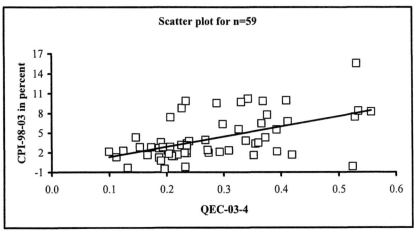

Figure 17: Scatter plot for QEC-03-4 versus CPI-98-03 without Romania, Tajikistan and Turkey (n=59)

The potential effect of central bank losses on average inflation is revisited in model 21. This time, however, with the outlier-adjusted sample of 59 countries. #LossespP-98-03 is again employed as independent variable while CPI-98-03 represents the dependent variable. The result remains in favour of chapter three's prediction: Central bank losses possess a statistically significant positive effect on average inflation. Model 22 shows that QEC-03-3 correlates weakly but significantly with central bank losses. QEC-03-4, however, is not significant anymore if the sample is adjusted for outliers. A high quality of eligible collateral still seems to help in avoiding central bank losses. Nevertheless the robustness of this result is slightly impaired as not all QEC-indices are statistically significant. Regression analyses concerning the main sample are herewith completed. In the following the sample is subdivided into high income countries and less developed countries also referred to as developing countries.

5.1.2 Results for subsamples

The 36 countries that form the sample of developing countries, i.e. those countries that for most of the years between 1998 and 2003 were not considered a high income country by the World Bank, are listed in table 1. Models 23a to 25 all contain the QEC-index and CPI-98-03 as independent and dependent variable respectively. Models 23 a and 23b additionally include all control variables introduced so far apart from Status-98-03 because this binary variable is already used to divide the main sample. Again the stepwise selection routine is employed and the main sample's result prevails. The variables QEC-03-4 and Pol-Stab-98-03 are simultaneously significant. Model 24 confirms these findings though significance levels are weaker if QEC-03-4, PolStab-98-03 and LogGDPpc-98-03 are integrated into the model. In model 25 the sample is again adjusted for the three outliers Romania, Tajikistan and Turkey as figure 18 reveals their potential to cause biased results. The results as well as figure 68 illustrate that the QEC-index remains weakly significant.[531] The variable #LossespP-98-03 is not significant in the sample of developing countries. To sum up, the QEC-index and political stability remain statistically significant and therefore robust predictors of average inflation – albeit with weaker significance levels – among developing countries while losses of central banks lose their predictive power in this sample.

The sample of high income economies consists of 26 countries – see table 1 – and is covered in models 26 to 32. Model 26 is formed by QEC-03-4 and all previously introduced control variables. Using the stepwise selection routine only LogGDPpc-98-03 is considered for the model. Following this analysis, a high per capita GDP in the group of high income countries correlates with low average inflation. However, if GDPdeflator-98-03 is employed as independent variable instead of CPI-98-03 – as implemented in models 27a and 27b – the QEC-index is again part of the model. Model 28 with GDPdeflator-98-03 as dependent and QEC-03-4, PolStab-98-03 and LogGDPpc-98-03 as independent variables confirms this result. Variables, LogGDPpc-98-03 and QEC-98-03, also possess a statistically significant effect on average inflation. Here GDP per capita dominates the QEC-index in the sense that it possesses a greater explanatory

---

531 Other models based on the sample of 33 countries that contain control variables are not listed as none of these satisfied the criterion of a model's minimum statistical significance level of $P = 0.1$.

power in this small sample whereas political stability cannot contribute to the 'explanation' of average inflation.

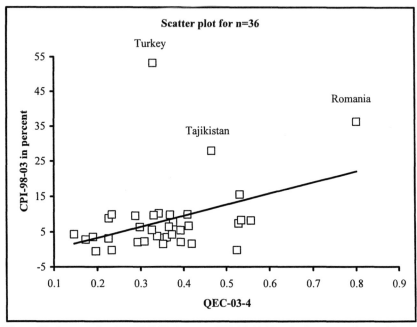

Figure 18: Scatter plot for QEC-03-4 versus CPI-98-03 (developing countries, n=36)

Central bank losses' effect on average inflation is revisited in model 29 for the sample of high income countries. #LossespP-98-03 is again employed as independent variable while GDPdeflator-98-03 represents the dependent one. The result confirms the finding with regard to the main sample: Central bank losses possess a statistically significant positive but rather weak effect on average inflation. Model 30 shows that QEC-03-3 correlates weakly but significantly with central bank losses. QEC-03-4, however, is not significant in this small sample. In this high income countries sample a high quality of eligible collateral seems to help somewhat in avoiding central bank losses. This result is, however, not very robust.

Figures 69 and 19 show the high-income countries sample with and without the outlier Slovenia. Correspondingly model 26 is rerun without Slovenia as model 31, i.e. including all control variables and CPI-98-03 as dependent variable. The QEC-index comes out as the only independent variable included in the model. The result of model 32 confirms this result as QEC-03-4 remains the most significant variable if LogGDPpc-98-03 and PolStab-98-03 enter the model. Thus, the QEC-index and the log of GDP per capita are robust predictors of average inflation among high income countries while central banks losses have only weak predictive power for this sample and political stability loses its.

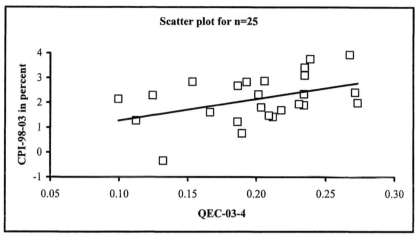

Figure 19: Scatter plot for QEC-03-4 versus CPI-98-03 without Slovenia (n=25)

5.1.3 Summary of results for the period 1998 to 2003

Summarising the regression results for the period 1998 to 2003 it can be stated that the QEC-index is throughout significantly correlated with average inflation. This correlation remains in particular robust

i)   if weightings used for its construction are modified (models 2 to 4) or the variable itself is transformed,[532]

ii)   if average inflation is operationalised employing different measures (models 6a to 9b and 27a to 28),

iii)   if the sample is divided into developing (models 23a to 25) and high income countries (models 26 to 28, 31 and 32),

iv)   if samples are adjusted for outliers (models 18a to 20, 25, 31 and 32) and

v)   if control variables are added to the model (models 6a to 13, 16a to 20, 23a to 24, 26 to 28, 31 and 32). Control variables employed measured the degree of a country's openness to trade, the degree of the rule of law, the degree of government effectiveness, the degree of regulatory quality, the degree of political stability and GDP per capita as an overall measure of a country's stage of development. The latter two variables are the only ones

---

532 The QEC-index has throughout been tested in the transformed form (QEC-03-4)^2, however, without delivering different results with regard to significance levels.

139

contributing to the explanation of average inflation. Political stability is, however, not significant in the subsample of high income countries while GDP per capita is only significant in the sub-sample of high income countries. These two variables possess accordingly no sub-sample validity.

A more technical interpretation of these results along the line of conventional statistics can be specified as follows: The null hypothesis stating that the QEC-Index is not correlated with average inflation in the period between 1998 and 2003 can be rejected. The QEC-Index possesses a statistically significant influence on inflation. The estimated equation of model 5 reads as follows (t-values in parentheses):

$$CPI\text{-}98\text{-}03 = -3.682 + 32.459 \; QEC\text{-}03\text{-}4$$
$$(-1.555) \quad (4.398) \qquad\qquad R^2 = 0.244$$

The QEC-index' coefficient is positive and hence consistent with the theoretical predictions. An index value of 0 represents the highest standards of the quality of eligible collateral while an index value of 1 represents maximum propensity for inflation. A high (low) value of the QEC-index is associated with a low (high) quality of eligible collateral and a high (low) rate of inflation. The constant is negative but not significantly different from zero. Given a QEC-index' value of 0.1 an average inflation of approximately 3.2 percent is to be expected (with the constant set to 0). This corresponds roughly to the observation of Canada (QEC-03-4: 0.10; CPI-98-03: 2.15) and even better if high inflation countries are excluded from the sample (n = 59) with predicted average inflation of 1.6 percent:

$$CPI\text{-}98\text{-}03 = -0.226 + 15.565 \; QEC\text{-}03\text{-}4$$
$$(-0.244 \quad (4.674) \qquad\qquad R^2 = 0.277$$

Models 33 to 35 allow for an interpretation of coefficients as elasticities. The elasticity of average inflation (CPI-98-03 plus 1) with respect to the quality of eligible collateral (QEC-03-4 plus 1) is 0.292, i.e. if the quality of eligible collateral increases by 1% – or equivalently the QEC-index decreases by 1% – average inflation is predicted to decrease by 0.3%. This elasticity increases to roughly 0.4% if only the QEC-index enters the model (model 34). However, assessing these elasticities one has to bear in mind that the logarithmised variables are transformed in order to be able to calculate the log. The elasticity of average inflation (CPI-98-03 plus 1) with respect to political stability (PolStab-98-03 plus 3) is -0.093, in other words, if political stability increases by 1% average inflation is predicted to decrease by 0.1%. The elasticity of average inflation with respect to central bank losses is 0.039 (model 35), i.e. if central bank losses

(#LossespP-98-03 plus 1) decrease by 1% average inflation (CPI-98-03 plus 1) is predicted to decrease by 0.04%.

Overall, the most prominent model to emerge from these regressions looks like model 6b:

$$CPI\text{-}98\text{-}03 = 0.601 + 22.600 \; QEC\text{-}03\text{-}4 - 3.312 \; PolStab\text{-}98\text{-}03$$
$$(\text{-}0.244) \quad (2.796) \qquad\qquad (\text{-}2.517) \quad R^2 = 0.317$$

This indicates that for the period 1998 to 2003 average inflation is best explained by the quality of eligible collateral and political stability.

Therefore, a robust, clearly negative and statistically significant correlation between the quality of eligible collateral and average inflation has been established for the period 1998 to 2003. The effect of central bank losses on average inflation is, however, less robust as significance levels are generally lower and central bank losses possess no explanatory power among the sub-sample of developing countries. Whether these results are robust to changes of the period under consideration is assessed in the following two sections.

5.2 Results of regression analyses for the period 1990 to 1997

The regression results for the period 1990 to 1997 are shown in table 6 and are based on the sample of 56 countries (see table 1). The results of a regression analysis with average inflation (CPI-90-97)[533] as dependent variable and the QEC-index' six constituent parts as independent variables are shown in model 1 of table 6. All variables have the signs that could be expected given hypotheses [H1], [H2] and [H3], though only a few explanatory variables in model 1 are statistically significant. What is more important, however, is that there are several significant correlations among the six constituent parts of the QEC-index. These correlations are presented in table 8 and render the use of these six variables as separate explanatory variables rather improper. Thus, the construction of an index of the quality of eligible collateral to evade the problems associated with multicollinearity is again well-founded.

Models 2 to 5 (see table 6) show results of regressions with CPI-90-97 as dependent and QEC-indices each representing a different weighting of its constituent parts as independent variable. All four QEC-indices possess a positive correlation with average inflation. These results correspond to the predictions made in chapter three, namely that a low (high) standard of eligible collateral – equivalent to high (low) values of the QEC-index – tends to go with high (low) average inflation. A positive correlation between average inflation and the QEC-

---

533 See table 4 in appendix B for detailed descriptions and sources of all employed variables.

index thus implies a negative correlation between average inflation and the quality of eligible collateral. According to the results presented in models 2 to 5 the QEC-index including all six components (QEC-90-4) is best in explaining average inflation followed by QEC-90-2 where CurrencyTA-90-97 is not part of the index as can be seen in table 3. All QEC-indices are, however, statistically significant, which entails that this result is fairly robust to changes of weightings of the QEC-index.

5.2.1 Results for the complete sample

The models 6 to 8 resemble model 5 except for the dependent variable: GDPdeflator-90-97 replaces CPI-90-97 in model 6, i.e. average inflation is measured with the GDP deflator instead of CPI. The result remains virtually unchanged. Average inflation is well explained by the quality of eligible collateral. Models 7 and 8 are again copies of the previous two except for the dependent variable: In models 7 and 8 average inflation is measured by the log of CPI (LogCPI-90-97) and the log of the GDP deflator (LogGDPdeflator-90-97) respectively. The log transformation has often been used in studies on the effect of central bank independence on average inflation and is supposed to lessen the potentially distorting influence of outliers.[534] The results, however, remain again almost unchanged apart from the coefficients' sizes, which are much smaller due to the log transformation. The quality of eligible collateral possesses a statistically significant negative effect on average inflation irrespective of the latter's operationalisation. The effect of the QEC-index on average inflation is therefore robust to variations in the dependent variable.

Model 9 comprises the dependent variable CPI-90-97 as measure of average inflation, the independent variable QEC-90-4 as measure of the quality of eligible collateral as well as other explanatory variables that can generally be expected to possess an effect on average inflation. The variables LogGDPpc-90-97, GDPpc-90-97 and Status-90-97 are each supposed to represent an overall measure of a country's stage of development. More precisely, GDPpc-90-97 measures average GDP per capita and LogGDPpc-90-97 is the average of the log of GDP per capita. GDP per capita was introduced by Campillo & Miron as a control variable to assess the explanatory power of central bank independence indices and is expected to possess a negative influence on inflation.[535] The log of GDP per capita represents a frequently employed transformation to lessen the influence of extreme values.[536]

The variable Status-90-97 represents a dummy variable with value one for developing countries and zero for high income countries respectively. The

---

534 Cf. Cukierman et al. (1992a).
535 Cf. Campillo & Miron (1997).
536 See for example Berger et al. (2001) Campillo & Miron (1997).

variables expected influence on inflation is accordingly positive. The variable Status-90-97 is employed as the most basic measure of a country's stage of development and serves also to subdivide the sample into developing and developed countries. Using the stepwise selection routine to reduce the number of potential explanatory variables, LogGDPpc-90-97 emerges as the sole independent variable to form the model. The coefficient is of the expected sign and statistically significant while none of the other potential explanatory variables can significantly contribute to explain average inflation over and above that, which is explained by LogGDPpc-90-97. If, however, model 9 is reproduced without LogGDPpc-90-97 as explanatory variable – as done in model 10 – the usual result prevails. The quality of eligible collateral possesses a statistically significant negative effect on average inflation while none of the other potential explanatory variables can significantly contribute to explain average inflation over and above that, which is explained by QEC-90-4. The result in model 9 is thus not robust to variations in the measurement of GDP per capita.

In model 11 two further control variables enter the model in addition to QEC-90-4 and GDPpc-90-97: Openness-90-97 and ProblCountry-90-97. The inclusion of Openness-90-97 necessitates the exclusion of Bahamas from the sample due to missing data, the same holds true for ProblCountry-90-97 and the United States respectively. Openness-90-97 is supposed to measure the degree of a country's openness to trade and represents annual averages of imports of goods and services as percentage of GDP. According to Romer this variable possesses a negative influence on inflation.[537] The variable ProblCountry-90-97 measures the likelihood of a state failure and represents averages of annual assessments based on numerous indicators.[538] According to Cukierman et al. political instability possesses a positive influence on inflation.[539] The result of model 11 supports the previous ones, i.e. QEC-90-4 possesses a correlation with average inflation, which, however, is not significant at conventional levels due to heteroskedasticity consistent standard errors. Measures of a country's stage of development (GDPpc-90-97), its degree of openness to trade (Openness-90-97), and its degree of political instability (ProblCountry-90-97) all cannot significantly contribute to the explanation of average inflation.

The potential effect of central bank losses on average inflation is assessed along the lines presented in section 5.1. The result, however, could not be confirmed for the period 1990 to 1997. Central bank losses (#LossespP-90-97) possess no statistically significant effect on average inflation. Furthermore, the quality of eligible collateral does not correlate significantly with central bank losses. A high quality of eligible collateral thus seems unapt to avoid central bank losses in this sample.

---

537 Cf. Romer (1993).
538 Cf. Goldstone et al. (2000).
539 Cf. Cukierman et al. (1992b).

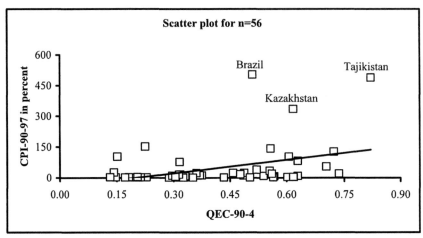

Figure 20: Scatter plot for QEC-90-4 versus CPI-90-97 (n=56)

Figure 20 depicts the scatter plot of QEC-90-4 versus CPI-90-97 for the complete sample. Obviously the sample includes three high-inflation countries – Brazil, Kazakhstan and Tajikistan feature pronounced above average inflation – that might possess an inadmissibly strong effect on the results presented so far. These three outliers are therefore excluded from the sample. Model 12 contains CPI-90-97 as dependent and QEC-90-4, LogGDPpc-90-97 and GDPpc-90-97 as independent variables to assess the explanatory power of the QEC-index after the exclusion of outliers and in the presence of its strongest explanatory variable rivals. The stepwise selection routine is employed as exercised above and the estimated equation confirms the result that the quality of eligible collateral possesses no statistically significant effect on average inflation if the log of GDP per capita forms part of the model. The size of coefficients in models 12 and 13 decreases distinctly as the maximum average inflation in the sample diminishes from more than 500% to roughly 160% as is also evident in figure 21.

Model 14 corresponds to model 9, i.e. CPI-90-97 is the dependent variable while QEC-90-4, GDPpc-90-97, Status-90-97 and LogGDPpc-90-97 potentially form part of the models as independent variables. With Openness-90-97, Probl-Country-90-97, PolStab-90-97 and PolInstab-90-97 four additional control variables are included, which necessitates the exclusion of Bahamas, Cape Verde, ECCB, Iceland, Malta and the United States from the sample due to missing data. The variable PolStab-90-97 measures the degree of political stability in a country and is supposed to possess a negative influence on inflation.[540] While the variable PolInstab-90-97 measures the degree of political instability in a

---

540 Cf. Cukierman *et al.* (1992b).

country and is supposed to possess a positive influence on inflation.[541] The step-wise selection routine is employed. Even after correcting for heteroskedasticity the QEC-index is the sole variable to enter the model, i.e. QEC-90-4 possesses a statistically significant effect on average inflation, whereas none of the other independent variables – including LogGDPpc-90-97 – contributes to the explanation of average inflation.

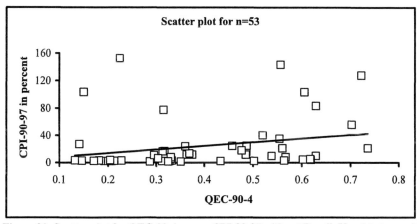

Figure 21: Scatter plot for QEC-90-4 versus CPI-90-97 without Brazil, Kazakhstan and Tajikistan (n=53)

Models 15 and 16 contain CPI-90-97 as dependent variable and QEC-90-4 as well as GDPpc-90-97 and Openness-90-97 as explanatory variables. Furthermore, PolStab-90-97 is included in model 15 and PolInstab-90-97 in model 16. These models give an idea of the explanatory power of the QEC-index relative to each of these four variables without inflating the number of independent variables. A large number of independent variables might raise the probability to encounter undesired side effects like over- or underestimated standard errors and the above mentioned problem of 'arbitrary' results. The results of models 15 and 16 reconfirm those of model 14, i.e. QEC-90-4 possesses a statistically significant correlation with average inflation while measures of a country's stage of development (GDPpc-90-97), its degree of political stability (PolStab-90-97), its degree of political instability (PolInstab-90-97) and its degree of openness to trade (Openness-90-97) all cannot significantly contribute to explain average inflation.

Model 17 is a copy of model 14 except for the sample: The outlier Brazil, Kazakhstan and Tajikistan are excluded. The log of GDP per capita is the only

541 Cf. Cukierman et al. (1992b).

variable to enter the model. The QEC-index does not contribute to the explanation of average inflation. To assess the QEC-index explanatory power relative to other independent variables only model 18 is shown as all other combinations do not result in a significant model. In model 18, however, where QEC-90-4 and ProblCountry-90-97 are included the QEC-index is insignificant due to heteroskedasticity. Therefore, it has to be concluded that in the main sample for the period 1990 to 1997 the QEC-index is not robust to the inclusion of the log of GDP per capita. Yet, it has to be kept in mind that there are only these two variables that have any significant effect on average inflation in this sample: QEC-90-4 and LogGDPpc-90-97. This implies, in turn, that the influence of GDP per capita depends on the log transformation and that LogGDPpc-90-97 is not robust to the inclusion of QEC-90-4. Obviously, small changes in the composition of the sample have strong effects on the presented results.

5.2.2 Results for subsamples

In the following the sample is subdivided into high income countries and those that are not, usually referred to as developing countries. The 39 countries that form the sample of developing countries, i.e. those countries that for most of the years between 1990 and 1997 were not considered a high income country by the World Bank, are listed in table 1. Models 19 to 28 all contain the QEC-index and CPI-90-97 as independent and dependent variable respectively. Model 19 includes in addition four control variables LogGDPpc-90-97, GDPpc-90-97, Openness-90-97 and ProblCountry-90-97. Status-90-97 is not included as this binary variable is used to divide the main sample. Again the stepwise selection routine is employed and the main sample's result prevails. The variable QEC-90-4 possesses a statistically significant effect on average inflation while none of the other variables – including LogGDPpc-90-97 – can contribute to the explanation of average inflation. Models 20 to 22 confirm this, though significance levels are weaker if GDPpc-90-97, Openness-90-97 and ProblCountry-90-97 enter the models directly. After adjusting the sample again for the three outliers Brazil, Kazakhstan and Tajikistan (see figure 22) there is no variable significantly correlated with average inflation.[542] This result is evident in figure 70 for the QEC-index.

Model 19 is reproduced in model 23, which additionally includes the control variables PolStab-90-97 and PolInstab-90-97. This necessitates the exclusion of Cape Verde, ECCB and Malta from the sample due to missing data. Using the stepwise selection routine to reduce the number of potential explanatory variables, QEC-90-4 emerges as the sole independent variable to form the model. Its coefficient reveals the expected relationship and is statistically significant while

---

542 Regression results are not shown as only statistically significant models are displayed.

none of the other potential explanatory variables can significantly contribute to explain average inflation over and above that, which is explained by QEC-90-4. Models 24 to 28 confirm this result: If potential explanatory variables are included directly in the models only the QEC-index is significantly correlated with average inflation. Thus, the QEC-index remains statistically significant and represents therefore a robust predictor of average inflation among developing countries. An adjustment of the developing country sample for outliers, however, reveals that this result depends on the three influential observations of Brazil, Kazakhstan and Tajikistan.

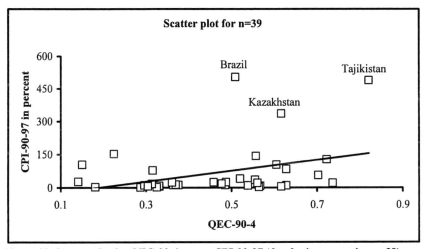

Figure 22: Scatter plot for QEC-90-4 versus CPI-90-97 (developing countries, n=39)

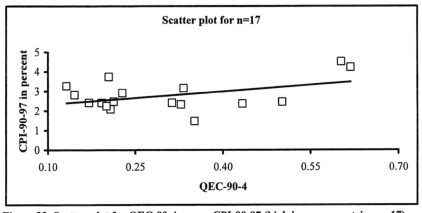

Figure 23: Scatter plot for QEC-90-4 versus CPI-90-97 (high income countries, n=17)

The sample of high income economies consists of 17 countries (see table 1) and is covered in model 29. Model 29 is formed by QEC-90-4 as independent and CPI-90-97 as dependent variable. Variables LogGDPpc-90-97 and GDPpc-90-97 possess no statistically significant effect on average inflation and there are no outliers (see figure 23). Only the QEC-index possesses explanatory power in this small sample of high income countries.

5.2.3 Summary of results for the period 1990 to 1997

Summarising the regression results for the period 1990 to 1997 it can be stated that the QEC-index is throughout significantly correlated with average inflation. In particular this correlation remains robust

i)   if weightings used for its construction are modified (models 2 to 4) or the variable itself is transformed,[543]

ii)   if average inflation is operationalised employing different measures (models 6 to 8),

iii)   if the sample is divided into high income (model 29) and developing countries (models 19 to 28),

iv)   if samples are adjusted for outliers (models 12 and 13 as well as 17 and 18) – only in the case of the developing countries sample adjusted for outliers was the QEC-index not statistically significant – and

v)   if control variables are added to the model (models 9 to 12 and 14 to 28). Control variables employed measured the degree of a country's openness to trade, the degree of political stability and GDP per capita as an overall measure of a country's stage of development. The latter variable is the only one that contributed to the explanation of average inflation. GDP per capita (LogGDPpc-90-97) is, however, not significant in the sub-sample of high income countries. Its effect depends furthermore on the log transformation and is not robust to the inclusion of the QEC-index. GDP per capita possesses thus no sub-sample validity. Both, GDP per capita and the QEC-index, are in various models not robust to the inclusion of the respectively other variable.

An interpretation of these results along statistical criteria can be specified as follows: The null hypothesis stating that the QEC-Index is not correlated with average inflation in the period between 1990 and 1997 can be rejected. The QEC-Index possesses a statistically significant influence on inflation. The estimated equation of model 5 reads as follows (t-values in parentheses):

$$CPI\text{-}90\text{-}97 = -43.574 + 220.600\ QEC\text{-}90\text{-}4$$
$$(-1.284)\quad (2.162)\qquad R^2 = 0.143$$

---

543 The QEC-index has throughout been tested in the transformed form $(QEC\text{-}90\text{-}4)^2$, however, without delivering different results with regard to significance levels.

The QEC-index' coefficient is positive and hence consistent with what was expected. An index value of 0 represents the highest standards to the quality of eligible collateral while an index value of 1 represents maximum propensity for inflation. A high (low) value of the QEC-index is associated with a low (high) quality of eligible collateral and a high (low) rate of inflation. The constant is negative but not significantly different from zero. Given a QEC-index' value of 0.2 an average inflation of approximately 0.5 percent is to be expected. This corresponds roughly to the observation of France (QEC-90-4: 0.20; CPI-90-97: 2.25).

Model 30 allows for an interpretation of the coefficient as elasticity. The elasticity of average inflation with respect to the quality of eligible collateral is 1.301, i.e. if the quality of eligible collateral increases by 1% – or equivalently the QEC-index decreases by 1% – average inflation is predicted to decrease by 1.3%. Therefore, a largely robust, clearly negative and statistically significant correlation between the quality of eligible collateral and average inflation has been established for the period 1997 to 1997. Central bank losses have no effect on average inflation in this period.

5.3 Results of regression analyses for the period 1995 to 1999

The regression results for the period 1995 to 1999 are shown in table 7 and are based on the sample of 46 countries (see table 1). This period was chosen for two reasons: Firstly this period and the reduced sample allow for the inclusion of important control variables such as measures of central bank independence, transparency and accountability. The use of these variables largely determined the period 1995 to 1999 as this is the one deemed most appropriate for the respective data to have a bearing on average inflation.[544] Assessing these concepts' explanatory power relative to the one of the QEC-index is clearly relevant from a policy perspective. Secondly the five years in the centre of the complete time span covered in this survey are thought to offer – in connection with the other two periods examined in the previous sections – a rough but nonetheless informative representation of potential special influences of different years on regression results.

The results of a regression analysis with average inflation (CPI-95-99) as dependent variable and the QEC-index' six constituent parts as independent variables are shown in model 1 of table 7. Qualitative variables that form part of the QEC-index are based on the data for the current framework and are thus identical to the values used for the 2003 framework as this better fits the actual

---

544 Cf. Chortareas et al. (2002b).

frameworks' prevalence in each country.[545] All variables apart from 3.1Creditworth-03 have the sign that could be expected given hypotheses [H1], [H2] and [H3], though none of these explanatory variables in model 1 is statistically significant. What is more important, however, is that there are several significant correlations among the six constituent parts of the QEC-index. These correlations are presented in table 8 and render the use of these six variables as separate explanatory variables rather improper. Thus, the construction of an index of the quality of eligible collateral to evade the problems associated with multicollinearity is once more well-founded.

Models 2 to 5 (see table 7) show results of regressions with CPI-95-99 as dependent and QEC-indices each representing a different weighting of its constituent parts as independent variable. All four QEC-indices possess a positive correlation with average inflation. These results correspond to the predictions made in chapter 3, namely that a low (high) standard of eligible collateral – equivalent to a high (low) value of the QEC-index – tends to go with high (low) average inflation. A positive correlation between average inflation and the QEC-index thus implies a negative correlation between average inflation and the quality of eligible collateral. According to the results presented in models 2 to 5 the QEC-index including all six components, QEC-99-4, is best in explaining average inflation followed by QEC-99-2 where CurrencyTA-95-99 is not part of the index as can be seen in table 3. All QEC-indices are, however, highly statistically significant, which entails that this result is fairly robust to changes of weightings of the QEC-index.

5.3.1 Results for the complete sample

Models 6a and 6b comprise the dependent variable CPI-95-99 as measure of average inflation, the independent variable QEC-99-4 as measure of the quality of eligible collateral as well as eleven other explanatory variables that can generally be expected to possess an effect on average inflation. The variable PolStab-96-98 is supposed to measure the degree of political stability or rather political violence in a country.[546] Index averages are based on annual data collected by Kaufmann et al. and were commissioned by the World Bank.[547] According to Cukierman et al. political stability possesses a negative influence on inflation.[548] The variables RuloLaw-96-98, RegQuality-96-98 and GovEffect-96-98 are supposed to measure respectively the degree of the rule of law, the degree of regu-

---

545 See sections 4.2 and 4.4 for an account of criteria guiding the selection of periods adequate given the collected data on central bank collateral frameworks and their duration.
546 See table 4 for descriptions and sources of all variables employed in these analyses.
547 Cf. Kaufmann et al. (2006).
548 Cf. Cukierman et al. (1992b).

latory quality and the degree of government effectiveness prevalent in a country. Index averages are based as well on annual data collected by Kaufmann *et al.*[549] These three variables suggest themselves to possess a negative influence on inflation and are considered here, to find out whether the QEC-index actually measures the quality of eligible collateral or if it represents merely a good instrument to detect different degrees of these three variables, i.e. the rule of law, the degree of regulatory quality and the degree of government effectiveness.[550]

The variables LogGDPpc-95-99, GDPpc-95-99 and Status-95-99 are each supposed to represent an overall measure of a country's stage of development. More precisely, GDPpc-95-99 measures average GDP per capita and LogGDPpc-95-99 is the average of the log of GDP per capita. GDP per capita was introduced by Campillo & Miron as a control variable to assess the explanatory power of central bank independence indices and is expected to possess a negative influence on inflation.[551] The log of GDP per capita represents a frequently employed transformation to lessen the influence of extreme values.[552] The variable Status-95-99 represents a dummy variable with value one for developing countries and zero for high income countries respectively. The variables expected influence on inflation is accordingly positive. The variable Status-95-99 is employed as the most basic measure of a country's stage of development and serves also to subdivide the sample into developing and developed countries.

A third group of control variables considered in models 6a and 6b are CBIndependence-98-1, CBIndependence-98-2, CBTransparency-98 and CBDeficit-Finance-98. The variables CBIndependence-98-1 and CBIndependence-98-2 are supposed to measure the degree of a central bank's independence from government.[553] Index values for the year 1998 are taken from the dataset on central bank monetary policy frameworks provided by Fry *et al.* and commissioned by the Bank of England.[554] According to Cukierman *et al.* central bank independence possesses a negative influence on inflation.[555] As the data collected by Fry *et al.* do not match exactly those collected by Cukierman *et al.* for the period 1950 to 1989 two different weightings are employed here: CBIndependence-98-1 is the index proposed by Fry *et al.* while in CBIndependence-98-2 weightings are manipulated in order to comply more closely with the ones used in Cukier-

549 Cf. Kaufmann *et al.* (2006). More detailed descriptions of these variables can be found in appendix B, table 4.
550 For the idea for this robustness test the author is indebted to participants of the Brown-Bag-Seminar in the Department of Economics at the University of Kiel in June 2005.
551 Cf. Campillo & Miron (1997).
552 See for example Berger *et al.* (2001) and Campillo & Miron (1997).
553 See table 4 for descriptions and sources of all variables employed in these analyses.
554 Cf. Fry *et al.* (2000).
555 Cf. Cukierman *et al.* (1992a).

man et al.[556] Table 9 in appendix B gives details of central bank independence index' constituent parts and weighting coefficients employed. The variable CBDeficitFinance-98 is supposed to measure the limits on a central bank's financing of the government deficit.[557] The degree with which a central bank finances its government's deficit usually represents a constituent part of indices of central bank independence. CBDeficitFinance-98 s expected influence on inflation is negative according to Fry and Chortareas et al.[558] Finally, the variable CBTransparency-98 is supposed to measure the transparency of a central bank's monetary policy by the detail of policy explanations combined in a Guttman-scale that was proposed by Chortareas et al.[559] According to Geraats and Chortareas et al. central bank transparency possesses a negative effect on inflation.[560]

Using the stepwise selection routine to reduce the number of potential explanatory variables, QEC-99-4 and PolStab-96-98 emerge as the sole independent variables to form the model. Their coefficients reveal the expected relationships and are statistically significant – the statistical insignificance of PolStab-96-98 is due to heteroskedasticity consistent standard errors – while none of the other potential explanatory variables can significantly contribute to explain average inflation over and above that, which is explained by QEC-99-4 and PolStab-96-98.

The models 7a and 7b resemble models 6a and 6b respectively except for the dependent variable: GDPdeflator-95-99 replaces CPI-95-99, i.e. average inflation is measured with the GDP deflator instead of CPI. The results remain virtually unchanged. Average inflation is best explained by the quality of eligible collateral and the degree of political stability. The significance of the coefficient of PolStab-96-98, however, is very weak due to the heteroskedasticity correction. Models 8a and 8b as well as 9a and 9b replicate the previous four except for the dependent variable: In models 8a and 8b average inflation is measured by the log of the GDP deflator (LogGDPdeflator-95-99) and the log of CPI (Log-CPI-95-99) in models 9a and 9b. The log transformation has often been used in studies on the effect of central bank independence on average inflation and is supposed to lessen the potentially distorting influence of outliers.[561] The results, however, remain again almost unchanged apart from the coefficients' sizes, which are much smaller due to the log transformation. The quality of eligible collateral and the degree of political stability each possess a statistically signifi-

556 Cf. Fry et al. (2000) and Cukierman et al. (1992a).
557 Cf. Fry et al. (2000).
558 Cf. Fry (1998) and Chortareas et al. (2002a).
559 Cf. Chortareas et al. (2002a). A Guttman-scale can be thought of as an index the values of which, however, remain interpretable with regard to its constituent parts.
560 Cf. Geraats (2002) and Chortareas et al. (2002a).
561 Cf. Cukierman et al. (1992a).

cant negative effect on average inflation irrespective of the latter's operationalisation. The effect of the QEC-index on average inflation is therefore robust to variations in the dependent variable.

Models 10 to 15 all contain CPI-95-99 as dependent variable and QEC-99-4 and LogGDPpc-95-99 as explanatory variables. Furthermore in each of the six models one of the following variables is included: PolStab-96-98, CBIndependence-98-1, CBIndependence-98-2, CBTransparency-98, CBDeficitFinance-98 and RegQuality-96-98. These models give an idea of the explanatory power of the QEC-index relative to each of these six variables and GDP per capita without inflating the number of independent variables. A large number of independent variables might raise the probability to encounter undesired side effects like over- or underestimated standard errors and the above mentioned problem of 'arbitrary' results. Model 10 confirms the results of models 6a to 9b, namely that the QEC-index and the degree of political stability both possess a negative effect on average inflation – PolStab-96-98 is insignificant due to heteroskedasticity consistent standard errors – while GDP per capita is not significant in this model.

The results of models 11 to 15 reconfirm those of models 6a to 9b, i.e. QEC-99-4 possesses a statistically significant correlation with average inflation while measures of a country's stage of development (LogGDPpc-95-99), a central bank's degree of independence (CBIndependence-98-1 and CBIndependence-98-2), its degree of central bank financing the government's deficit (CBDeficitFinance-98) and a country's degree of regulatory quality (RegQuality-95-99) all cannot significantly contribute to explain average inflation. The only exception is model 13 in which CBTransparency-98 possesses a statistically significant negative effect on average inflation. The degree of transparency in monetary policy explanations therefore contributes to the explanation of average inflation over and above what the quality of eligible collateral offers. Thus the negative correlation found in Chortareas *et al.* between central bank transparency and average inflation is confirmed.

The potential effect of central bank losses on average inflation is assessed along the lines presented in section 5.1. The result, however, could not be confirmed for the period 1995 to 1999. Central bank losses (#LossespP-95-99) possess no statistically significant effect on average inflation. Furthermore, the quality of eligible collateral does not correlate significantly with central bank losses. A high quality of eligible collateral thus seems unapt to avoid central bank losses in this sample.

Models 16 and 17 correspond to models 10 to 15, i.e. CPI-95-99 is the dependent variable while QEC-99-4 and LogGDPpc-95-99 form part of the models as independent variables. With Openness-95-99 and CBAccountability-98 two additional control variables are included, which necessitate the exclusion of Bahamas and Japan respectively from the sample due to missing data. Openness-

95-99 is supposed to measure the degree of a country's openness to trade and represents annual averages of imports of goods and services as percentage of GDP. According to Romer this variable possesses a negative influence on inflation.[562]

Again the stepwise selection routine is employed to reduce the number of explanatory variables. CBAccountability-98 measures the degree of a central bank's accountability vis-à-vis the government.[563] Its expected influence on inflation is negative. The results of models 16 and 17 confirm the previous results: Neither a country's openness to trade nor a central bank's degree of accountability possesses explanatory power regarding average inflation if the quality of eligible collateral forms part of the model. Thus, the QEC-index' statistical significance is robust to the inclusion of control variables.

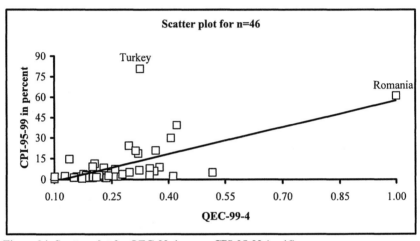

Figure 24: Scatter plot for QEC-99-4 versus CPI-95-99 (n=46)

Figure 24 depicts the scatter plot of QEC-99-4 versus CPI-95-99 for the complete sample of 46 central banks. The sample includes two high-inflation countries – Romania and Turkey feature pronounced above average inflation – that might possess an inadmissibly strong effect on the results presented so far. These two outliers are therefore excluded from the sample. Model 18 contains CPI-95-99 as dependent and QEC-99-4, PolStab-96-98, LogGDPpc-95-99, CBIndependence-98-1, CBIndependence-98-2, CBTransparency-98 and CBDeficitFinance-98 as independent variables to assess the explanatory power of the QEC-index after the exclusion of outliers and in the presence of its strongest ex-

562 Cf. Romer (1993).
563 Cf. Fry *et al.* (2000).

planatory variable rivals. For this task the stepwise selection routine is employed as exercised above. The result of model 18 refutes the previous ones in so far as the only and most significant explanatory variable to enter the model is LogGDPpc-95-99. Thus, no other variable apart from GDP per capita is able to contribute to the explanation of average inflation in this outlier reduced sample. If, however, LogGDPpc-95-99 is removed from the list of potential independent variables – as was done in models 19a and 19b – then estimated equations confirm the result that the quality of eligible collateral and central bank transparency possess statistically significant effects on average inflation. The size of coefficients, however, decreases distinctly as the maximum average inflation in the sample drops from more than 80% per year to less than 40% as is also evident in figure 25.

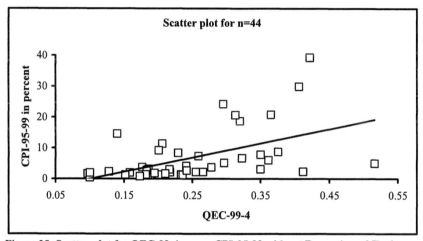

Figure 25: Scatter plot for QEC-99-4 versus CPI-95-99 without Romania and Turkey (n=44)

Models 20 to 22 all contain CPI-95-99 as dependent variable and QEC-99-4 and CBTransparency-98 as explanatory variables. In model 20 PolStab-96-98 is entered to appraise these variables combined explanatory power. Models 21 and 22 contain Openness-95-99 and CBAccountability-98 respectively as these variables did not form part of potential variables in models 19a and 19b due to missing data. Models 20 to 22 give an idea of the explanatory power of the QEC-index relative to these three variables and central bank transparency without inflating the number of independent variables. Models 20 to 22 confirm the results of models 19a and 19b, namely that the QEC-index and the degree of central bank transparency both possess a statistically significant negative effect on average inflation. One has to bear in mind, however, that no variable is able to contribute to the explanation of average inflation delivered by GDP per capita in the outlier reduced sample. In other words, average inflation in the outlier reduced sample is best explained by GDP per capita alone.

5.3.2 Results for subsamples

In the following the sample is subdivided into high income countries and less developed countries also referred to as developing countries. The 25 countries that form the sample of developing countries, i.e. those countries that for most of the years between 1995 and 1999 were not considered a high income country by the World Bank, are listed in table 1. Models 23a to 23c all contain CPI-95-99 as dependent variable and all control variables introduced so far apart from Status-95-99 as this binary variable is used to divide the main sample. Again the stepwise selection routine is employed and the main sample's result prevails. The variables QEC-99-4 and CBTransparency-98 are simultaneously significant while PolStab-96-98 becomes insignificant after correcting for heteroskedasticity. In model 24 the sample is again adjusted for the two outliers Romania and Turkey as figure 71 reveals their potential to cause biased results. Only LogGDPpc-95-99 is considered as explanatory variable since no other variable can significantly contribute to the explanation of average inflation in this sample. This result as well as figure 26 illustrate that the QEC-index becomes statistically insignificant in this outlier adjusted sample. Thus, the QEC-index, central bank transparency and political stability remain statistically significant and therefore robust predictors of average inflation among developing countries. An adjustment of the developing country sample for outliers, however, reveals that this result depends on the two influential observations of Romania and Turkey.

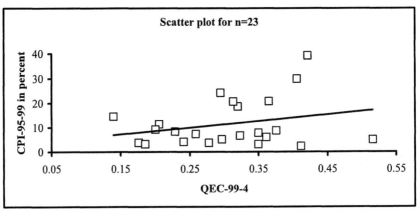

Figure 26: Scatter plot for QEC-99-4 versus CPI-95-99 without Romania and Turkey (n=23)

The sample of high income economies consists of 21 countries (see table 1) and is covered in models 25a to 30. Models 25a and 26b contain QEC-99-4 and most previously introduced control variables: PolStab-96-98, LogGDPpc-95-99, GDPpc-95-99, CBIndependence-98-1, CBIndependence-98-2, RegQuality-96-98, CBTransparency-98 and CBDeficitFinance-98. Using the stepwise selection routine LogGDPpc-95-99 and CBTransparency-98 emerge as best explanation of average inflation, which is measured by CPI-95-99. This result, however, entails a certain drawback as central bank transparency is statistically significant but wrongly signed, which clearly invalidates its contribution to the explanation of average inflation in this case. Thus, a higher per capita GDP in the group of high income countries seems to go with lower average inflation. However, if GDPdeflator-95-99 is employed as independent variable instead of CPI-95-99 – as implemented in models 26a to 26d – the QEC-index is again the variable most strongly correlated with average inflation. This sensitivity of results to different operationalisations of the dependent variable is – as figures 27 and 72 show – obviously due to the increased variance in average inflation measured with the GDP deflator since the dispersion of CPI-95-99 is more compressed than the one of GDPdeflator-95-99 – lowest and highest inflation rates are 0.44% to 2.99% versus -0.49% to 3.86% respectively. Figure 27 and 72 show furthermore that there are no potential unduly influential observations in the high-income sample. There are certain drawbacks to the results of models 26b to 26d as CBTransparency-98 and RegQuality-96-98 are statistically significant but wrongly signed. The quality of eligible collateral and political stability, however, possess a statistically significant negative effect on average inflation in the high-income sample. Model 27 with GDPdeflator-95-99 as dependent and QEC-99-4 and PolStab-96-98 as independent variables confirms this result while political stability is insignificant if LogGDPpc-95-99 is included (see model 28).

Model 29 and 30 replicate model 28 except for the third explanatory variable: LogGDPpc-95-99 is exchanged for Openness-95-99 and CBAccountability-98 respectively that had not been part of any model for the high-income sample. The result confirms the previous ones: Neither a country's openness to trade nor a central bank's degree of accountability possesses explanatory power regarding average inflation if the quality of eligible collateral and political stability form part of the model. Thus, the QEC-index' statistical significance is robust to the inclusion of control variables. The QEC-index and – to a lesser degree – political stability are robust predictors of average inflation among high income countries while GDP per capita has only weak predictive power and central bank transparency loses its.

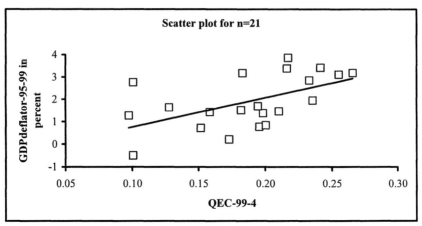

Figure 27: Scatter plot for QEC-99-4 versus GDPdeflator-95-99 (high income countries, n = 21)

5.3.3 Summary of results for the period 1995 to 1999

Summarising the regression results for the period 1995 to 1999 it can be stated that the QEC-index is throughout significantly correlated with average inflation. This correlation remains in particular robust

i) if weightings used for its construction are modified (models 2 to 4) or the variable itself is transformed,[564]

ii) if average inflation is operationalised employing different measures (models 6a to 9b and 26a to 30) – only in the sample of high income countries does the measure of inflation matter,

iii) if the sample is divided into developing (models 23a to 24) and high income countries (models 25 to 30),

iv) if samples are adjusted for outliers (models 18 to 22 and 24) – only in the case of the developing countries sample adjusted for outliers was the QEC-index not statistically significant – and

v) if control variables are added to the model (models 6a to 31). Control variables employed measured the degree of a country's openness to trade, the degree of the rule of law, the degree of government effectiveness, the degree of regulatory quality, a central bank's independence from government, a central bank's accountability and limits on financing the government deficit. Control variables were furthermore central bank transparency the degree of political stability and GDP per capita as an overall measure of

---

564 The QEC-index has throughout been tested in the transformed form $(QEC-99-4)^2$, however, without delivering different results with regard to significance levels.

a country's stage of development. The latter three variables are the only ones that contributed to the explanation of average inflation. Political Stability is, however, not significant in the sub-sample of developing countries while central bank transparency is not significant or possesses a wrongly signed coefficient in the sub-sample of high-income countries. These two variables possess accordingly no sub-sample validity.

A more technical interpretation of these results along the line of conventional statistics can be specified as follows: The null hypothesis stating that the QEC-Index is not correlated with average inflation in the period between 1995 and 1999 can be rejected. The QEC-Index possesses a statistically significant influence on inflation. The estimated equation of model 5 reads as follows (t-values in parentheses):

$$CPI\text{-}95\text{-}99 = -7.812 + 65.196\ QEC\text{-}99\text{-}4$$
$$(-1.978)\quad (5.014)\qquad R^2 = 0.364$$

The QEC-index' coefficient is positive and hence consistent with what was expected. An index value of 0 represents the highest standards to the quality of eligible collateral while an index value of 1 represents maximum propensity for inflation. A high (low) value of the QEC-index is associated with a low (high) quality of eligible collateral and a high (low) rate of inflation. The constant is negative and weakly significant. Given a QEC-index' value of 0.15 an average inflation of approximately 2 percent is to be expected. This corresponds roughly to the observation of Germany (QEC-99-4: 0.15; CPI-95-99: 1.30). If high inflation countries are excluded from the sample (n = 44) predicted average inflation of Japan (QEC-99-4: 0.10; CPI-95-99: 0.44) is -0.02 percent:

$$CPI\text{-}95\text{-}99 = -4.614 + 45.928\ QEC\text{-}99\text{-}4$$
$$(-1.205)\quad (2.509)\qquad R^2 = 0.262$$

Models 31 and 32 allow for an interpretation of coefficients as elasticities. The elasticity of average inflation (CPI-95-99 plus 1) with respect to the quality of eligible collateral (QEC-99-4 plus 1) is 0.633, i.e. if the quality of eligible collateral increases by 1% – or equivalently the QEC-index decreases by 1% – average inflation is predicted to decrease by 0.6%. This elasticity increases to roughly 0.7% if only the QEC-index enters the model (model 32). However, assessing these elasticities one has to bear in mind that the logarithmised variables are transformed in order to be able to calculate the log. The elasticity of average inflation (CPI-95-99 plus 1) with respect to political stability (PolStab-95-99 plus 3) is -0.224, i.e. if political stability increases by 1% average inflation is predicted to decrease by 0.2%. The elasticity of average inflation with respect to central bank transparency is -0.040, i.e. if central bank transparency (CBTransparency-98 plus 1) increases by 1% average inflation (CPI-95-99 plus 1) is predicted to decrease by 0.04%.

Overall, the most prominent model to emerge from these regressions looks like model 6b:

$$CPI\text{-}95\text{-}99 = \underset{(0.638)}{11.892} + \underset{(3.562)}{54.847\ QEC\text{-}99\text{-}4} - \underset{(-2.047)}{2.705\ CBTransparency\text{-}98}$$
$$\underset{(-0.642)}{-\ 1.214\ LogGDPpc\text{-}95\text{-}99} \qquad R^2 = 0.448$$

This indicates that for the period 1995 to 1999 average inflation is best explained by the quality of eligible collateral and central bank transparency. Therefore, a robust, clearly negative and statistically significant correlation between the quality of eligible collateral and average inflation has been established for the period 1995 to 1999. Central bank losses have no effect on average inflation in this period.

5.4 Summary of results for the period 1990 to 2003

The following summarises the regression results for the periods 1998 to 2003, 1990 to 1997 and 1995 to 1999. The overall result of this survey is that the QEC-index is significantly correlated with average inflation. To assess the validity of this result, six different robustness-tests were employed.

i)   The result holds true regardless of the vector of weights used for the QEC-index' elements. Similarly, employing the squared QEC-index has no noteworthy effect on significance levels.

ii)   The dependent variable, average inflation, has been operationalised in a way that corresponds to this paper's research questions as different ways of operationalising the dependent variable had no effect on results. The measure of average inflation matters only in the sample of high income countries for the period 1995 to 1999.

iii)   The results are valid for the main sample as well as for subsamples of high income and developing countries respectively.

iv)   The results depend not unduly on a few influential observations, i.e. there is no outlier problem except for the developing countries samples adjusted for outliers for the periods 1995 to 1999 and 1990-1997.

v)   Additional explanatory variables, i.e. control variables, were incorporated to reveal the explanatory power of the QEC-index relative to other potentially relevant independent variables. In total eleven additional explanatory variables were included in the different regression analyses. These variables measured the degree of a country's openness to trade, the degree of the rule of law, the degree of government effectiveness, the degree of regulatory quality, the degree of political stability, the degree of a central bank's independence from government, the degree of a central bank's accountability, the degree to which the financing of the government deficit by the central bank is limited, the degree of central bank transparency and GDP per capita as an overall measure of a country's stage of development. The QEC-index' statistical significance is robust to the inclusion of all these control variables except for the log of GDP per capita in some samples of the period 1990 to 1997.

vi)   Finally, the result that the QEC-index possesses a statistically significant effect on average inflation is robust to variations of examined periods as significant correlations are found in all three periods, i.e. 1998 to 2003, 1990 to 1997 and 1995 to 1999.

Therefore, a robust, clearly negative and statistically significant correlation between the quality of eligible collateral and average inflation has been established for the period 1990 to 2003. An effect of central bank losses on average inflation could only be detected for the period 1998 to 2003 and even in this period central bank losses possess no explanatory power among the sub-sample of developing countries. However, central bank losses have no effect on average inflation in the periods 1990 to 1997 and 1995 to 1999.

Variables that contribute to the explanation of average inflation over and above that, which is explained by the QEC-index, are political stability, GDP per capita and central bank transparency. Political stability is, however, not significant in the sub-sample of high income countries for the period 1998 to 2003, in the sub-sample of developing countries for the period 1995 to 1999 and in all samples of the period 1990 to 1997. GDP per capita is not significant in the main and in the sub-sample of developing countries for the period 1998 to 2003 and in the sub-sample of high income countries for the period 1990 to 1997. The latter effect depends furthermore on the log transformation, i.e. without this transformation the variable GDP per capita is insignificant. Central bank transparency is not significant or possesses a wrongly signed coefficient in the sub-sample of high-income countries for the period 1995 to 1999. The three variables, political stability, GDP per capita and central bank transparency, possess accordingly no sub-sample validity. Moreover, the correlations of these three variables are in numerous cases not robust to the inclusion of the QEC-index and lack therefore robustness with regard to control variables. Variables that measured the degree of a country's openness to trade, the degree of the rule of law, the degree of government effectiveness, the degree of regulatory quality, the degree of a central bank's independence from government, the degree of a central bank's accountability and the degree to which the financing of the government deficit by the central bank is limited did all not contribute to the explanation of average inflation over and above that, which is explained by the QEC-index.

6 Discussion of regression results

This survey's results provide new evidence on the significance of institutional determinants of inflation. A discussion of these results, however, would be incomplete without reference to what these can deliver and what represents an invalid interpretation of results. In other words, results have to be interpreted with regard to the usual problems of cross-section analyses.[565] The sizes of the samples employed in this regression analysis are sufficiently large to be considered representative – albeit in a narrow sense. Sample sizes between 20 and 62 are nevertheless commonly accepted to be meaningful.[566] Notably developed countries are well represented in the sample for the period 1998 to 2003. To interpret the results in terms of a universal validity seems not indicated though. The sample might be biased in the sense that predominantly those central banks contributed to this survey that recently have had some success in fighting inflation. Moreover, it can generally not be ruled out that the control variables employed managed to deliver only crude measures of what was intended to be measured. These caveats, however, apply to all cross-section analyses – including the literature on institutional determinants of inflation and are thus not unique to this survey.

An additional – though unwarranted – objection might exist with regard to the generation of hypotheses. The accomplished and comparatively simple analysis is, like the theory of Property Economics, not based on a mathematical model. In the economics literature of today, however, a mathematical model of a thesis, as simple as the one that a more transparent monetary policy would be desirable, evidently seems to be some kind of compulsory exercise.[567] In consideration of this fact it must be stressed that, whether a mathematical model of a theory exists or not, cannot be seen as a criterion for methodological invulnerability. Caldwell finds no evidence for the thesis that a theory based on a mathematical model possesses advantages vis-à-vis a verbal analysis except for an appearance that resembles the one of the science par excellence, physics.[568] Blaug criticises an excessive mathematical formalism in today's economics while Boland interprets this as a shift of emphasis in economics away from theses being – at least in principle – empirically confutable to theses being logically

565 Cf. Campillo & Miron (1997) p. 355.
566 Cf. Berger *et al.* (2001) p. 16-25. In their meta-study of empirical surveys on central bank independence the median of sample sizes of 35 reported studies was 19, the average sample size 31, the minimum sample size 9 and the maximum sample size 97.
567 See for example Chortareas *et al.* (2002b).
568 Cf. Caldwell (1991).

invulnerable.[569] An interesting interpretation is delivered by McCloskey who regards mathematical formalism as the rhetoric of modern economists.[570]

According to Popper it is crucial that a theory generates hypotheses, which are at least in principle falsifiable.[571] In the case of the theories of money and central banks, which form major elements of the theory of Property Economics, this clearly applies, taking into account its classification of good creditor's and bad debtor's money. Despite the mentioned caveats the results of this survey shed some new light on the significance of potential determinants of the interrelation between the institutional framework of monetary policy and inflation. The following will illustrate the results' significance with regard to the theory of Property Economics and the current theory of central banking.

6.1 Implications of results for the theory of Property Economics

According to the major result of the previous chapter, there is a robust negative and statistically significant correlation between the quality of eligible collateral and average inflation, which supports the theses of Property Economics. Given an index like the QEC-index it is, other than in the case of, for instance, a Guttman scale, not possible to interpret single index values.[572] The result illustrated in chapter five supports especially hypotheses [H1] and [H2].

[H1] *The collateralisation of a central bank's issuance of money directly limits inflation through the scarceness of eligible assets.*

[H2] *Ensuring the preservation of the principle of creditor's liability in the collateralisation of the issuance of money limits in particular government's demand for credit in such a way that a threat to monetary stability can be ruled out.*

For hypothesis [H1] and the tested samples this indicates that a central bank, which secures its issuance of money, limits its room for an expansionary monetary policy by the scarceness of assets needed for the collateralisation and thereby ultimately limits inflation. Evidence supporting the validity of this interpretation can also be found in the trend of transition countries' inflation rates from the early 1990s. The twelve transition countries in the sample experienced some years of extreme inflation at the beginning of the 1990s and all of these –

---

569 Cf. Blaug (1998) and Boland (1998) respectively.
570 Cf. McCloskey (1983).
571 Cf. Popper (2002) p. 14 ff and chapter IV.
572 Cf. Chortareas *et al.* (2002a) p. 148.

except for Romania and Tajikistan – feature single-digit inflation rates today.[573] These countries are – in this respect – representative of most high-inflation countries in the 1990s that successfully managed to achieve disinflation. Transition countries inflation performance, however, is particularly indicative: Central bank officials in these countries conducted monetary policy for the first time in a capitalist environment at the beginning of the 1990s. Not surprisingly, central bank officials were rather inexperienced, resulting in ill-suited early monetary frameworks: The survey data reveal that often collateralisation of central bank credits was not required at the beginning of the 1990s. Moreover, inflation performances of these countries seem to reflect the trends of learning curves. Slovenia, for instance, adapted very quickly to the new rules of the game and features a low value in the QEC-index, indicating a high quality of eligible collateral, whereas countries like Romania and Tajikistan show a low quality of eligible collateral and still suffer from high inflation.

Suboptimal inflation records, however, might also be due to a lack of developed markets for government bonds. This could explain the inadequate collateralisation of central bank credits observed in many transition countries during the 1990s. Moreover, the pervasive trend that central banks are to a certain extent involved in the development of government debt markets might also represent an attempt to secure an adequate collateralisation of the issuance of money since currency is usually backed by government bonds.[574]

Hypothesis [H2] states that adherence to the principle of creditor's liability with respect to a central bank's issuance of money limits government's demand for central bank credit and thereby eliminates a threat to monetary stability. The results of this survey support this hypothesis. Good stable money must be backed by the property of at least three proprietors: The central bank's property, the commercial bank's property and the property of commercial banks' debtors. The issuance of money is limited by the commercial banks' readiness to accept liability with their property and vis-à-vis the central bank for potential losses accruing from debt instruments issued by commercial banks' debtors that serve as collateral. Especially in the case of government's demand for credit the principle of creditor's liability has to be followed strictly. That is, a counterparty of the central bank must be willing to accept liability with its property vis-à-vis the central bank for the potential losses accruing from debt instruments issued by government before these debt instruments can be accepted as eligible collateral with the central bank. Therefore, government's debt instruments always have to be evaluated on the asset market first. If the principle of creditor's liability is not adhered to, the financing of the government's deficit will – without much doubt – be resolved by printing money.

---

573 These transition countries comprise China, Croatia, Czech Republic, Estonia, Hungary, Kazakhstan, Latvia, Macedonia, Mongolia, Romania, Slovenia, Tajikistan.
574 Cf. Martínez-Resano (2004).

165

To what extent this quality of collateral not only guarantees its scarceness but also protects a central bank from suffering losses is the subject matter of hypothesis [H3].

[H3] *A high quality of eligible assets helps to limit excessive central bank losses and thereby safeguards monetary stability.*

A high standard for eligible collateral helps to prevent excessive central bank losses and thereby shields a currency from the threat of inflation. Evidently, it is not possible here to come to a concluding appraisal of this hypothesis. The evidence for the period 1998 to 2003 is in favour of the hypothesis while no correlation between the frequency of central bank losses and average inflation could be found for the periods 1990 to 1997 and 1995 to 1999.

In case a central bank suffers losses from its granting of credit, e.g. in consequence of a banking crisis, a respective share of the money issued would not be backed by the property of the central bank's debtors. This, in turn, would imply that money circulated, which the central bank could not absorb with the help of collateral designated for that end. Now, given the central bank decided that there was too much liquidity in the market and consequently had to be absorbed, it would have to use its capital and reserves. But even this option would be in vain if losses reached a magnitude that surmounted the central bank's capital resulting in negative capital. In such a case the central bank would have to refrain from absorbing unbacked money since financial help from government usually cannot be counted on.[575] On the contrary, the central bank would be forced to try to replenish its capital through greater profits from an increased issuance of money. In light of this evidence it seems possible, however, that a test of hypothesis [H3] based on more advanced statistical methods could deliver conclusive results.

The hypotheses [H1] and [H2] are interpreted here as being in line with the results of this survey. The corroboration of hypothesis [H1] highlights the importance of a collateralisation of the issuance of money and the associated scarceness of eligible assets that limits inflation. Hypothesis [H2] additionally puts the quality of eligible collateral at centre stage. The readiness of a central bank's counterparty to accept liability with its property for potential losses of a not self-issued debt instrument pledged to the central bank as collateral represents the pivotal quality of an eligible asset. If this quality is missing, i.e. government possesses the option of using its own self-issued debt instruments as collateral to acquire credit directly from the central bank, the scarceness of eligible assets existing under normal circumstances is eliminated. As highlighted by the corroboration of [H1] it is exactly the fixation of the issuance of money to

---

575 See the literature reviewed in section 2.3.

an anchor that is not arbitrarily augmentable and thus scarce, i.e. collateral representing scarce property, which would be eliminated if government had the option to directly pledge self-issued debt instruments to the central bank. This is due to the fact that debt instruments, i.e. the issuance of claims against oneself, are in principle infinitely augmentable. The scarceness of debt instruments cannot be secured by the issuers of such titles but only by those who buy these titles on the asset market. That is the reason why all collateral and especially the one originally issued by government must take the scarceness guaranteeing loop way across the asset market. However, the standards for the quality of eligible collateral go still one step further: The marketability of an eligible asset alone, i.e. the existence of a potential buyer for that asset, is not sufficient to guarantee a genuine anchor for the issuance of money. The quality of an eligible asset consists in the readiness of its buyer to accept liability for potential losses from an asset, the occurrence of which generally cannot be influenced by the buyer. Therefore, good central bank money, creditor's money, is based on the property of liable creditors. Given this surveys result it has to be concluded that only Property Economics' creditor's money can guarantee monetary stability. Thus, it can be stated that the theory of Property Economics has successfully passed this test. The next section provides an interpretation of regression results with regard to the central banking literature.

6.2 Implications of results for the theory of central banking

There exists a broad consensus in the central banking literature on the overriding objectives of a central bank. There is also a consensus concerning the institutional framework that should be in place to ensure the achievement of those objectives: a stable financial system and monetary stability.[576] Central banks ought to be independent and follow a transparent monetary policy. The empirical evidence supporting this latter consensus (see section 2.1), however, is rather weak: The reported correlations between central bank independence and inflation are typically not robust to the inclusion of control variables and periods covered – if such correlation is found at all. The most influential surveys, e.g. by Cukierman et al., suggesting that central bank independence possesses an effect on inflation did not test for the robustness of their results.[577] The evidence on the missing robustness of these surveys' results is substantial.[578] Surveys on the effects of central bank independence cover only the period 1950 to 1995. More recent data to test for the effect of central bank independence on inflation exist, but are surprisingly either not used to test for effects on inflation or are ignored as in the

576 See the literature reviewed in section 2.1.
577 Cf. Cukierman et al. (1992a). See also Alesina & Summers (1993).
578 Cf. inter alia Fujiki (1996), Fuhrer (1997) and Campillo & Miron (1997).

case of the most comprehensive survey on monetary policy framework characteristics to date.[579] Therefore, the current consensus on the institutional framework of central banks' independence and transparency has to be regarded as not well-founded.

The results of this survey represent further evidence on the influence of the institutional framework of monetary policy on inflation. Three variables have been found to contribute to the explanation of average inflation over and above that, which is explained by the QEC-index: Political stability, GDP per capita and central bank transparency. The results of Cukierman et al. concerning political stability's negative effect on inflation are thus confirmed.[580] This statement needs to be qualified, however, as political stability is neither significant in several of the sub-samples tested nor consistently robust to the inclusion of the QEC-index. Nevertheless, political stability can be regarded as one of the determinants of inflation alongside the quality of eligible collateral.

The effect of central bank transparency on average inflation could only be assessed for the period 1995 to 1999 due to data constraints. The results of Chortareas et al. are largely confirmed, i.e. central bank transparency possesses a significant negative effect on average inflation.[581] Again, however, this result is not very robust as central bank transparency possesses neither sub-sample validity nor is it consistently robust to the inclusion of the QEC-index. Nonetheless, central bank transparency can be regarded as one of the determinants of inflation alongside the quality of eligible collateral since it was only possible to use roughly half of the data provided in Fry et al. and used by Chortareas et al.[582]

GDP per capita is found to possess a negative effect on average inflation, which largely confirms the results of Campillo & Miron.[583] This result is, however, not robust to the inclusion of the QEC-index and lacks sub-sample validity. Moreover, the main result concerning GDP per capita crucially depends on the log transformation. Despite these caveats, the strong influence of variables measuring the degree of a country's stage of development, like GDP per capita, on inflation during the 1990s represents a novelty in the literature on central

---

579 Cf. Arnone et al. (2006b) as well as Fry et al. (2000). The two comprehensive reviews on central bank independence, Berger et al. (2001) and Arnone et al. (2006a) do not even mention the Bank of England's survey by Fry et al. (2000), which covers almost 100 central banks.

580 Cf. Cukierman et al. (1992b). It has to be mentioned here that the index of political instability employed in this survey does not measure the same construct as the one used in Cukierman et al. Notwithstanding, a strong correlation between the two indices of political instability can be assumed. See Kaufmann et al. (2006) and Goldstone et al. (2000).

581 Cf. Chortareas et al. (2002b).

582 Cf. Fry et al. (2000) and Chortareas et al. (2002b).

583 Cf. Campillo & Miron (1997).

banking. Developed countries and especially the Euro-area have recently been very successful in fighting inflation with rates between zero and four percent. The same holds true of most developing countries in this sample where inflation is only slightly higher (up to ten percent). This difference, however, is, due to the homogeneity in each group regarding inflation rates, sufficient to bring about a significant effect of a country's stage of development on inflation measured by GDP per capita and even the dummy variable Status.

Variables that measured the degree of the rule of law, the degree of government effectiveness, the degree of regulatory quality and the degree of a central bank's independence from government did not contribute to the explanation of average inflation over and above that, which is explained by the QEC-index. The results strengthen the position of those who doubt that central bank independence is the key to monetary stability.[584] Furthermore, the findings of this survey challenge the result of Romer regarding the negative effect of openness on inflation.[585] The variable measuring a country's openness to trade is, just like central bank independence, not robust to the inclusion of control variables like the QEC-index, indices of political stability and GDP per capita. Based on the results of this survey the negative correlation between inflation and central bank independence as established by Alesina & Summers as well as Cukierman *et al.* can therefore not be confirmed.[586] Given the unambiguity of results it even seems prudent to regard the thesis that central bank independence possesses a negative effect on average inflation as refuted by the data for the years 1990 and at least until 2003.

Finally, it should be kept in mind when assessing these results that apart from central bank transparency and the quality of eligible collateral no institutional variable with a demonstrated effect on inflation remains that can be regarded as a potentially adjustable parameter. All other variables have either been shown not to possess any significant effect on inflation or cannot really be regarded as parameters adjustable for the purposes of monetary stability, like political stability and the level of GDP per capita. After all, nobody would want to argue that, for instance, political stability was desirable first and foremost because it possesses a negative effect on inflation.

One might object that both the central bank independence index of Cukierman *et al.* and the QEC-index used in this survey derive a considerable part of their variance from the criterion, whether government is allowed to borrow from the central bank or not.[587] Obviously, the general problem is identified and attempted to be measured by both indices. The Cukierman *et al.* index' criterion of government borrowing, however, fails in most cases to grasp the problem that

---

584 See, for instance, Posen (1998) or Fuhrer (1997).
585 Cf. Romer (1993).
586 Cf. Alesina & Summers (1993) and Cukierman *et al.* (1992a).
587 Cf. Cukierman *et al.* (1992a).

ultimately brings about the practice of 'printing money'. If a government is allowed to borrow directly from the central bank, is an issue of minor importance, since there might exist a less obvious but nonetheless efficient channel through which government could gain access to central bank credit. This channel would be open, for instance, if a central bank's counterparty is linked to a public entity and is allowed to pledge debt titles issued by that public entity which are not traded on the asset market, i.e. nonmarketable assets.[588] The crucial criterion, therefore, is not whether direct government access to central bank credit is explicitly ruled out or not, but if the credit in question is collateralised with scarce property. That is, whether central bank credit is collateralised with infinitely augmentable IOU notes or debt titles that have been bought on the asset market. This criterion is employed in the QEC-index and rules out both direct and indirect government access to central bank credit. Thus, the criterion employed in the Cukierman *et al.* index cannot be seen as measuring the same construct as was attempted in this survey regarding the second hypothesis [H2].

A bold interpretation of this survey's results would be to claim that an issuance of money only on the basis of good collateral ultimately amounts to a rule bound monetary policy. Such a view would help to renew the fame of Kydland and Prescott's thesis but it ignores that monetary policy with a given rate of interest does not entail a fully elastic supply of money.[589] A central bank usually announces the discount rate and issues money in tender operations according to quotas decided beforehand.[590] Insofar there exists a rather discretionary monetary policy regime even if the money issue is adequately collateralised, but of course only with regard to issuing less than what is demanded.

A last point to note is that the findings of the literature on collateral (see subsection 2.4.2) are somewhat inadequate with regard to the collateralisation of central bank credits. The microeconomic literature on collateral considers collateral only in some cases as an optimal ingredient of credit contracts and, if it does so, thinks of external collateral. By contrast, in this dissertation full collateralisation of all central bank credits is shown to represent best practice with regard to monetary stability. In addition, commercial banks pledge only internal collateral to the central bank. Central banks, however, do not demand internal collateral to be able to enforce their claims first in case of default since central banks credit contracts commonly rank the creditor central bank first in this respect.

---

588 In a German example such link of central bank counterparty and public entity would correspond to a Landesbank and the respective Bundesland. Cf. Heinsohn & Steiger (2002).

589 Cf. Steiger (2006b).

590 Cf. for instance ECB (2005).

7 Summary and conclusion

This dissertation provides an answer to the question if and to what extent the quality of a central bank's eligible collateral is able to explain inflation. The motivation for this endeavour has been to provide a first systematic empirical test of the theory of Property Economics. The literature following Kydland and Prescott on institutional determinants of monetary stability has been reviewed as well as the literature on a central bank's raison d'être, on causes of and remedies for central bank losses, on collateral in economic analyses and on the neoclassical theory of money. None of these strands of economic literature has anything to say on the quality of eligible collateral while the findings of the literature on collateral are shown to be completely at odds with central bank practice. Property Economics' theory of money and central banking has been explained and on its basis three hypotheses have been formulated.

Data on the quality of eligible collateral and central bank losses have been collected employing an online questionnaire answered by central bank officials.[591] With these data the dissertation delivers the first comprehensive dataset suitable for assessing the significance of central bank losses and the quality of eligible collateral for monetary stability. Overall, data for 62 countries were gathered and combined in an index of the quality of eligible collateral (QEC-index). The influence of the QEC-Index on inflation has been examined using OLS regression analysis. For the period 1990 to 2003 a robust negative and statistically significant correlation between the quality of eligible collateral and average inflation has been found. This result has in particular been shown to be robust to the use of control variables from the literature on institutional determinants of monetary stability.

The results of this survey enhance the evidence on the influence of the institutional framework of monetary policy on inflation. This survey's findings have to be regarded as establishing the quality of eligible collateral as one pivotal element of a theory of central banking. Collateralisation of the issuance of money and the elimination of financing the government deficit directly via the central bank can be seen as necessary conditions for achieving monetary stability. The crucial quality of eligible collateral consists in the readiness of a central bank's counterparty to accept liability with its property vis-à-vis the central bank for potential losses stemming from pledged assets. This quality of eligible collateral guarantees that money is fixed most tightly to its property base. Good central bank money should therefore be backed by the liable property of credi-

---

591 The survey of Berger *et al.* (2001) clearly reveals that the generation of new data for testing hypotheses is rather an exception in the empirical literature on the theory of central banks.

tors to safeguard monetary stability. This finding can be utilized by policy makers especially in less-developed and transition countries on their way towards a more stable economic development. In addition, adapting monetary policy frameworks accordingly would represent a rather minor reform compared to the time and effort necessary to make a central bank independent from government. Given the robustness of the available results, further research on eligible collateral seems promising. In any case it can be stated that the theory of Property Economics has successfully passed the first comprehensive empirical test.

Moreover, it has been argued that a high standard for eligible collateral helps to prevent excessive central bank losses and thereby shields a currency from the threat of inflation. The theory of Property Economics has been shown to be consistent with this thesis, whereas the literature following Kydland and Prescott so far ignores the phenomenon of central bank losses. The evidence on the effect of central bank losses, however, is inconclusive. A high quality of eligible collateral has been found to be negatively correlated with the frequency of central bank losses and at the same time central bank losses have been shown to be positively correlated with average inflation. Yet, this finding holds true only for the sub-period 1998 to 2003.

The recent crisis of the international banking system in July and August 2007 has shown that the quality of eligible collateral is a current and most eminent issue.[592] In the course of this liquidity crisis central banks all over the world were forced to act as lender of last resort.[593] The crisis had been triggered by the default of so called subprime mortgages, i.e. credits to low income individuals who have no capital.[594] Alarmingly, the Fed felt forced to accept mortgage-backed securities as collateral for its emergency credits.[595] Thus, the Fed accepted assets as collateral that are based on those that had triggered the crisis. Whether such collateralisation still deserves its name seems questionable.[596] The Fed's behaviour, however, reveals that the quality of eligible collateral is still not fully understood even by central bankers.

Finally, this survey's results strengthen the evidence on the influence of central bank framework characteristics on monetary stability. Central bank independence and transparency represents the consensus in the literature following Kydland and Prescott. This consensus is shown to stand on shaky ground. Since the results of this survey show that the quality of eligible collateral 'trumps' all

---

592 Cf. Economist (2007a).
593 The ECB, for instance, injected more liquidity into the market on August 9th 2007 alone than it did after the terrorist attacks of September 11th 2001. Cf. Economist (2007c).
594 Cf. Heinsohn & Steiger (2007b) p. 216-218.
595 Cf. Economist (2007c).
596 Heinsohn & Steiger (2007b) make clear that mortgage-backed securities should never be considered as eligible collateral.

alternative explanations of average inflation. Notably, this finding holds true regarding the evidence on central bank independence.

The theory of Property Economics as an alternative to neoclassical General Equilibrium theory provides a variety of hypotheses awaiting further critical review and empirical tests. In light of the inconclusive evidence on the effect of central bank losses on inflation it seems worthwhile to make use of panel data. A test based on such data might deliver conclusive results. Such test and corresponding results would represent a crucial step ahead on the way to the crest of the theory of central banking.

Appendix A

Questionnaire on Eligible Collateral

The following questions are organized under five headings. The major part of the questions will ask for information regarding the current framework of your central bank as well as the framework of 1990 or an alternative year, on which you can provide information, possibly close to 1990. The answering of the questions should not take more than 30 minutes. Any additional information and comments are welcome. If you have questions, please feel free to contact us: lehmbecker@uni-bremen.de.

1 Basic information

1.1 If you were to categorise your monetary policy framework as one of the following, would you describe your framework as: (Please tick)

Targeted variable	Current framework	Framework of 1990 or other 19☐ ☐
Money targeting	☐	☐
Inflation targeting	☐	☐
Discretionary	☐	☐
Exchange rate targeting	☐	☐
Balance of payments targeting	☐	☐
Other (please specify)	☐	☐
Cannot be summarised as targeting one variable	☐	☐
Please provide details for current framework:		
Please provide details for framework of 1990 or another year:		

Please note: If you do not have information on the framework of 1990, please provide information for an alternative year close to 1990 and state for which year you provide information.

1.2 Since when are the current terms and conditions of your central bank on eligible collateral for monetary policy operations valid? (Please enter year)

☐☐☐☐

1.3 How many times have the guidelines on eligible collateral been changed since 1990?

```
┌─────────────┐
│             │
└─────────────┘
```

2 Quality of eligible assets

2.1 Does your central bank provide liquidity if the receiving institution is not pledging sufficient collateral to secure the credit, e.g. for short-term liquidity shortages? (Please tick)

Current framework:	Framework of 1990 or other 19☐ ☐
Yes ☐ / No ☐	Yes ☐ / No ☐

2.2 Does your central bank provide advances (non-collateralized lending) to the government? (Please tick)

Current framework:	Framework of 1990 or other 19☐ ☐
Yes ☐ / No ☐	Yes ☐ / No ☐

2.3 Does your central bank accept assets as collateral from institutions that are the issuers of those assets? That is, do issuers of assets that would be accepted as collateral have the right to pledge these assets as collateral? (Please tick)

Current framework:	Framework of 1990 or other 19☐ ☐
Yes ☐ / No ☐	Yes ☐ / No ☐

2.4 Does your central bank accept assets as collateral from institutions that have close ties with the issuers of those assets? (Please tick)

Current framework:	Framework of 1990 or other 19☐ ☐
Yes ☐ / No ☐	Yes ☐ / No ☐

2.5 Which assessment procedure or assessment criteria are used to evaluate those assets accepted as collateral? (Please tick)

Assessment procedure / criteria to evaluate accepted collateral	Current framework	Framework of 1990 or other 19☐☐
Evaluation always with lowest value	☐	☐
Evaluation with market value	☐	☐
Evaluation with market value and evaluation haircuts	☐ minimum haircut ☐ % maximum haircut ☐ %	☐ minimum haircut ☐ % maximum haircut ☐ %
If other procedure / criteria under current framework, please specify:		
If other procedure / criteria under framework of 1990 or another year, please specify:		

2.6 What is the minimum percentage eligible collateral has to satisfy relative to an amount of credit? That is, what is the minimum sufficient cover? (Please tick)

Minimum sufficient cover	Current framework	Framework of 1990 or other 19☐☐
No backing by collateral needed	☐	☐
Less than 50% of the amount of credit	☐	☐
50% or more of the amount of credit	☐	☐
100% of the amount of credit	☐	☐
More than 100% of the amount of credit	☐	☐

3 Creditworthiness

3.1 Which is the minimum degree of creditworthiness that issuers of assets eligible as collateral at your central bank have to satisfy?

Issuer's degree of creditworthiness		Current framework	Framework of 1990 or other 19☐☐
Standard & Poor's	Moody's		
AAA / most creditworthy	Aaa	☐	☐
AA / highly creditworthy	Aa	☐	☐
A / creditworthy	A	☐	☐

177

BBB / less creditworthy but investment-grade	Baa	☐	☐
BB / low-risk speculative	Ba	☐	☐
B / moderate-risk speculative	B	☐	☐
C / high-risk speculative	C	☐	☐
None		☐	☐

3.2 Which is the minimum degree of creditworthiness that eligible counterparties that pledge collateral to your central bank have to satisfy?

Counterparty's degree of creditworthiness		Current framework	Framework of 1990 or other 19☐☐
Standard & Poor's	Moody's		
AAA / most creditworthy	Aaa	☐	☐
AA / highly creditworthy	Aa	☐	☐
A / creditworthy	A	☐	☐
BBB / less creditworthy but investment-grade	Baa	☐	☐
BB / low-risk speculative	Ba	☐	☐
B / moderate-risk speculative	B	☐	☐
C / high-risk speculative	C	☐	☐
None		☐	☐

4 Capital and reserves

4.1 What was the amount of bad debts as percentage of the total amount of credits granted by your central bank in each year?

Bad debts as percentage of credits granted				
2003	2002	2001	2000	1999
1998	1997	1996	1995	1994
1993	1992	1991	1990	

4.2 Please complete the following balance sheets for your central bank.

Please feel free to choose a convenient unit of measurement and use this unit for all of the balance sheet entries.

Balance sheets for the years 2003 to 1990					
Assets	2003	2002	Liabilities	2003	2002
Gold and gold receivables			Banknotes in circulation		
Foreign assets			Liabilities in domestic currency		
Claims on government			Liabilities in foreign currency		
Claims on domestic banks			Provisions for possible losses		
Other assets			Other liabilities		
Total assets			Revaluation accounts		
			Capital and reserves		
			Total liabilities		
Loss for the year			Profit for the year		
Major reason(s) for loss			Major reason(s) for profit		

Please note: If your central bank provides the information asked for in this table, i.e data on balance sheets and profits and losses for the years 1990 to 2003, on its homepage and in English language, please provide the corresponding link(s) here:
Otherwise, please complete the following tables as well.

179

180

Balance sheets for the years 2001 to 1999

Assets	2001	2000	1999	Liabilities	2001	2000	1999
Gold and gold receivables				Banknotes in circulation			
Foreign assets				Liabilities in domestic currency			
Claims on government				Liabilities in foreign currency			
Claims on domestic banks				Provisions for possible losses			
Other assets				Other liabilities			
Total assets				Revaluation accounts			
				Capital and reserves			
				Total liabilities			
Loss for the year				Profit for the year			
Major reason(s) for loss				Major reason(s) for profit			

Balance sheets for the years 1998 to 1996

Assets	1998	1997	1996
Gold and gold receivables			
Foreign assets			
Claims on government			
Claims on domestic banks			
Other assets			
Total assets			
Loss for the year			
Major reason(s) for loss			

Liabilities	1998	1997	1996
Banknotes in circulation			
Liabilities in domestic currency			
Liabilities in foreign currency			
Provisions for possible losses			
Other liabilities			
Revaluation accounts			
Capital and reserves			
Total liabilities			
Profit for the year			
Major reason(s) for profit			

Balance sheets for the years 1995 to 1993

Assets	1995	1994	1993	Liabilities	1995	1994	1993
Gold and gold receivables				Banknotes in circulation			
Foreign assets				Liabilities in domestic currency			
Claims on government				Liabilities in foreign currency			
Claims on domestic banks				Provisions for possible losses			
Other assets				Other liabilities			
Total assets				Revaluation accounts			
				Capital and reserves			
				Total liabilities			
Loss for the year				Profit for the year			
Major reason(s) for loss				Major reason(s) for profit			

182

Balance sheets for the years 1992 to 1990

Assets	1992	1991	1990	Liabilities	1992	1991	1990
Gold and gold receivables				Banknotes in circulation			
Foreign assets				Liabilities in domestic currency			
Claims on government				Liabilities in foreign currency			
Claims on domestic banks				Provisions for possible losses			
Other assets				Other liabilities			
Total assets				Revaluation accounts			
				Capital and reserves			
				Total liabilities			
Loss for the year				Profit for the year			
Major reason(s) for loss				Major reason(s) for profit			

4.3 In each of the following years, what was the amount of profits transferred to government (Please indicate transfers received from government with a minus)?

Profits transferred to government				
2003	2002	2001	2000	1999
1998	1997	1996	1995	1994
1993	1992	1991	1990	

5 Publications and address

5.1 Which publication/act/law contains the relevant guidelines on eligible collateral?

5.2 Please provide your central bank's official title.

5.3 Please provide your email address if you are interested in the results of our survey.

Fax: + 49 421 218 4336

Email: lehmbecker@uni-bremen.de

We thank you very much for your time and effort.

184

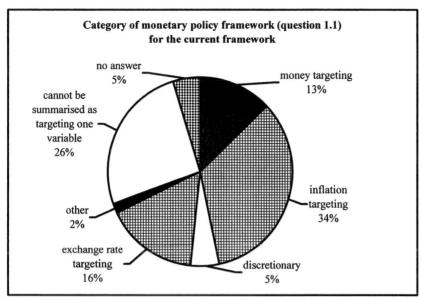

Figure 28: Distribution of answers to question 1.1 for the current framework

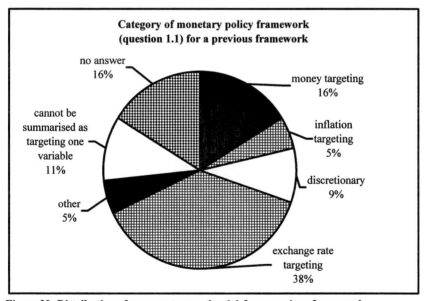

Figure 29: Distribution of answers to question 1.1 for a previous framework

185

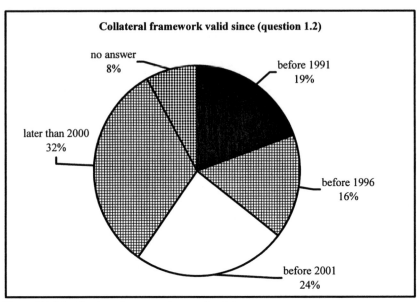

Figure 30: Distribution of answers to question 1.2

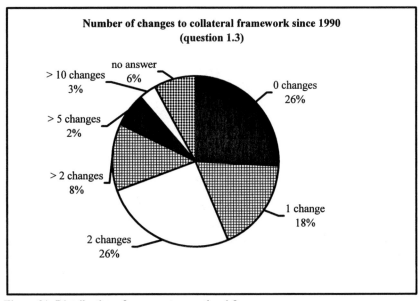

Figure 31: Distribution of answers to question 1.3

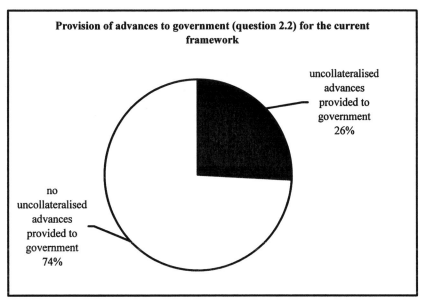

Figure 32: Distribution of answers to question 2.2 for the current framework

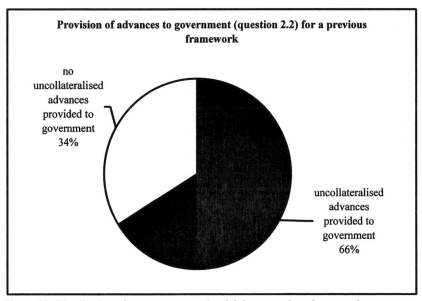

Figure 33: Distribution of answers to question 2.2 for a previous framework

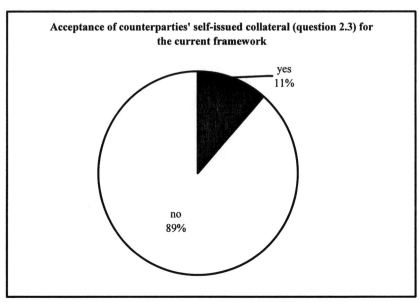

Figure 34: Distribution of answers to question 2.3 for the current framework

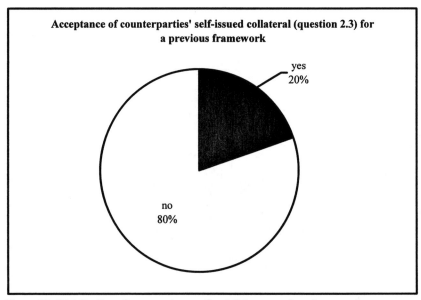

Figure 35: Distribution of answers to question 2.3 for a previous framework

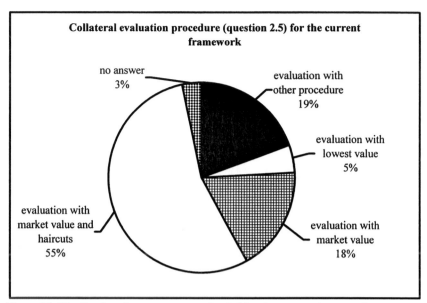

Figure 36: Distribution of answers to question 2.5 for the current framework

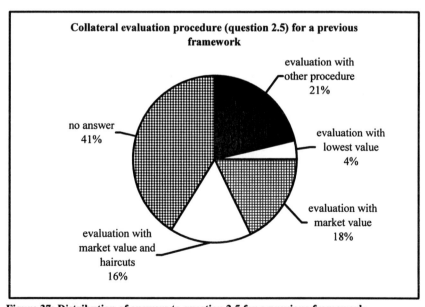

Figure 37: Distribution of answers to question 2.5 for a previous framework

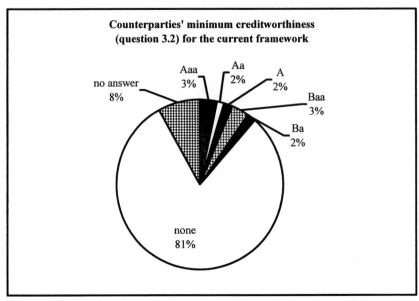

Figure 38: Distribution of answers to question 3.2 for the current framework

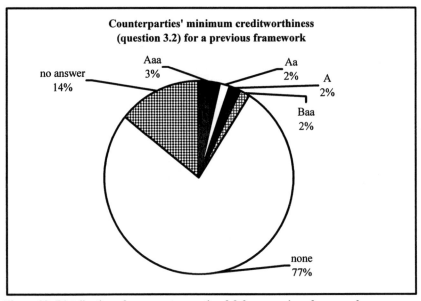

Figure 39: Distribution of answers to question 3.2 for a previous framework

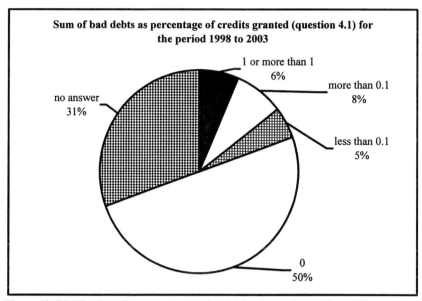

Figure 40: Distribution of answers to question 4.1 for the period 1998 to 2003

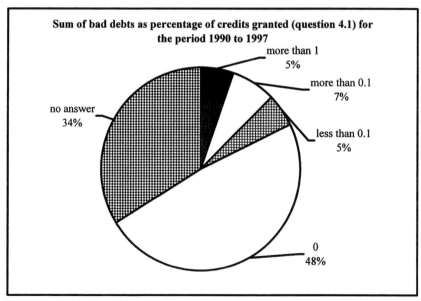

Figure 41: Distribution of answers to question 4.1 for the period 1990 to 1997

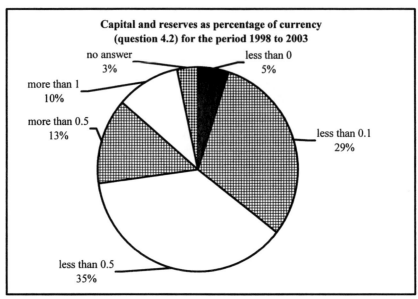

Figure 42: Distribution of answers to question 4.2 for the period 1998 to 2003

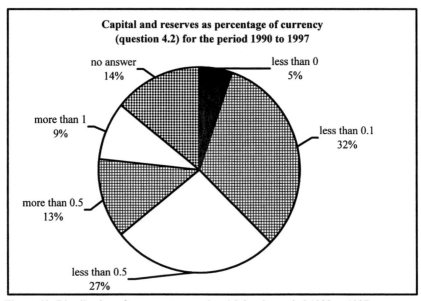

Figure 43: Distribution of answers to question 4.2 for the period 1990 to 1997

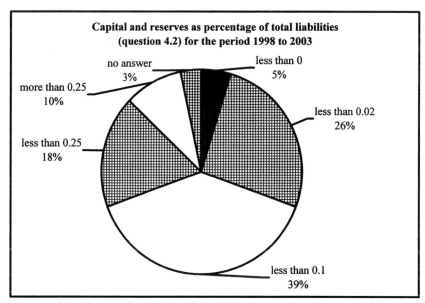

Figure 44: Distribution of answers to question 4.2 for the period 1998 to 2003

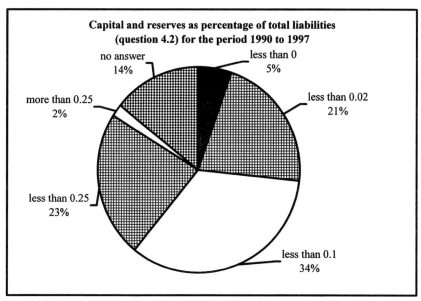

Figure 45: Distribution of answers to question 4.2 for the period 1990 to 1997

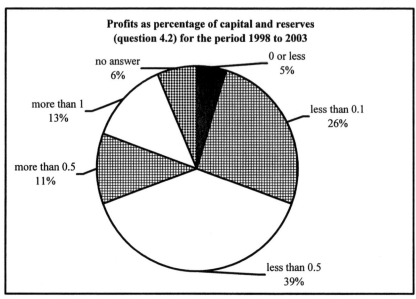

Figure 46: Distribution of answers to question 4.2 for the period 1998 to 2003

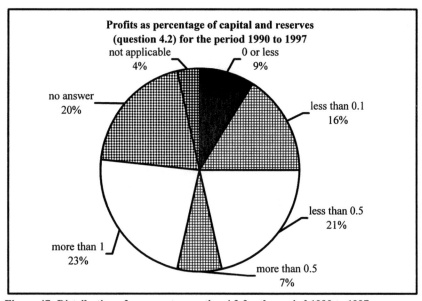

Figure 47: Distribution of answers to question 4.2 for the period 1990 to 1997

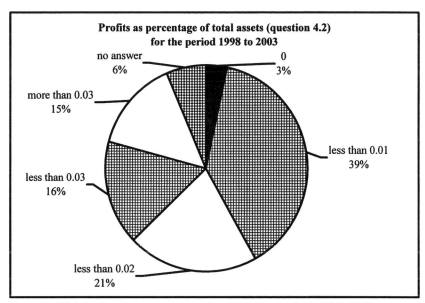

Figure 48: Distribution of answers to question 4.2 for the period 1998 to 2003

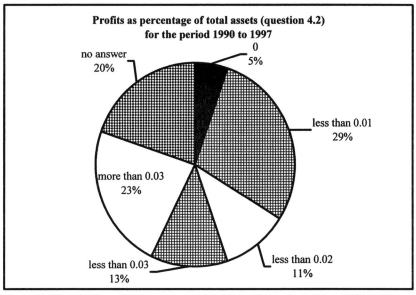

Figure 49: Distribution of answers to question 4.2 for the period 1990 to 1997

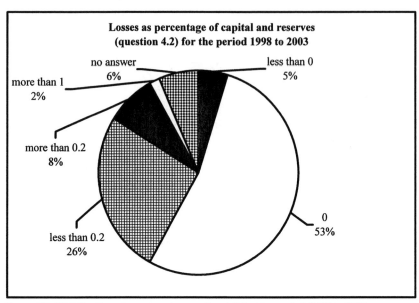

Figure 50: Distribution of answers to question 4.2 for the period 1998 to 2003

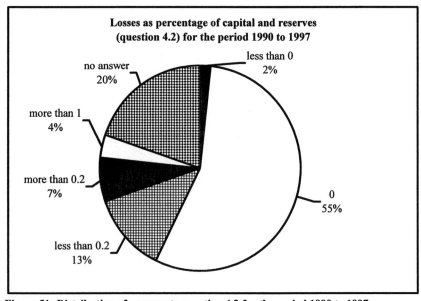

Figure 51: Distribution of answers to question 4.2 for the period 1990 to 1997

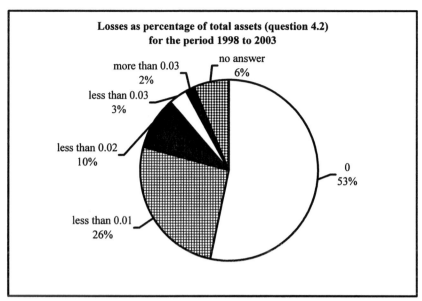

Figure 52: Distribution of answers to question 4.2 for the period 1998 to 2003

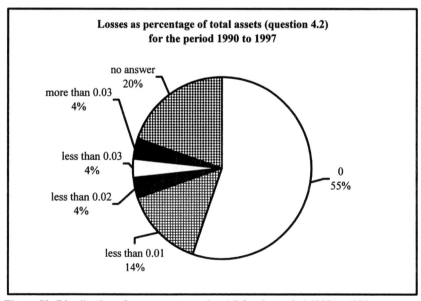

Figure 53: Distribution of answers to question 4.2 for the period 1990 to 1997

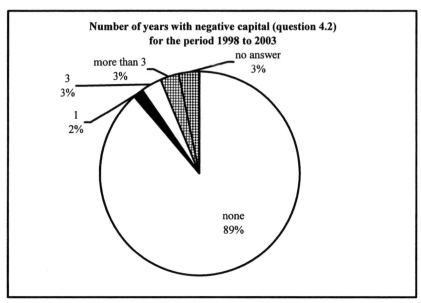

Figure 54: Distribution of answers to question 4.2 for the period 1998 to 2003

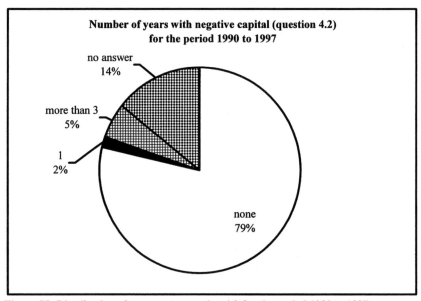

Figure 55: Distribution of answers to question 4.2 for the period 1990 to 1997

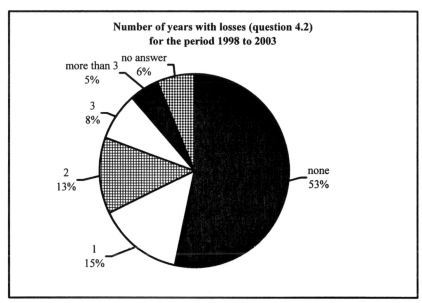

Figure 56: Distribution of answers to question 4.2 for the period 1998 to 2003

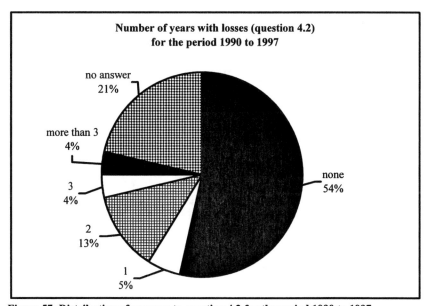

Figure 57: Distribution of answers to question 4.2 for the period 1990 to 1997

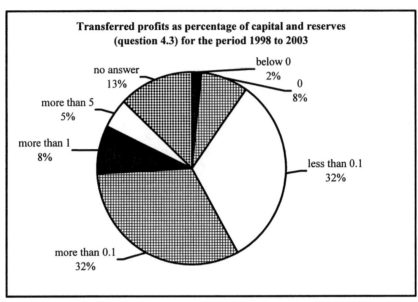

Figure 58: Distribution of answers to question 4.3 for the period 1998 to 2003

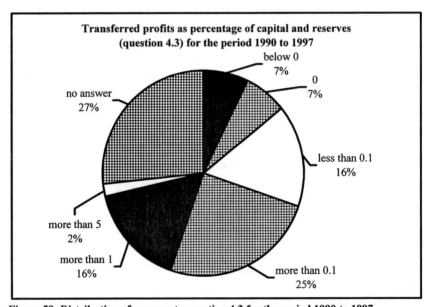

Figure 59: Distribution of answers to question 4.3 for the period 1990 to 1997

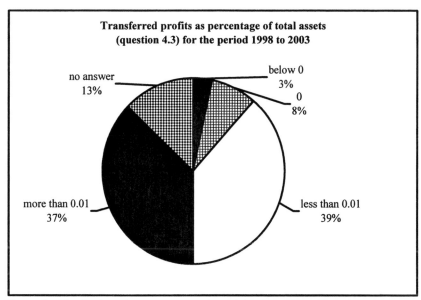

Figure 60: Distribution of answers to question 4.3 for the period 1998 to 2003

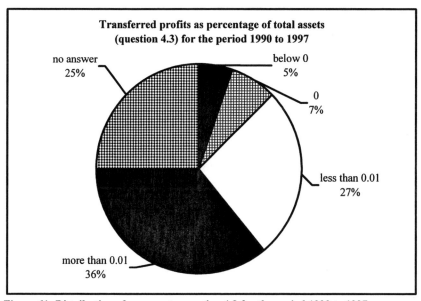

Figure 61: Distribution of answers to question 4.3 for the period 1990 to 1997

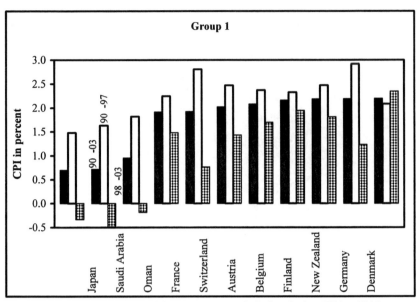

Figure 62: Group of countries with lowest average inflation during 1990 to 2003

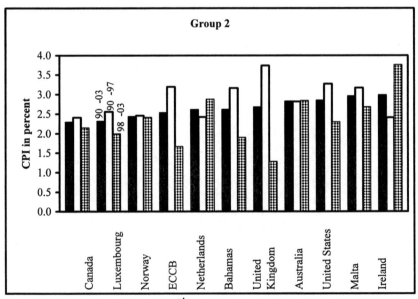

Figure 63: Group of countries with 2nd lowest average inflation during 1990 to 2003

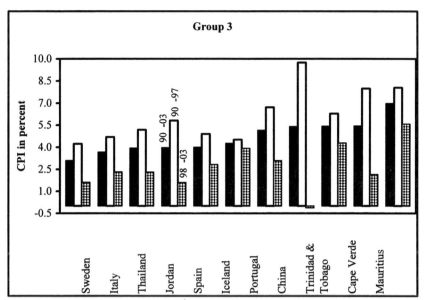

Figure 64: Group of countries with 3rd lowest average inflation during 1990 to 2003

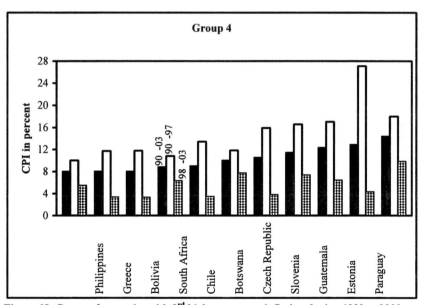

Figure 65: Group of countries with 3rd highest average inflation during 1990 to 2003

203

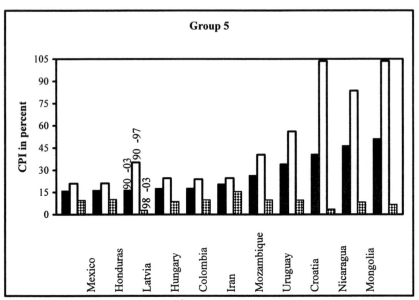

Figure 66: Group of countries with 2nd highest average inflation during 1990 to 2003

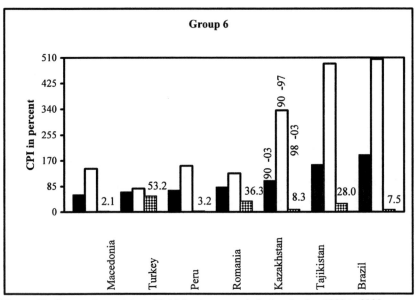

Figure 67: Group of countries with highest average inflation during 1990 to 2003

Appendix B

Table 4: Descriptions and sources of variables

Variable	Description and source
2.1Liquidity-03 2.1Liquidity-90	The variables 2.1Liquidity-03 and 2.1Liquidity-90 are dummy variables with value '1' for an affirming answer to question 2.1 of the questionnaire and '0' otherwise: "Does your central bank provide liquidity if the receiving institution is not pledging sufficient collateral to secure the credit, e.g. for short-term liquidity shortages?". The variables expected influence on inflation is positive and they form part of the index of the quality of eligible collateral for the periods 1998 to 2003 and 1990 to 1997 respectively. Data source: own survey, available at: http://www.wiwi.uni-bremen.de/empwifo/forschung/central_bank.html[597]
2.4CloseTies-03 2.4CloseTies-90	The variables 2.4CloseTies-03 and 2.4CloseTies-90 are dummy variables with value '1' for an affirming answer to question 2.4 of the questionnaire and '0' otherwise: "Does your central bank accept assets as collateral from institutions that have close ties with the issuers of those assets?" The variables expected influence on inflation is positive and they form part of the index of the quality of eligible collateral for the periods 1998 to 2003 and 1990 to 1997 respectively. Data source: own survey, available at: http://www.wiwi.uni-bremen.de/empwifo/forschung/central_bank.html
2.6Sufficient-Cover-03 2.6Sufficient-Cover-90	The variables 2.6SufficientCover-03 and 2.6SufficientCover-90 measure the minimum sufficient cover, i.e. the minimum percentage eligible collateral has to satisfy relative to an amount of credit. The variables expected influence on inflation is negative and they form part of the index of the quality of eligible collateral for the periods 1998 to 2003 and 1990 to 1997 respectively. Data source: own survey, available at: http://www.wiwi.uni-bremen.de/empwifo/forschung/central_bank.html

---

597 Data will be downloadable from the project's homepage from February 2008.

Table 4 (continued): Descriptions and sources of variables

Variable	Description and source
3.1Credit-worth-03 3.1Credit-worth-90	The variables 3.1Creditworth-03 and 3.1Creditworth-90 measure the creditworthiness of issuers of eligible assets. These variables expected influence on inflation is negative and they form part of the index of the quality of eligible collateral for the periods 1998 to 2003 and 1990 to 1997 respectively. Data source: own survey, available at: http://www.wiwi.uni-bremen.de/empwifo/forschung/central_bank.html
#Losses-pP-90-97 #Losses-pP-95-99 #Losses-pP-98-03	The variables #LossespP-90-97, #LossespP-95-99 and #LossespP-98-03 measure the frequency of central bank losses. The variables expected influence on inflation is positive. The number of years in which a central bank recorded losses per period for the periods 1990 to 1997, 1995 to 1999 and 1998 to 2003 respectively. Data source: own survey, available at: http://www.wiwi.uni-bremen.de/empwifo/forschung/central_bank.html[598]
BadDebtsX-90-97 BadDebtsX-95-99 BadDebtsX-98-03	The variables BadDebtsX-90-97, BadDebtsX-95-99 and BadDebtsX-98-03 measure the effectiveness of a central bank's eligible collateral framework. The expected influence on inflation is positive. Index values of a central bank's bad debts are based on the number of years in which bad debts have been recorded, the percentage sum of bad debts and the average bad debts for the periods 1990 to 1997, 1995 to 1999 and 1998 to 2003 respectively. Data source: own survey, available at: http://www.wiwi.uni-bremen.de/empwifo/forschung/central_bank.html
CBAccounta-bility-98	The variable CBAccountability-98 measures the degree of a central bank's accountability vis-à-vis the government.[599] The expected influence on inflation is negative. Index values of a central bank's accountability for the year 1998. Data source: Fry *et al.* (2000) Table A.6 p. 149 f. Available at: http://www.bankofengland.co.uk/education/ccbs/publications/mpfagc.htm

---

598 Data will be downloadable from the project's homepage from February 2008.
599 Cf. Fry *et al.* (2000).

Table 4 (continued): Descriptions and sources of variables

Variable	Description and source
CBDeficit-Finance-98	The variable CBDeficitFinance-98 measures the limits of central bank's financing of the government deficit.[600] The expected influence on inflation is negative.[601] Index values of a central bank's accountability for the year 1998. Data source: Fry et al. (2000) Table A.5, item 4, p. 149 f. Available at: http://www.bankofengland.co.uk/education/ ccbs/publications/mpfagc.htm
CBIndependence-98-1	The variable CBIndependence-98-1 measures the degree of a central bank's independence.[602] The expected influence on inflation is negative. Index values of a central bank's independence for the year 1998 with the index weights proposed in Fry et al. (2000). Data source: Fry et al. (2000) Table A.5 p. 149 f. Available at: http://www.bankofengland.co.uk/education/ccbs/ publications/mpfagc.htm
CBIndependence-98-2	The variable CBIndependence-98-1 measures the degree of a central bank's independence.[603] The expected influence on inflation is negative. Index values of a central bank's independence for the year 1998 with index weights in compliance with the ones used in Cukierman et al. (1992a). Data source: Fry et al. (2000) Table A.5 p. 149 f. Available at: http://www.bankofengland.co.uk/education/ccbs/ publications/mpfagc.htm
CBTranspa-rency-98	The variable CBTransparency-98 measures the degree of a central bank's transparency by the detail of a central bank's explanations in forecasts and forward-looking analyses. The expected influence on inflation is negative.[604] Index values of a central bank's transparency for the year 1998 from Fry et al. (2000) are transformed into a Guttman-scale.[605] Source: Chortareas et al. (2002b), Data source: Fry et al. (2000) Table A.7.ii p. 153 f. Available at: http://www.bankofengland.co.uk/education/ccbs/ publications/mpfagc.htm

---

600 Cf. Fry et al. (2000).
601 Cf. Chortareas et al. (2002a).
602 Cf. Fry et al. (2000).
603 Cf. Fry et al. (2000).
604 Cf. Chortareas et al. (2002b).
605 Cf. Chortareas et al. (2002b).

Table 4 (continued): Descriptions and sources of variables

Variable	Description and source
CPI-90-97 CPI-95-99 CPI-98-03	The variables CPI -90-97, CPI -95-99 and CPI -98-03 measure inflation. Geometrical average of the annual consumer price inflation for the periods 1990 to 1997, 1995 to 1999 and 1998 to 2003 respectively. Data source: World Development Indicators on CD-ROM, World Bank (2006)
CurrencyTA-90-97 CurrencyTA-95-99 CurrencyTA-98-03	The variables CurrencyTA-90-97, CurrencyTA-95-99 and CurrencyTA-98-03 measure the extent to which a central bank's balance sheet is burdened with quasi fiscal activities. These are thought to represent obstacles to the pursuit of monetary policy's goal of price stability. The expected influence on inflation is positive.[606] Average of a central bank's issue of currency as percentage of total assets in the annual balance sheet for the periods 1990 to 1997, 1995 to 1999 and 1998 to 2003 respectively. Data source: own survey, available at: http://www.wiwi.uni-bremen.de/empwifo/forschung/central_bank.html
GDPdeflator-90-97 GDPdeflator-95-99 GDPdeflator-98-03	The variables GDPdeflator-90-97, GDPdeflator-95-99 and GDPdeflator-98-03 measure inflation. Geometrical average of changes of the annual GDP deflator for the periods 1990 to 1997, 1995 to 1999 and 1998 to 2003 respectively. Data source: World Development Indicators on CD-ROM, World Bank (2006)
GDPpc-90-97 GDPpc-05-99 GDPpc-98-03	The variables GDPpc-90-97, GDPpc-05-99 and GDPpc-98-03 are used as an overall measure of a country's stage of development. The variables are expected to possess a negative influence on inflation.[607] Average of annual GDP per capita in constant US$ of 2000 for the periods 1990 to 1997, 1995 to 1999 and 1998 to 2003 respectively. Data source: World Development Indicators on CD-ROM, World Bank (2006)

---

606 Cf. Gros (2004).
607 Cf. Campillo & Miron (1997).

Table 4 (continued): Descriptions and sources of variables

Variable	Description and source
GovEffect-96-98 GovEffect-98-03	The variables GovEffect-96-98 and GovEffect-98-03 measure the degree of government effectiveness in a country. "Government effectiveness, the quality of public services, the quality of the civil service and the degree of its independence from political pressures, the quality of policy formulation and implementation, and the credibility of the government's commitment to such policies"[608], is expected to possess a negative influence on inflation. Average of annual index values for government effectiveness for the periods 1996 to 1998 and 1998 to 2003 respectively. Source: Kaufmann *et al.* (2006), data available at: http://www.worldbank.org/wbi/governance/wp-governance.htm
LogCPI-90-97 LogCPI-95-99 LogCPI-98-03	The variables LogCPI-90-97, LogCPI-95-99 and LogCPI-98-03 measure inflation. Average of the log of annual consumer price inflation plus 1 – to be able to calculate the log – for the periods 1990 to 1997, 1995 to 1999 and 1998 to 2003 respectively. Data source: World Development Indicators on CD-ROM, World Bank (2006)
LogGDP-deflator-90-97 LogGDP-deflator-95-99 LogGDP-deflator-98-03	The variables LogGDPdeflator-90-97, LogGDPdeflator-95-99 and LogGDPdeflator-98-03 measure inflation. Average of the log of the annual change in the GDP deflator plus 1– to be able to calculate the log – for the periods 1990 to 1997, 1995 to 1999 and 1998 to 2003 respectively. Data source: World Development Indicators on CD-ROM, World Bank (2006)
LogGDPpc-90-97 LogGDPpc-95-99 LogGDPpc-98-03	The variables LogGDPpc-90-97, LogGDPpc-05-99 and LogGDPpc-98-03 measure the Gross Domestic Product per capita and are used as a proxy for a country's stage of development. The variables are expected to possess a negative influence on inflation.[609] Average of the log of annual GDP per capita in constant US$ of 2000 for the periods 1990 to 1997, 1995 to 1999 and 1998 to 2003 respectively. Data source: World Development Indicators on CD-ROM, World Bank (2006)

608 Cf. Kaufmann *et al.* (2006) p. 4.
609 Cf. Campillo & Miron (1997).

Table 4 (continued): Descriptions and sources of variables

Variable	Description and source
Log#LossespP-98-03	The variable Log#LossespP-98-03 measures the frequency of central bank losses. The variables expected influence on inflation is positive The log of the number of years in which a central bank recorded losses between 1998 and 2003 plus 1 to be able to calculate the log. Data source: own survey, available at: http://www.wiwi.uni-bremen.de/empwifo/forschung/central_bank.html[610]
LogPolStab-96-98 LogPolStab-98-03	The variables LogPolStab-96-98 and LogPolStab-98-03 measure the degree of political stability or, more precisely, political violence in a country.[611] According to Cukierman *et al*. political stability possesses a negative influence on inflation.[612] Log of the average of annual index values for political stability plus 3 – to be able to calculate the log – (range of index values from -2.5 to 2.5) for the periods 1996 to 1998 and 1998 to 2003 respectively. Source: Kaufmann *et al*. (2006), data available at: http://www.worldbank.org/wbi/governance/wp-governance.htm
LogQEC-03-4 LogQEC-90-4 LogQEC-99-4	The variables LogQEC-03-4, LogQEC-90-4 and QEC-99-4 measure the quality of eligible collateral pledged to central banks. These variables are expected to possess a positive influence on inflation. Log of index values of the quality of eligible collateral weighted with weighting-vector 4 plus 1 – to avoid negative values – for the period 1998 to 2003, 1990 to 1997 and 1995 to 1999 respectively. Data source: own survey, available at: http://www.wiwi.uni-bremen.de/empwifo/forschung/central_bank.html

---

610 Data will be downloadable from the project's homepage from February 2008.
611 Cf. Kaufmann *et al*. (2006).
612 Cf. Cukierman *et al*. (1992b).

Table 4 (continued): Descriptions and sources of variables

Variable	Description and source
LogTranspa-rency-98	The variable LogTransparency-98 measures the degree of a central bank's transparency based on how detailed central bank's explanations in forecasts and forward-looking analyses are. Its expected influence on inflation is negative. Log of Guttman-scale values of a central bank's transparency plus 1 to be able to calculate the log for the year 1998 from Fry *et al.* (2000).[613] Source: Chortareas *et al.* (2002b), data source: Fry *et al.* (2000) Table A.7.ii p. 153 f. Available at: http://www.bankofengland.co.uk/education/ccbs/publications/mpfagc.htm
Openness-90-97 Openness-95-99 Openness-98-03	The variables Openness-90-97, Openness-95-99 and Openness-98-03 measure the degree of a country's openness to trade. According to Romer this variable possesses a negative influence on inflation.[614] Average of imports of goods and services as percentage of annual GDP in percent for the periods 1990 to 1997, 1995 to 1999 and 1998 to 2003 respectively. Source: Romer (1993), data source: World Development Indicators on CD-ROM, World Bank (2006)
PolStab-96-98 PolStab-98-03	The variables PolStab-96-98 and PolStab-98-03 measure the degree of political stability or rather political violence in a country.[615] According to Cukierman *et al.* political stability possesses a negative influence on inflation.[616] Average of annual index values for political stability for the periods 1996 to 1998 and 1998 to 2003 respectively. Source: Kaufmann *et al.* (2006), data available at: http://www.worldbank.org/wbi/governance/wp-governance.htm

---

613 Cf. Chortareas *et al.* (2002b).
614 Cf. Romer (1993).
615 Cf. Kaufmann *et al.* (2006).
616 Cf. Cukierman *et al.* (1992b).

Table 4 (continued): Descriptions and sources of variables

Variable	Description and source
PolStab-90-97	The variable PolStab-90-97 measures the degree of political stability in a country.[617] According to Cukierman *et al.* political stability possesses a negative influence on inflation.[618] Average of annual index values for political stability for the period 1990 to 1997. Source: Goldstone *et al.* (2000), data available at: http://globalpolicy.gmu.edu/pitf/pitfdata.htm
PolInstab90-97	The variable PolInstab-90-97 measures the degree of political instability and political violence in a country.[619] According to Cukierman *et al.* political instability possesses a positive influence on inflation.[620] Average of annual index values for political stability for the period 1990 to 1997. Source: Goldstone *et al.* (2000), data available at: http://globalpolicy.gmu.edu/pitf/pitfdata.htm
ProblCountry-90-97	The variable ProblCountry-90-97 measures the likelihood of a state failure.[621] According to Cukierman *et al.* political instability possesses a positive influence on inflation.[622] The variable has the value one for countries that face the risk of a state failure and zero otherwise. Average of annual values for the likelihood of state failure for the period 1990 to 1997. Source: Goldstone *et al.* (2000), data source: http://globalpolicy.gmu.edu/pitf/pitfdata.htm
QEC-03-1 QEC-03-2 QEC-03-3 QEC-03-4	The variables QEC03-1, QEC03-2, QEC03-3 and QEC03-4 measure the quality of eligible collateral pledged to central banks. The variables are expected to possess a positive influence on inflation. Index values of the quality of eligible collateral weighted with weighting-vectors 1, 2, 3 and 4 for the period 1998 to 2003. Data source: own survey, available at: http://www.wiwi.uni-bremen.de/empwifo/forschung/central_bank.html[623]

---

617 Cf. Goldstone *et al.* (2000).
618 Cf. Cukierman *et al.* (1992b).
619 Cf. Goldstone *et al.* (2000).
620 Cf. Cukierman *et al.* (1992b).
621 Cf. Goldstone *et al.* (2000).
622 Cf. Cukierman *et al.* (1992b).
623 Data will be downloadable from the project's homepage from February 2008.

Table 4 (continued): Descriptions and sources of variables

Variable	Description and source
QEC-90-1 QEC-90-2 QEC-90-3 QEC-90-4	The variables QEC-90-1, QEC-90-2, QEC-90-3 and QEC-90-4 measure the quality of eligible collateral pledged to central banks. The variables are expected to possess a positive influence on inflation. Index values of the quality of eligible collateral weighted with weighting-vectors 1, 2, 3 and 4 for the period 1990 to 1997. Data source: own survey, available at: http://www.wiwi.uni-bremen.de/empwifo/forschung/central_bank.html
QEC-99-1 QEC-99-2 QEC-99-3 QEC-99-4	The variables QEC-99-1, QEC-99-2, QEC-99-3 and QEC-99-4 measure the quality of eligible collateral pledged to central banks. The variables are expected to possess a positive influence on inflation. Qualitative information is based on the data for the current framework – these are identical to the values used for the 2003 framework. Index values of the quality of eligible collateral weighted with weighting-vectors 1, 2, 3 and 4 for the period 1995 to 1999. Data source: own survey, available at: http://www.wiwi.uni-bremen.de/empwifo/forschung/central_bank.html[624]
RegQuality-95-99 RegQuality-98-03	The variables RegQuality-95-99 and RegQuality-98-03 measure the degree of regulatory quality in a country. "Regulatory quality, the ability of the government to formulate and implement sound policies and regulations that permit and promote private sector development"[625], is expected to possess a negative influence on inflation. Average of annual index values for regulatory quality for the periods 1996 to 1998 and 1998 to 2003 respectively. Source: Kaufmann *et al.* (2006), data available at: http://www.worldbank.org/wbi/governance/wp-governance.htm

---

624 Data will be downloadable from the project's homepage from February 2008.
625 Cf. Kaufmann *et al.* (2006) p. 4.

Table 4 (continued): Descriptions and sources of variables

Variable	Description and source
RuloLaw-95-99 RuloLaw-98-03	The variables RuloLaw-95-99 and RuloLaw-98-03 measure the degree of the rule of law in a country. "Rule of law, the extent to which agents have confidence in and abide by the rules of society, and in particular the quality of contract enforcement, the police, and the courts, as well as the likelihood of crime and violence"[626], is expected to possess a negative influence on inflation. Average of annual index values for rule of law for the periods 1996 to 1998 and 1998 to 2003 respectively. Source: Kaufmann et al. (2006), data available at: http://www.worldbank.org/wbi/governance/wp-governance.htm
Status-90-97 Status-95-99 Status-98-03	The variables Status-90-07, Status-95-99 and Status-98-03 are dummy variables with value one for developing countries and zero for developed countries. The variables expected influence on inflation is positive. A developed country is defined as one that is classified as high income country by the World Bank for most years of the periods 1990 to 1997, 1995 to 1999 and 1998 to 2003 respectively. Data source: World Development Indicators, World Bank (2007), available at: http://www.worldbank.org/.

Table 4: Descriptions and sources of variables employed

---

626 Cf. Kaufmann et al. (2006) p. 4.

Table 5: OLS results for the period 1998 to 2003

Model	Included variables	adjust-ted R^2	F-Value	Coefficient	Standard Error	Standardised β	t-Value
Dependent variable: CPI-98-03, n = 62				Explanatory variables:	2.1Liquidity-03, 2.4CloseTies-03, 2.6SufficientCover-03, 3.1Creditworth-03, BadDebtsX-98-03, CurrencyTA-98-03		
Method: All variables enter the regression model							
Model 1	2.1Liquidity-03	0.394	7.606***	5.590	3.463	0.179	1.614
	2.4CloseTies-03			0.004	2.609	0.000	0.001
	2.6SufficientCover-03			3.494***	1.299	0.288***	2.690
	3.1Creditworth-03			0.976***	0.366	0.291***	2.668
	BadDebtsX-98-03			9.461***	3.254	0.316***	2.908
	CurrencyTA-98-03			-9.316*	4.976	-0.196*	-1.872
	Constant			-11.877*	6.408		-1.854
Dependent variable: CPI-98-03, n = 62				Explanatory variables:	QEC-03-1		
Method: All variables enter the regression model							
Model 2	QEC-03-1	0.059	4.832**	15.834**	7.203	0.273**	2.198
	Constant			2.316	1.924		1.204
Dependent variable: CPI-98-03, n = 62				Explanatory variables:	QEC-03-2		
Method: All variables enter the regression model							
Model 3	QEC-03-2	0.165	13.045***	25.340***	7.016	0.423***	3.612
	Constant			0.824	1.710		0.482
Dependent variable: CPI-98-03, n = 62				Explanatory variables:	QEC-03-3		
Method: All variables enter the regression model							
Model 4	QEC-03-3	0.116	9.023***	24.297***	8.056	0.362***	3.004
	Constant			-3.011	3.123		-0.964
Dependent variable: CPI-98-03, n = 62				Explanatory variables:	QEC-03-4		
Method: All variables enter the regression model							
Model 5	QEC-03-4	0.231	19.345***	32.459***	7.380	0.494***	4.398
	Constant			-3.682	2.368		-1.555

Note: ***, **, and * indicate statistical significance at the 1%, 5% and 10% levels respectively.

Table 5 (continued): OLS results for the period 1998 to 2003

Model	Included variables	adjusted R²	F-Value	Coefficient	Standard Error	Standardised β	t-Value
Dependent variable: CPI-98-03, n = 62				Explanatory variables:	QEC-03-4, PolStab-98-03, RuloLaw-98-03, RegQuality-98-03, GovEffect-98-03, LogGDPpc-98-03, GDPpc-98-03, Status-98-03		
Method: Stepwise selection (include if significance of F-Value ≤ 0.05, exclude if significance of F-Value ≥ 0.10)							
Model 6a	QEC-03-4	0.231	19.345***	32.459***	7.380	0.494***	4.398
	Constant			-3.682	2.368		-1.555
Model 6b	QEC-03-4	0.294	13.699***	22.600***	8.085	0.344***	2.796
	PolStab-98-03			-3.312**	1.316	-0.310**	-2.517
	Constant			0.601	2.837		0.212
Dependent variable: GDPdeflator-98-03, n = 62				Explanatory variables:	QEC-03-4, PolStab-98-03, RuloLaw-98-03, RegQuality-98-03, GovEffect-98-03, LogGDPpc-98-03, GDPpc-98-03, Status-98-03		
Method: Stepwise selection (include if significance of F-Value ≤ 0.05, exclude if significance of F-Value ≥ 0.10)							
Model 7a	QEC-03-4	0.266	23.099***	34.884***	7.258	0.527***	4.806
	Constant			-3.986*	2.329		-1.711
Model 7b[w]	QEC-03-4	0.343	16.905***	24.116*	12.565		1.919
	PolStab-98-03			-3.617	2.193		-1.649
	Constant			0.692	4.378		0.158
Dependent variable: LogGDPdeflator-98-03, n = 62				Explanatory variables:	QEC-03-4, PolStab-98-03, RuloLaw-98-03, RegQuality-98-03, GovEffect-98-03, LogGDPpc-98-03, GDPpc-98-03, Status-98-03		
Method: Stepwise selection (include if significance of F-Value ≤ 0.05, exclude if significance of F-Value ≥ 0.10)							
Model 8a	QEC-03-4	0.288	25.689***	0.303***	0.060	0.548***	5.068
	Constant			-0.031	0.019		-1.622
Model 8b[w]	QEC-03-4	0.370	18.902***	0.211**	0.102		2.067
	PolStab-98-03			-0.031*	0.018		-1.768
	Constant			0.009	0.035		0.255

Note: ***, **, and * indicate statistical significance at the 1%, 5% and 10% levels respectively. [w] indicates heteroskedasticity consistent standard errors.

Table 5 (continued): OLS results for the period 1998 to 2003

Model	Included variables	adjusted R²	F-Value	Coefficient	Standard Error	Standardised β	t-Value
Dependent variable: LogCPI-98-03, n = 62				Explanatory variables:	QEC-03-4, PolStab-98-03, RuloLaw-98-03, RegQuality-98-03, GovEffect-98-03, LogGDPpc-98-03, GDPpc-98-03, Status-98-03		
Method: Stepwise selection (include if significance of F-Value ≤ 0.05, exclude if significance of F-Value ≥ 0.10)							
Model 9a	QEC-03-4	0.257	22.102***	0.284***	0.060	0.519***	4.701
	Constant			-0.029	0.019		-1.510
Model 9b	QEC-03-4	0.324	15.602***	0.200***	0.066	0.365***	3.036
	PolStab-98-03			-0.028**	0.011	-0.317**	-2.631
	Constant			0.007	0.023		0.312
Dependent variable: CPI-98-03, n = 62				Explanatory variables:	QEC-03-4, PolStab-98-03, LogGDPpc-98-03		
Method: All variables enter the regression model							
Model 10	QEC-03-4	0.289	9.260***	26.437***	9.557	0.402***	2.766
	PolStab-98-03			-4.130**	1.704	-0.386**	-2.424
	LogGDPpc-98-03			0.886	1.166	0.142	0.760
	Constant			-7.826	11.452		-0.683
Dependent variable: CPI-98-03, n = 62				Explanatory variables:	QEC-03-4, RegQuality-98-03, LogGDPpc-98-03		
Method: All variables enter the regression model							
Model 11	QEC-03-4	0.224	6.864***	24.267**	10.296	0.369**	2.357
	RegQuality-98-03			-1.905	2.639	-0.162	-0.722
	LogGDPpc-98-03			-0.153	1.401	-0.025	-0.109
	Constant			1.299	12.225		0.106
Dependent variable: CPI-98-03, n = 62				Explanatory variables:	QEC-03-4, RuloLaw-98-03, LogGDPpc-98-03		
Method: All variables enter the regression model							
Model 12	QEC-03-4	0.227	6.979***	24.974**	10.041	0.380**	2.487
	RuloLaw-98-03			-2.041	2.312	-0.237	-0.883
	LogGDPpc-98-03			0.364	1.714	0.058	0.212
	Constant			-3.371	14.799		-0.228

Note: ***, **, and * indicate statistical significance at the 1%, 5% and 10% levels respectively.

Table 5 (continued): OLS results for the period 1998 to 2003

Model	Included variables	adjusted R²	F-Value	Coefficient	Standard Error	Standardised β	t-Value
Dependent variable: CPI-98-03, n = 62	Explanatory variables:				QEC-03-4, GovEffect-98-03, LogGDPpc-98-03		
Method: All variables enter the regression model							
Model 13		0.234	7.196***				
	QEC-03-4			24.561**	10.013	0.374**	2.453
	GovEffect-98-03			-2.581	2.297	-0.292	-1.124
	LogGDPpc-98-03			0.639	1.660	0.103	0.385
	Constant			-5.033	14.217		-0.354
Dependent variable: CPI-98-03, n = 62	Explanatory variables:				#LossespP-98-03		
Method: All variables enter the regression model							
Model 14		0.057	4.691**				
	#LossespP-98-03			1.822**	0.841	0.269**	2.166
	Constant			4.293***	1.278		3.359
Dependent variable: #LossespP-98-03, n = 62	Explanatory variables:				QEC-03-4		
Method: All variables enter the regression model							
Model 15		0.070	5.611**				
	QEC-03-4			2.841**	1.199	0.292**	2.369
	Constant			0.021	0.385		0.053
Dependent variable: CPI-98-03, n = 61	Explanatory variables:				QEC-03-4, PolStab-98-03, Status-98-03, RuloLaw-98-03, RegQuality-98-03, GovEffect-98-03, LogGDPpc-98-03, GDPpc-98-03, Openness-98-03		
	Excluded country:				Bahamas		
Method: Stepwise selection (include if significance of F-Value ≤ 0.05, exclude if significance of F-Value ≥ 0.10)							
Model 16a	QEC-03-4	0.229	18.842***	32.340***	7.450	0.492***	4.341
	Constant			-3.614	2.400		-1.506
Model 16b	QEC-03-4	0.292	13.343***	22.547***	8.156	0.343***	2.764
	PolStab-98-03			-3.303**	1.328	-0.309**	-2.488
	Constant			0.636	2.866		0.222

Note: ***, **, and * indicate statistical significance at the 1%, 5% and 10% levels respectively.

Table 5 (continued): OLS results for the period 1998 to 2003

Model	Included variables	adjusted R²	F-Value	Coefficient	Standard Error	Standardised β	t-Value
Dependent variable: CPI-98-03, n = 61				Explanatory variables:	QEC-03-4, Openness-98-03, LogGDPpc-98-03		
				Excluded country:	Bahamas		
Method: All variables enter the regression model							
Model 17	QEC-03-4	0.216	6.521***	25.724**	10.137	0.391**	2.538
	Openness-98-03			-0.019	0.046	-0.048	-0.420
	LogGDPpc-98-03			-0.939	0.966	-0.151	-0.972
	Constant			7.251	11.033		0.657
Dependent variable: CPI-98-03, n = 59				Explanatory variables:	QEC-03-4, PolStab-98-03, GDPpc-98-03		
				Excluded countries:	Romania, Tajikistan, Turkey		
Method: Stepwise selection (include if significance of F-Value ≤ 0.05, exclude if significance of F-Value ≥ 0.10)							
Model 18a^w	QEC-03-4	0.264	21.844***	15.565***	4.222		3.686
	Constant			-0.226	1.053		-0.215
Model 18b^w	QEC-03-4	0.319	14.573***	11.148**	4.458		2.501
	PolStab-98-03			-1.314**	0.534		-2.459
	Constant			1.652	1.344		1.229
Dependent variable: CPI-98-03, n = 59				Explanatory variables:	QEC-03-4, PolStab-98-03, GDPpc-98-03		
Method: All variables enter the regression model							
Excluded countries:					Romania, Tajikistan, Turkey		
Model 19^w	QEC-03-4	0.324	10.279***	9.281*	4.960		1.871
	PolStab-98-03			-0.884	0.673		-1.315
	GDPpc-98-03			-5.38E-05	0.000		-1.538
	Constant			2.612	1.626		1.607

Note: ***, **, and * indicate statistical significance at the 1%, 5% and 10% levels respectively. ^w indicates heteroskedasticity consistent standard errors.

Table 5 (continued): OLS results for the period 1998 to 2003

Model	Included variables	adjusted R^2	F-Value	Coefficient	Standard Error	Standardised β	t-Value
Dependent variable: CPI-98-03, n = 59				Explanatory variables:	QEC-03-4, PolStab-98-03, LogGDPpc-98-03		
				Excluded countries:	Romania, Tajikistan, Turkey		
Method: All variables enter the regression model							
Model 20[w]	QEC-03-4	0.327	10.398***	7.891	5.548		1.422
	PolStab-98-03			-0.804	0.705		-1.140
	LogGDPpc-98-03			-0.607	0.439		-1.383
	Constant			7.614	4.768		1.597
Dependent variable: CPI-98-03, n = 59				Explanatory variables:	#LossespP-98-03		
				Excluded countries:	Romania, Tajikistan, Turkey		
Method: All variables enter the regression model							
Model 21	#LossespP-98-03	0.078	5.922**	0.815**	0.335	0.307**	2.433
	Constant			3.508***	0.495		7.082
Dependent variable: #LossespP-98-03, n = 59				Explanatory variables:	QEC-03-3		
				Excluded countries:	Romania, Tajikistan, Turkey		
Method: All variables enter the regression model							
Model 22	QEC-03-3	0.043	3.603*	2.413*	1.271	0.244*	1.898
	Constant			-0.072	0.485		-0.149

Note: ***, **, and * indicate statistical significance at the 1%, 5% and 10% levels respectively. [w] indicates heteroskedasticity consistent standard errors.

Table 5 (continued): OLS results for the period 1998 to 2003

Model	Included variables	adjusted R²	F-Value	Coefficient	Standard Error	Standardised β	t-Value
Dependent variable: CPI-98-03, n = 36							
Method: Stepwise selection (include if significance of F-Value ≤ 0.05, exclude if significance of F-Value ≥ 0.10)							
Model 23a	QEC-03-4	0.124	5.975**	31.230**	12.776	0.387**	2.444
	Constant			-2.890	4.893		-0.591
				Explanatory variables:	QEC-03-4, PolStab-98-03, RuloLaw-98-03, RegQuality-98-03, GovEffect-98-03, LogGDPpc-98-03, GDPpc-98-03, Openness-98-03		
Model 23b	QEC-03-4	0.199	5.357***	26.945**	12.395	0.334**	2.174
	PolStab-98-03			-4.555**	2.228	-0.314**	-2.045
	Constant			-1.538	4.725		-0.325
Dependent variable: CPI-98-03, n = 36							
Method: All variables enter the regression model							
Model 24	QEC-03-4	0.177	3.511**	28.610**	13.558	0.354**	2.110
	PolStab-98-03			-4.870*	2.456	-0.335*	-1.083
	LogGDP-98-03			0.671	2.051	0.060	0.327
	Constant			-7.296	18.233		-0.400
				Explanatory variables:	QEC-03-4		
				Excluded countries:	Romania, Tajikistan, Turkey		
Dependent variable: CPI-98-03, n = 33							
Method: All variables enter the regression model							
Model 25	QEC-03-4	0.076	3.641*	11.105*	5.820	0.324*	1.908
	Constant			1.743	2.104		0.828
Dependent variable: CPI-98-03, n = 26							
Method: Stepwise selection (include if significance of F-Value ≤ 0.05, exclude if significance of F-Value ≥ 0.10)				Explanatory variables:	QEC-03-4, PolStab-98-03, GDPpc-98-03, LogGDPpc-98-03, RuloLaw-98-03, RegQuality-98-03, GovEffect-98-03		

Note: ***, **, and * indicate statistical significance at the 1%, 5% and 10% levels respectively.

221

Table 5 (continued): OLS results for the period 1998 to 2003

Model	Included variables	adjusted R²	F-Value	Coefficient	Standard Error	Standardised β	t-Value
Model 26	LogGDP-98-03	0.232	8.538***	-1.637***	0.560	-0.512***	-2.922
	Constant			18.673***	5.590		3.341

Dependent variable: GDPdeflator-98-03, n = 26
Method: Stepwise selection (include if significance of F-Value ≤ 0.05, exclude if significance of F-Value ≥ 0.10)

Explanatory variables: QEC-03-4, PolStab-98-03, GDPpc-98-03, LogGDPpc-98-03, RuloLaw-98-03, RegQuality-98-03, GovEffect-98-03

Model	Included variables	adjusted R²	F-Value	Coefficient	Standard Error	Standardised β	t-Value
Model 27a	LogGDP-98-03	0.242	8.981***	-1.866***	0.623	-0.522***	-2.997
	Constant			21.088***	6.215		3.393
Model 27b	QEC-03-4	0.364	8.151***	12.532**	5.296	0.378**	2.366
	LogGDP-98-03			-1.806***	0.571	-0.505***	-3.162
	Constant			17.964***	5.844		3.074

Dependent variable: GDPdeflator-98-03, n = 26
Method: All variables enter the regression model
Explanatory variables: QEC-03-4, PolStab-98-03, LogGDPpc-98-03

Model	Included variables	adjusted R²	F-Value	Coefficient	Standard Error	Standardised β	t-Value
Model 28	QEC-03-4	0.335	5.203***	12.297**	5.921	0.371**	2.077
	PolStab-98-03			0.093	0.945	0.018	0.098
	LogGDP-98-03			-1.828***	0.627	-0.511***	-2.917
	Constant			18.136***	6.226		2.913

Dependent variable: GDPdeflator-98-03, n = 26
Method: All variables enter the regression model
Explanatory variables: #LossespP-98-03

Model	Included variables	adjusted R²	F-Value	Coefficient	Standard Error	Standardised β	t-Value
Model 29	#LossespP-98-03	0.093	3.570*	0.695*	0.368	0.360*	1.889
	Constant			2.213***	0.323		6.855

Dependent variable: #LossespP-98-03, n = 26
Method: All variables enter the regression model
Explanatory variables: QEC-03-3

Model	Included variables	adjusted R²	F-Value	Coefficient	Standard Error	Standardised β	t-Value
Model 30	QEC-03-3	0.084	3.287*	4.105*	2.264	0.347*	1.813
	Constant			-0.746	0.642		-1.163

Note: ***, **, and * indicate statistical significance at the 1%, 5% and 10% levels respectively.

Table 5 (continued): OLS results for the period 1998 to 2003

Model	Included variables	adjusted R²	F-Value	Coefficient	Standard Error	Standardised β	t-Value
Dependent variable: CPI-98-03, n = 25				Explanatory variables:	QEC-03-4, PolStab-98-03, GDPpc-98-03, LogGDPpc-98-03, RuloLaw-98-03, RegQuality-98-03, GovEffect-98-03		
				Excluded countries:	Slovenia		
Method: Stepwise selection (include if significance of F-Value ≤ 0.05, exclude if significance of F-Value ≥ 0.10)							
Model 31	QEC-03-4	0.156	5.421**	8.665**	3.721	0.437**	2.328
	Constant			0.414	0.767		0.540
Dependent variable: CPI-98-03, n = 25				Explanatory variables:	QEC-03-4, PolStab-98-03, LogGDPpc-98-03		
				Excluded countries:	Slovenia		
Method: All variables enter the regression model							
Model 32	QEC-03-4	0.226	3.338**	8.715**	3.902	0.439**	2.233
	PolStab-98-03			-0.129	0.627	-0.043	-0.206
	LogGDP-98-03			-0.799*	0.448	-0.347*	-1.786
	Constant			8.536*	4.445		1.920
Dependent variable: LogCPI-98-03, n = 62				Explanatory variables:	LogQEC-03-4, LogPolStab-98-03, LogGDPpc-98-03		
Method: All variables enter the regression model							
Model 33	LogQEC-03-4	0.315	10.334***	0.292***	0.108	0.393***	2.692
	LogPolStab-98-03			-0.093**	0.036	-0.373**	-2.585
	LogGDPpc-98-03			0.004	0.009	0.082	0.466
	Constant			0.055	0.087		0.637
Dependent variable: LogCPI-98-03, n = 62				Explanatory variables:	LogQEC-03-4		
Method: All variables enter the regression model							
Model 34	LogQEC-03-4	0.245	20.783***	0.377***	0.083	0.507***	4.559
	Constant			-0.041*	0.022		-1.841

Note: ***, **, and * indicate statistical significance at the 1%, 5% and 10% levels respectively.

Table 5 (continued): OLS results for the period 1998 to 2003

Model	Included variables	adjusted R²	F-Value	Coefficient	Standard Error	Standardised β	t-Value
Dependent variable: LogCPI-98-03, n = 62				Explanatory variables:	Log#LossespP-98-03		
Method: All variables enter the regression model							
Model 35	Log#LossespP-98-03	0.086	6.742**	0.039**	0.015	0.318**	2.597
	Constant			0.037***	0.011		3.403

Note: ***, **, and * indicate statistical significance at the 1%, 5% and 10% levels respectively.

Table 5: OLS regression results for the period 1998 to 2003

Table 6: OLS results for the period 1990 to 1997

Model	Included variables	adjusted R²	F-Value	Coefficient	Standard Error	Standardised β	t-Value
Dependent variable: CPI-90-97, n = 56				Explanatory variables:	2.1Liquidity-90, 2.4CloseTies-90, 2.6SufficientCover-90, 3.1Creditworth-90, CurrencyTA-90-97, BadDebtsX-90		
Method: All variables enter the regression model							
Model 1ʷ	2.1Liquidity-90	0.223	3.633***	16.021	39.735		0.403
	2.4CloseTies-90			93.745*	54.376		1.724
	2.6SufficientCover-90			9.394	9.230		1.010
	3.1Creditworth-90			-1.865	3.814		-0.489
	CurrencyTA-90-97			-82.627	62.281		-1.327
	BadDebtsX-90			117.260*	68.298		1.717
	Constant			13.365	44.141		0.303
Dependent variable: CPI-90-97, n = 56				Explanatory variables:	QEC-90-1		
Method: All variables enter the regression model							
Model 2	QEC-90-1	0.062	4.605**	121.942**	56.822	0.280**	2.146
	Constant			-4.467	27.503		-0.162

Note: ***, **, and * indicate statistical significance at the 1%, 5% and 10% levels respectively. ʷ indicates heteroskedasticity consistent standard errors.

Table 6 (continued): OLS results for the period 1990 to 1997

Model	Included variables	adjusted R^2	F-Value	Coefficient	Standard Error	Standardised β	t-Value
Dependent variable: CPI-90-97, n = 56				Explanatory variables:	QEC-90-2		
Method: All variables enter the regression model							
Model 3^w	QEC-90-2	0.107	7.591***	174.152*	88.668		1.964
	Constant			-15.332	25.094		-0.611
Dependent variable: CPI-90-97, n = 56				Explanatory variables:	QEC-90-3		
Method: All variables enter the regression model							
Model 4	QEC-90-3	0.076	5.514***	166.522**	70.915	0.304**	2.348
	Constant			-36.441	37.969		-0.960
Dependent variable: CPI-90-97, n = 56				Explanatory variables:	QEC-90-4		
Method: All variables enter the regression model							
Model 5^w	QEC-90-4	0.127	9.023***	220.600**	102.019		2.162
	Constant			-43.574	33.923		-1.284
Dependent variable: GDPdeflator-90-97, n = 56				Explanatory variables:	QEC-90-4		
Method: All variables enter the regression model							
Model 6	QEC-90-4	0.081	5.843**	159.585***	66.020	0.312**	2.417
	Constant			-18.834	29.512		-0.638
Dependent variable: LnCPI-90-97, n = 56				Explanatory variables:	QEC-90-4		
Method: All variables enter the regression model							
Model 7^w	QEC-90-4	0.154	10.996***	0.963**	0.374		2.577
	Constant			-0.129	0.133		-0.968
Dependent variable: LnGDPdeflator-90-97, n = 56				Explanatory variables:	QEC-90-4		
Method: All variables enter the regression model							
Model 8	QEC-90-4	0.106	7.541***	0.796***	0.290	0.350***	2.746
	Constant			-0.049	0.130		-0.376

Note: ***, **, and * indicate statistical significance at the 1%, 5% and 10% levels respectively. ^{w} indicates heteroskedasticity consistent standard errors.

225

Table 6 (continued): OLS results for the period 1990 to 1997

Model	Included variables	adjusted R²	F-Value	Coefficient	Standard Error	Standardised β	t-Value
Dependent variable: CPI-90-97, n = 56				Explanatory variables:	QEC-90-4, Status-90-97, GDPpc-90-97, LogGDPpc-90-97		
Method: Stepwise selection (include if significance of F-Value ≤ 0.05, exclude if significance of F-Value ≥ 0.10)							
Model 9	LogGDPpc-90-97	0.142	10.084***	-30.607***	9.638	-0.397***	-3.176
	Constant			302.440***	81.439		3.714
Dependent variable: CPI-90-97, n = 56				Explanatory variables:	QEC-90-4, Status-90-97, GDPpc-90-97		
Method: Stepwise selection (include if significance of F-Value ≤ 0.05, exclude if significance of F-Value ≥ 0.10)							
Model 10^w	QEC-90-4	0.127	9.023***	220.600**	102.019		2.162
	Constant			-43.574	33.923		-1.284
Dependent variable: CPI-90-97, n = 54				Explanatory variables:	QEC-90-4, ProblCountry-90-97, Openness-90-97, GDPpc-90-97		
				Excluded countries:	Bahamas, United States		
Method: All variables enter the regression model							
Model 11^w	QEC-90-4	0.124	2.868**	174.326	113.619		1.534
	Openness-90-97			-0.677	1.258		-0.538
	GDPpc-90-97			-0.003	0.002		-1.327
	ProblCountry-90-97			0.215	66.042		0.003
	Constant			24.534	105.612		0.232
Dependent variable: CPI-90-97, n = 53				Explanatory variables:	QEC-90-4		
				Excluded countries:	Brazil, Kazakhstan, Tajikistan		
Method: Stepwise selection (include if significance of F-Value ≤ 0.05, exclude if significance of F-Value ≥ 0.10)							
Model 12^w	LogGDP-90-97	0.197	13.760***	-13.333***	3.282		-4.063
	Constant			136.958***	31.666		4.325

Note: ***, **, and * indicate statistical significance at the 1%, 5% and 10% levels respectively. ^w indicates heteroskedasticity consistent standard errors.

Table 6 (continued): OLS results for the period 1990 to 1997

Model	Included variables	adjusted R²	F-Value	Coefficient	Standard Error	Standardised β	t-Value
Dependent variable: CPI-90-97, n = 53				Explanatory variables:	QEC-90-4, LogGDP-90-97, GDPpc-90-97		
				Excluded countries:	Brazil, Kazakhstan, Tajikistan		
Method: Stepwise selection (include if significance of F-Value ≤ 0.05, exclude if significance of F-Value ≥ 0.10)							
Model 13	QEC-90-4	0.040	3.169*	53.759*	30.198	0.242*	1.780
	Constant			3.247	13.036		0.249
Dependent variable: CPI-90-97, n = 50				Explanatory variables:	QEC-90-4, ProblCountry-90-97, PolStab-90-97, PolInstab-90-97, Openness-90-97, LogGDPpc-90-97, GDPpc-90-97, Status-90-97		
				Excluded countries:	Bahamas, Cape Verde, ECCB, Iceland, Malta, United States		
Method: Stepwise selection (include if significance of F-Value ≤ 0.05, exclude if significance of F-Value ≥ 0.10)							
Model 14^w	QEC-90-4	0.146	9.350***	249.300**	112.860		2.209
	Constant			-50.649	38.083		-1.330
Dependent variable: CPI-90-97, n = 50				Explanatory variables:	QEC-90-4, PolStab-90-97, Openness-90-97, GDPpc-90-97		
				Excluded countries:	Bahamas, Cape Verde, ECCB, Iceland, Malta, United States		
Method: All variables enter the regression model							
Model 15^w	QEC-90-4	0.146	3.088**	201.213*	111.129		1.811
	PolStab-90-97			-2.528	3.608		-0.701
	Openness-90-97			-0.564	1.186		-0.476
	GDPpc-90-97			-0.002	0.002		-1.157
	Constant			20.551	67.322		0.305

Note: ***, **, and * indicate statistical significance at the 1%, 5% and 10% levels respectively. ^w indicates heteroskedasticity consistent standard errors.

Table 6 (continued): OLS results for the period 1990 to 1997

Model	Included variables	adjusted R²	F-Value	Coefficient	Standard Error	Standardised β	t-Value
Dependent variable: CPI-90-97, n = 50				Explanatory variables:	QEC-90-4, PolInstab-90-97, Openness-90-97, GDPpc-90-97		
				Excluded countries:	Bahamas, Cape Verde, ECCB, Iceland, Malta, United States		
Method: All variables enter the regression model							
Model 16[w]	QEC-90-4	0.144	3.056**	203.225*	113.356		1.793
	PolInstab-90-97			33.322	49.854		0.668
	Openness-90-97			-0.578	1.178		-0.491
	GDPpc-90-97			-0.002	0.002		-1.145
	Constant			-4.628	90.216		-0.051
Dependent variable: CPI-90-97, n = 47				Explanatory variables:	QEC-90-4, ProblCountry-90-97, PolStab-90-97, PolInstab-90-97, Openness-90-97, LogGDPpc-90-97, GDPpc-90-97		
				Excluded countries:	Bahamas, Brazil, Cape Verde, ECCB, Iceland, Kazakhstan, Malta, Tajikistan, United States		
Method: Stepwise selection (include if significance of F-Value ≤ 0.05, exclude if significance of F-Value ≥ 0.10)							
Model 17[w]	LogGDPpc-90-97	0.197	12.301***	-14.025***	3.509		-3.997
	Constant			144.337***	33.662		4.288
Dependent variable: CPI-90-97, n = 47				Explanatory variables:	QEC-90-4, ProblCountry-90-97		
				Excluded countries:	Bahamas, Brazil, Cape Verde, ECCB, Iceland, Kazakhstan, Malta, Tajikistan, United States		
Method: All variables enter the regression model							
Model 18[w]	QEC-90-4	0.071	2.756*	59.637	43.028		1.386
	ProblCountry-90-97			21.133	20.273		1.042
	Constant			-0.931	14.378		-0.065

Note: ***, **, and * indicate statistical significance at the 1%, 5% and 10% levels respectively. [w] indicates heteroskedasticity consistent standard errors.

Table 6 (continued): OLS results for the period 1990 to 1997

Model	Included variables	adjusted R²	F-Value	Coefficient	Standard Error	Standardised β	t-Value
Dependent variable: CPI-90-97, n = 39							
Method: Stepwise selection (include if significance of F-Value ≤ 0.05, exclude if significance of F-Value ≥ 0.10)							
Model 19	QEC-90-4	0.098	5.113**	246.272**	108.917	0.348**	2.261
	Constant			-46.238	53.011		-0.872
	Explanatory variables:				QEC-90-4, LogGDPpc-90-97, GDPpc-90-97, Openness-90-97, ProblCountry-90-97		
Dependent variable: CPI-90-97, n = 39							
Method: All variables enter the regression model							
Model 20	QEC-90-4	0.091	2.903*	206.189*	118.958	0.292*	1.733
	GDPpc-90-97			-0.007	0.008	-0.144	-0.854
	Constant			-6.479	70.684		-0.092
	Explanatory variables:				QEC-90-4, GDPpc-90-97		
Dependent variable: CPI-90-97, n = 39							
Method: All variables enter the regression model							
Model 21[w]	QEC-90-4	0.083	2.718*	236.231	148.645		1.589
	Openness-90-97			-0.597	1.090		-0.548
	Constant			-16.830	90.980		-0.185
	Explanatory variables:				QEC-90-4, Openness-90-97		
Dependent variable: CPI-90-97, n = 39							
Method: All variables enter the regression model							
Model 22	QEC-90-4	0.080	2.648*	249.650**	110.174	0.353**	2.266
	ProblCountry-90-97			23.966	45.131	0.083	0.531
	Constant			-54.389	55.690		-0.977
	Explanatory variables:				QEC-90-4, ProblCountry-90-97, PolStab-90-97, PolInstab-90-97, GDPpc-90-97, LogGDPpc-90-97, Openness-90-97		
	Excluded countries:				Cape Verde, ECCB, Malta		
Dependent variable: CPI-90-97, n = 36							
Method: Stepwise selection (include if significance of F-Value ≤ 0.05, exclude if significance of F-Value ≥ 0.10)							
Model 23	QEC-90-4	0.107	5.177**	266.518**	117.130	0.364**	2.275
	Constant			-50.798	57.134		-0.889

Note: ***, **, and * indicate statistical significance at the 1%, 5% and 10% levels respectively. [w] indicates heteroskedasticity consistent standard errors.

Table 6 (continued): OLS results for the period 1990 to 1997

Model	Included variables	adjusted R²	F-Value	Coefficient	Standard Error	Standardised β	t-Value
Dependent variable: CPI-90-97, n = 36				Explanatory variables:	QEC-90-4, PolStab-90-97		
				Excluded countries:	Cape Verde, ECCB, Malta		
Method: All variables enter the regression model							
Model 24	QEC-90-4	0.102	2.996*	269.299**	117.447	0.367**	2.293
	PolStab-90-97			-3.032	3.310	-0.147	-0.916
	Constant			-38.318	58.868		-0.651
Dependent variable: CPI-90-97, n = 36				Explanatory variables:	QEC-90-4, PolInstab-90-97		
				Excluded countries:	Cape Verde, ECCB, Malta		
Method: All variables enter the regression model							
Model 25	QEC-90-4	0.101	2.957*	272.421**	117.719	0.372**	2.314
	PolInstab-90-97			41.047	46.761	0.141	0.878
	Constant			-69.956	61.342		-1.140
Dependent variable: CPI-90-97, n = 36				Explanatory variables:	QEC-90-4, ProblCountry-90-97		
				Excluded countries:	Cape Verde, ECCB, Malta		
Method: All variables enter the regression model							
Model 26	QEC-90-4	0.083	2.590*	269.511**	118.933	0.368**	2.266
	ProblCountry-90-97			17.307	47.344	0.059	0.366
	Constant			-57.340	60.580		-0.947
Dependent variable: CPI-90-97, n = 36				Explanatory variables:	QEC-90-4, GDPpc-90-97		
				Excluded countries:	Cape Verde, ECCB, Malta		
Method: All variables enter the regression model							
Model 27	QEC-90-4	0.099	2.921*	229.897*	125.423	0.314*	1.833
	GDPpc-90-97			-0.007	0.009	-0.144	-0.842
	Constant			-12.160	73.482		-0.165

Note: ***, **, and * indicate statistical significance at the 1%, 5% and 10% levels respectively.

Table 6 (continued): OLS results for the period 1990 to 1997

Model	Included variables	adjusted R²	F-Value	Coefficient	Standard Error	Standardised β	t-Value
Dependent variable: CPI-90-97, n = 36				Explanatory variables:	QEC-90-4, Openness-90-97		
				Excluded countries:	Cape Verde, ECCB, Malta		
Method: All variables enter the regression model							
Model 28	QEC-90-4	0.084	2.613*	263.549**	118.789	0.359**	2.219
	Openness-90-97			-0.486	1.161	-0.068	-0.418
	Constant			-30.610	75.333		-0.406
Dependent variable: CPI-90-97, n = 17				Explanatory variables:	QEC-90-4		
Method: All variables enter the regression model							
Model 29	QEC-90-4	0.135	3.493*	2.231*	1.194	0.435*	1.869
	Constant			2.106***	0.405		5.206
Dependent variable: CPI-90-97, n = 56				Explanatory variables:	LogQEC-90-4		
Method: All variables enter the regression model							
Model 30[w]	LogQEC-90-4	0.139	9.857***	1.301**	0.518		2.511
	Constant			-0.171	0.153		-1.119

Note: ***, **, and * indicate statistical significance at the 1%, 5% and 10% levels respectively. [w] indicates heteroskedasticity consistent standard errors.

Table 6: OLS regression results for the period 1990 to 1997

Table 7: OLS results for the period 1995 to 1999

Model	Included variables	adjusted R²	F-Value	Coefficient	Standard Error	Standardised β	t-Value
Dependent variable: CPI-95-99, n = 46				Explanatory variables:	2.1Liquidity-03, 2.4CloseTies-03, 2.6SufficientCover-03, 3.1Creditworth-03, BadDebtsX-95-99, CurrencyTA-95-99		
Method: All variables enter the regression model							
Model 1	2.1Liquidity-03	0.369	5.387***	14.320	10.502	0.227	1.364
	2.4CloseTies-03			7.305	6.020	0.146	1.213
	2.6SufficientCover-03			4.500	2.862	0.224	1.573
	3.1Creditworth-03			2.001**	0.920	0.293**	2.176
	BadDebtsX-95-99			10.066	6.120	0.264	1.645
	CurrencyTA-95-99			-14.880	9.843	-0.192	-1.512
	Constant			-15.057	14.523		-1.037
Dependent variable: CPI-95-99, n = 46				Explanatory variables:	QEC-99-1		
Method: All variables enter the regression model							
Model 2	QEC-99-1	0.125	7.418***	43.149***	15.843	0.380***	2.724
	Constant			0.784	3.904		0.201
Dependent variable: CPI-95-99, n = 46				Explanatory variables:	QEC-99-2		
Method: All variables enter the regression model							
Model 3	QEC-99-2	0.280	18.506***	55.141***	12.818	0.544***	4.302
	Constant			-0.312	3.036		-0.103
Dependent variable: CPI-95-99, n = 46				Explanatory variables:	QEC-99-3		
Method: All variables enter the regression model							
Model 4[w]	QEC-99-3	0.204	12.532***	60.660***	22.582		2.686
	Constant			-10.740*	6.059		-1.773
Dependent variable: CPI-95-99, n = 46				Explanatory variables:	QEC-99-4		
Method: All variables enter the regression model							
Model 5	QEC-99-4	0.349	25.135***	65.196***	13.004	0.603***	5.014
	Constant			-7.812*	3.950		-1.978

Note: ***, **, and * indicate statistical significance at the 1%, 5% and 10% levels respectively. [w] indicates heteroskedasticity consistent standard errors.

Table 7 (continued): OLS results for the period 1995 to 1999

Model	Included variables	adjusted R²	F-Value	Coefficient	Standard Error	Standardised β	t-Value
Dependent variable: CPI-95-99, n = 46				Explanatory variables:	QEC-99-4, PolStab-96-98, RuloLaw-96-98, RegQuality-96-98, GovEffect-96-98, LogGDPpc-95-99, GDPpc-95-99, Status-95-99, CBIndependence-98-1, CBIndependence-98-2, CBTransparency-98, CBDeficitFinance-98		
Method: Stepwise selection (include if significance of F-Value ≤ 0.05, exclude if significance of F-Value ≥ 0.10)							
Model 6a	QEC-99-4	0.349	25.135***	65.196***	13.004	0.603***	5.014
	Constant			-7.812*	3.950		-1.978
Model 6b[w]	QEC-99-4	0.470	20.943***	51.086***	13.330		3.832
	PolStab-96-98			-9.130	5.803		-1.573
	Constant			0.977	6.702		0.146
Dependent variable: GDPdeflator-95-99, n = 46				Explanatory variables:	QEC-99-4, PolStab-96-98, RuloLaw-96-98, RegQuality-96-98, GovEffect-96-98, LogGDPpc-95-99, GDPpc-95-99, Status-95-99, CBIndependence-98-1, CBIndependence-98-2, CBTransparency-98, CBDeficitFinance-98		
Method: Stepwise selection (include if significance of F-Value ≤ 0.05, exclude if significance of F-Value ≥ 0.10)							
Model 7a	QEC-99-4	0.365	26.855***	63.010***	12.159	0.616***	5.182
	Constant			-7.454**	3.693		-2.018
Model 7b[w]	QEC-99-4	0.486	22.236***	49.678***	14.400		3.450
	PolStab-96-98			-8.627	5.321		-1.621
	Constant			0.850	6.451		0.132

Note: ***, **, and * indicate statistical significance at the 1%, 5% and 10% levels respectively. [w] indicates heteroskedasticity consistent standard errors.

Table 7 (continued): OLS results for the period 1995 to 1999

Model	Included variables	adjusted R²	F-Value	Coefficient	Standard Error	Standardised β	t-Value
Dependent variable: LogGDPdeflator-95-99, n = 46				Explanatory variables:	QEC-99-4, PolStab-96-98, RuloLaw-96-98, RegQuality-96-98, GovEffect-96-98, LogGDPpc-95-99, GDPpc-95-99, Status-95-99, CBIndependence-98-1, CBIndependence-98-2, CBTransparency-98, CBDeficitFinance-98		
Method: Stepwise selection (include if significance of F-Value ≤ 0.05, exclude if significance of F-Value ≥ 0.10)							
Model 8a	QEC-99-4	0.376	28.140***	0.498***	0.094	0.625***	5.305
	Constant			-0.051*	0.029		-1.778
Model 8b^w	QEC-99-4	0.506	24.052***	0.391***	0.104		3.773
	PolStab-96-98			-0.069*	0.038		-1.840
	Constant			0.016	0.046		0.351
Dependent variable: LogCPI-95-99, n = 46				Explanatory variables:	QEC-99-4, PolStab-96-98, RuloLaw-96-98, RegQuality-96-98, GovEffect-96-98, LogGDPpc-95-99, GDPpc-95-99, Status-95-99, CBIndependence-98-1, CBIndependence-98-2, CBTransparency-98, CBDeficitFinance-98		
Method: Stepwise selection (include if significance of F-Value ≤ 0.05, exclude if significance of F-Value ≥ 0.10)							
Model 9a	QEC-99-4	0.367	27.127***	0.516***	0.099	0.618***	5.208
	Constant			-0.054*	0.030		-1.804
Model 9b^w	QEC-99-4	0.493	22.918***	0.405***	0.096		4.239
	PolStab-96-98			-0.072*	0.040		-1.775
	Constant			0.015	0.047		0.316
Dependent variable: CPI-95-99, n = 46				Explanatory variables:	QEC-99-4, PolStab-96-98, LogGDPpc-95-99		
Method: All variables enter the regression model							
Model 10^w	QEC-99-4	0.464	13.989***	56.660***	12.277		4.615
	PolStab-96-98			-10.844	8.457		-1.282
	LogGDPpc-95-99			1.606	3.141		0.511
	Constant			-13.727	25.012		-0.549

Note: ***, **, and * indicate statistical significance at the 1%, 5% and 10% levels respectively. ^{w} indicates heteroskedasticity consistent standard errors.

Table 7 (continued): OLS results for the period 1995 to 1999

Model	Included variables	adjusted R²	F-Value	Coefficient	Standard Error	Standardised β	t-Value
Dependent variable: CPI-95-99, n = 46					QEC-99-4, CBIndependence-98-1, LogGDPpc-95-99		
Method: All variables enter the regression model				Explanatory variables:			
Model 11	QEC-99-4	0.352	9.142***	53.018***	16.486	0.490***	3.216
	CBIndependence-98-1			5.490	15.396	0.045	0.357
	LogGDPpc-95-99			-2.664	1.843	-0.215	-1.446
	Constant			14.538	23.053		0.631
Dependent variable: CPI-95-99, n = 46					QEC-99-4, CBIndependence-98-2, LogGDPpc-95-99		
Method: All variables enter the regression model				Explanatory variables:			
Model 12	QEC-99-4	0.352	9.143***	50.271***	16.508	0.465***	3.045
	CBIndependence-98-2			-6.568	18.385	-0.049	-0.357
	LogGDPpc-95-99			-2.466	1.907	-0.199	-1.293
	Constant			23.145	22.256		1.040
Dependent variable: CPI-95-99, n = 46					QEC-99-4, CBTransparency-98, LogGDPpc-95-99		
Method: All variables enter the regression model				Explanatory variables:			
Model 13	QEC-99-4	0.409	11.374***	54.847***	15.399	0.507***	3.562
	CBTransparency-98			-2.705**	1.321	-0.255**	-2.047
	LogGDPpc-95-99			-1.214	1.892	-0.098	-0.642
	Constant			11.892	18.642		0.638
Dependent variable: CPI-95-99, n = 46					QEC-99-4, CBDeficitFinance-98, LogGDPpc-95-99		
Method: All variables enter the regression model				Explanatory variables:			
Model 14	QEC-99-4	0.388	10.526***	42.629**	16.544	0.394**	2.577
	CBDeficitFinance-98			-19.749	12.143	-0.235	-1.626
	LogGDPpc-95-99			-1.742	1.873	-0.140	-0.930
	Constant			31.075	20.022		1.552

Note: ***, **, , and * indicate statistical significance at the 1%, 5% and 10% levels respectively.

Table 7 (continued): OLS results for the period 1995 to 1999

Model	Included variables	adjusted R²	F-Value	Coefficient	Standard Error	Standardised β	t-Value
Dependent variable: CPI-95-99, n = 46				Explanatory variables:	QEC-99-4, RegQuality-96-98, LogGDPppc-95-99		
Method: All variables enter the regression model							
Model 15	QEC-99-4	0.353	9.200***	53.315***	16.386	0.493***	3.254
	RegQuality-96-98			2.917	6.056	0.102	0.482
	LogGDPppc-95-99			-3.558	2.645	-0.287	-1.345
	Constant			24.664	22.356		1.103
Dependent variable: CPI-95-99, n = 45				Explanatory variables:	QEC-99-4, Openness-95-99, LogGDPppc-95-99		
				Excluded country:	Bahamas		
Method: All variables enter the regression model							
Model 16	QEC-99-4	0.360	9.265***	50.313***	16.148	0.466***	3.116
	Openness-95-99			-0.095	0.101	-0.116	-0.939
	LogGDPppc-95-99			-2.965	1.896	-0.239	-1.564
	Constant			26.223	20.863		1.257
Dependent variable: CPI-95-99, n = 45				Explanatory variables:	QEC-99-4, CBAccountability-98, LogGDPppc-95-99		
				Excluded country:	Japan		
Method: All variables enter the regression model							
Model 17	QEC-99-4	0.349	8.857***	51.897***	16.239	0.475***	3.196
	CBAccountability-98			-3.779	8.072	-0.057	-0.468
	LogGDPppc-95-99			-2.742	1.875	-0.217	-1.462
	Constant			22.589	20.457		1.104

Note: ***, **, and * indicate statistical significance at the 1%, 5% and 10% levels respectively.

Table 7 (continued): OLS results for the period 1995 to 1999

Model	Included variables	adjusted R²	F-Value	Coefficient	Standard Error	Standardised β	t-Value
Dependent variable: CPI-95-99, n = 44				Explanatory variables:	QEC-99-4, PolStab-96-98, LogGDPpc-95-99, CBIndependence-98-1, CBIndependence-98-2, CBTransparency-98, CBDeficitFinance-98		
				Excluded country:	Romania, Turkey		
Method: Stepwise selection (include if significance of F-Value ≤ 0.05, exclude if significance of F-Value ≥ 0.10)							
Model 18^w	LogGDPpc-95-99	0.414	31.388***	-4.387***	0.969		-4.529
	Constant			45.730***	9.412		4.859
Dependent variable: CPI-95-99, n = 44				Explanatory variables:	QEC-99-4, PolStab-96-98, CBIndependence-98-1, CBIndependence-98-2, CBTransparency-98, CBDeficitFinance-98		
				Excluded country:	Romania, Turkey		
Method: Stepwise selection (include if significance of F-Value ≤ 0.05, exclude if significance of F-Value ≥ 0.10)							
Model 19a^w	QEC-99-4	0.244	14.881***	45.928**	18.304		2.509
	Constant			-4.614	3.829		-1.205
Model 19b^w	QEC-99-4	0.312	10.770***	41.355**	16.054		2.576
	CBTransparency-98			-1.689***	0.733		-2.303
	Constant			0.517	3.839		0.135
Dependent variable: CPI-95-99, n = 44				Explanatory variables:	QEC-99-4, PolStab-96-98, CBTransparency-98		
				Excluded countries:	Romania, Turkey		
Method: All variables enter the regression model							
Model 20^w	QEC-99-4	0.330	8.072***	34.137*	17.034		2.004
	PolStab-96-98			-2.907	1.976		-1.471
	CBTransparency-98			-1.391*	0.811		-1.716
	Constant			3.354	4.302		0.779

Note: ***, **, and * indicate statistical significance at the 1%, 5% and 10% levels respectively. ^w indicates heteroskedasticity consistent standard errors.

Table 7 (continued): OLS results for the period 1995 to 1999

Model	Included variables	adjusted R^2	F-Value	Coefficient	Standard Error	Standardised β	t-Value
Dependent variable: CPI-95-99, n = 43				Explanatory variables: Excluded countries:	QEC-99-4, CBTransparency-98, Openness-95-99 Bahamas, Romania, Turkey		
Method: All variables enter the regression model							
Model 21[w]	QEC-99-4	0.298	6.930***	41.091**	16.650		2.470
	CBTransparency-98			-1.715**	0.751		-2.285
	Openness-95-99			-0.001	0.055		-0.024
	Constant			0.827	3.853		0.215
Dependent variable: CPI-95-99, n = 43				Explanatory variables: Excluded countries:	QEC-99-4, CBTransparency-98, CBAccountability-98 Japan, Romania, Turkey		
Method: All variables enter the regression model							
Model 22[w]	QEC-99-4	0.308	7.232***	42.327**	17.712		2.390
	CBTransparency-98			-1.729**	0.720		-2.402
	CBAccountability-98			5.284	3.740		1.413
	Constant			-3.544	5.846		-0.606

Note: ***, **, and * indicate statistical significance at the 1%, 5% and 10% levels respectively. [w] indicates heteroskedasticity consistent standard errors.

Table 7 (continued): OLS results for the period 1995 to 1999

Model	Included variables	adjusted R^2	F-Value	Coefficient	Standard Error	Standardised β	t-Value
Dependent variable: CPI-95-99, n = 25				Explanatory variables:	QEC-99-4, PolStab-96-98, LogGDPpc-95-99, GDPpc-95-99, CBIndependence-98-1, CBIndependence-98-2, RegQuality-96-98, Openness-95-99, CBTransparency-98, CBDeficitFinance-98, CBAccountability-98		
Method: Stepwise selection (include if significance of F-Value ≤ 0.05, exclude if significance of F-Value ≥ 0.10)							
Model 23a	QEC-99-4	0.215	7.577***	57.353**	20.835	0.498**	2.753
	Constant			-2.940	7.746		-0.380
Model 23b	QEC-99-4	0.326	6.794***	64.720***	19.605	0.562***	3.301
	CBTransparency-98			-5.287**	2.421	-0.372**	-2.184
	Constant			3.479	7.759		0.448
Model 23c[w]	QEC-99-4	0.416	6.691***	62.412***	10.971		5.689
	CBTransparency-98			-4.850***	2.190		-2.214
	PolStab-96-98			-9.679	7.239		-1.337
	Constant			5.075	7.893		0.643
Dependent variable: CPI-95-99, n = 23				Explanatory variables:	LogGDPpc-95-99		
				Excluded countries:	Romania, Turkey		
Method: All variables enter the regression model							
Model 24	LogGDPpc-95-99	0.122	4.052*	-4.035*	2.004	-0.402*	-2.013
	Constant			43.278***	15.913		2.720

Note: ***, **, and * indicate statistical significance at the 1%, 5% and 10% levels respectively. [w] indicates heteroskedasticity consistent standard errors.

Table 7 (continued): OLS results for the period 1995 to 1999

Model	Included variables	adjusted R²	F-Value	Coefficient	Standard Error	Standardised β	t-Value
Dependent variable: CPI-95-99, n = 21				Explanatory variables:	QEC-99-4, PolStab-96-98, LogGDPpc-95-99, GDPpc-95-99, CBIndependence-98-1, CBIndependence-98-2, RegQuality-96-98, CBTransparency-98, CBDeficitFinance-98		
Method: Stepwise selection (include if significance of F-Value ≤ 0.05, exclude if significance of F-Value ≥ 0.10)							
Model 25a	LogGDPpc-95-99	0.152	4.573**	-0.856**	0.400	-0.440**	-2.138
	Constant			10.246***	3.982		2.573
Model 25b	LogGDPpc-95-99	0.308	5.452**	-0.947***	0.363	-0.487***	-2.605
	CBTransparency-98			0.214***	0.093	0.431**	2.301
	Constant			10.503***	3.598		2.919
Dependent variable: GDPdeflator-95-99, n = 21				Explanatory variables:	QEC-99-4, PolStab-96-98, LogGDPpc-95-99, GDPpc-95-99, CBIndependence-98-1, CBIndependence-98-2, RegQuality-96-98, CBTransparency-98, CBDeficitFinance-98		
Method: Stepwise selection (include if significance of F-Value ≤ 0.05, exclude if significance of F-Value ≥ 0.10)							
Model 26a	QEC-99-4	0.265	8.206***	13.146***	4.589	0.549***	2.865
	Constant			-0.554	0.889		-0.624
Model 26b	QEC-99-4	0.384	7.238***	13.807***	4.212	0.577***	3.278
	CBTransparency-98			0.344**	0.159	0.381**	2.163
	Constant			-1.726*	0.978		-1.766
Model 26c	QEC-99-4	0.637	12.699***	17.128***	3.357	0.716***	5.102
	CBTransparency-98			0.476***	0.127	0.527***	3.740
	PolStab-96-98			-2.472***	0.672	-0.532***	-3.679
	Constant			-0.248	0.851		-0.291
Model 26d[w]	QEC-99-4	0.713	13.450***	19.282***	2.851		6.764
	CBTransparency-98			0.471***	0.110		4.269
	PolStab-96-98			-3.113***	0.572		-5.439
	RegQuality-96-98			1.326*	0.711		1.865
	Constant			-1.464	1.044		-1.402

Note: ***, **, and * indicate statistical significance at the 1%, 5% and 10% levels respectively. [w] indicates heteroskedasticity consistent standard errors.

Table 7 (continued): OLS results for the period 1995 to 1999

Model	Included variables	adjusted R²	F-Value	Coefficient	Standard Error	Standardised β	t-Value
Dependent variable: GDPdeflator-95-99, n = 21				Explanatory variables:	QEC-99-4, PolStab-96-98		
Method: All variables enter the regression model							
Model 27	QEC-99-4	0.375	7.001***	15.335***	4.360	0.641***	3.517
	PolStab-96-98			-1.764*	0.846	-0.380*	-2.086
	Constant			0.821	1.052		0.780
Dependent variable: GDPdeflator-95-99, n = 21				Explanatory variables:	QEC-99-4, PolStab-96-98, LogGDPpc-95-99		
Method: All variables enter the regression model							
Model 28	QEC-99-4	0.375	5.001**	13.419**	4.762	0.561**	2.818
	PolStab-96-98			-1.453	0.901	-0.313	-1.612
	LogGDPpc-95-99			-0.703	0.703	-0.199	-1.000
	Constant			7.862	7.116		1.105
Dependent variable: GDPdeflator-95-99, n = 20				Explanatory variables:	QEC-99-4, PolStab-96-98, Openness-95-99		
Method: All variables enter the regression model				Excluded countries:	Bahamas		
Model 29	QEC-99-4	0.359	4.545**	14.150**	4.905	0.588***	2.885
	PolStab-96-98			-2.036**	0.931	-0.430***	-2.186
	Openness-95-99			0.016	0.015	0.213	1.062
	Constant			0.784	1.083		0.724
Dependent variable: GDPdeflator-95-99, n = 20				Explanatory variables:	QEC-99-4, PolStab-96-98, CBAccountability-98		
Method: All variables enter the regression model				Excluded countries:	Japan		
Model 30	QEC-99-4	0.365	4.641**	12.269**	4.339	0.530**	2.827
	PolStab-96-98			-1.486*	0.798	-0.358*	-1.862
	CBAccountability-98			1.256	0.778	0.304	1.615
	Constant			0.254	1.270		0.200

Note: ***, **, and * indicate statistical significance at the 1%, 5% and 10% levels respectively.

241

Table 7 (continued): OLS results for the period 1995 to 1999

Model	Included variables	adjusted R^2	F-Value	Coefficient	Standard Error	Standardised β	t-Value
Dependent variable: LogCPI-95-99, n = 46 Method: All variables enter the regression model				Explanatory variables:	LogQEC-99-4, LogTransparency-98, LogPolStab-96-98, LogGDPpc-95-99		
Model 31[w]		0.518	13.094***				
	LogQEC-99-4			0.633***	0.194		3.258
	LogTransparency-98			-0.040	0.024		-1.653
	LogPolStab-96-98			-0.224	0.165		-1.361
	LogGDPpc-95-99			0.011	0.024		0.464
	Constant			0.163	0.154		1.053
Dependent variable: LogCPI-95-99, n = 46 Method: All variables enter the regression model				Explanatory variables:	LogQEC-99-4		
Model 32	LogQEC-99-4	0.362	26.512***	0.734***	0.143	0.613***	5.149
	Constant			-0.086**	0.036		-2.395

Note: ***, **, and * indicate statistical significance at the 1%, 5% and 10% levels respectively. [w] indicates heteroskedasticity consistent standard errors.

Table 7: OLS regression results for the period 1995 to 1999

Table 8: Correlations among constituent parts of the QEC-index

Method: Pearson	2.1Liquidity-03	2.4CloseTies-03	2.6SufficientCover-03	3.1Creditworth-03	BadDebtsX-98-03
			Period 1998 to 2003		
2.4CloseTies-03	0.063				
2.6SufficientCover-03	-0.285**	-0.013			
3.1Creditworth-03	0.175	0.180	0.120		
BadDebtsX-98-03	0.284**	0.002	0.100	0.232*	
CurrencyTA-98-03	0.127	0.103	0.000	0.242*	0.143

Method: Pearson	2.1Liquidity-90	2.4CloseTies-90	2.6SufficientCover-90	3.1Creditworth-90	BadDebtsX-90-97
			Period 1990 to 1997		
2.4CloseTies-90	0.225*				
2.6SufficientCover-90	-0.430***	0.047			
3.1Creditworth-90	-0.309**	0.064	0.037		
BadDebtsX-90-97	0.226*	-0.007	-0.027	0.196	
CurrencyTA-90-97	-0.219	0.006	0.242*	-0.150	-0.154

Method: Pearson	2.1Liquidity-03	2.4CloseTies-03	2.6SufficientCover-03	3.1Creditworth-03	BadDebtsX-95-99
			Period 1995 to 1999		
2.4CloseTies-03	-0.092				
2.6SufficientCover-03	-0.330**	0.043			
3.1Creditworth-03	0.303**	-0.160	-0.191		
BadDebtsX-95-99	0.542***	-0.070	0.179	0.234	
CurrencyTA-95-99	-0.042	0.040	-0.041	-0.326**	-0.152

Note: ***, **, and * indicate statistical significance at the 1%, 5% and 10% levels respectively.
Table 8: Correlations among constituent parts of the QEC-index

Table 9: Employed weightings for central bank independence indices

Index	Weighting coefficients				
	(1.) Statutory/legal objectives focus on price stability?	(2.) Target Independence	(3.) Instrument independence	(4.) Central Bank financing of government deficit	(5.) Term of Office of Governor
CBIndependence-98-1	0.154	0.154	0.308	0.308	0.077
CBIndependence-98-2	0.150	0.075	0.075	0.500	0.200

Sources:
Fry *et al.* (2000), table A.5 p. 149 f. for data and weighting coefficients of CBIndependence-98-1.
Cukierman *et al.* (1992a), table 1 page 358 f. for the weighting coefficients of CBIndependence-98-2.
Table 9: Employed weightings for central bank independence indices

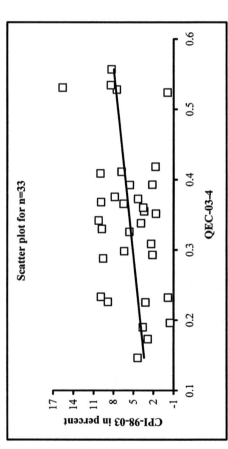

Scatter plot for n=33

Figure 68: Scatter plot for QEC-03-4 versus CPI-98-03 without Romania, Tajikistan and Turkey (n=33)

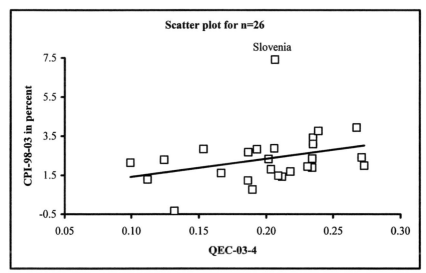

Figure 69: Scatter plot for QEC-03-4 versus CPI-98-03 (high income countries, n=26)

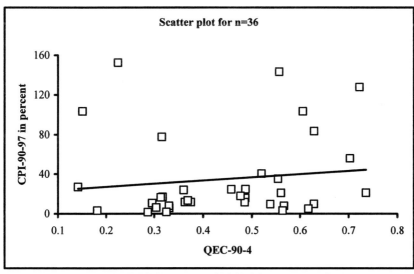

Figure 70: Scatter plot for QEC-90-4 versus CPI-90-97 without Brazil, Kazakhstan and Tajikistan (n=36)

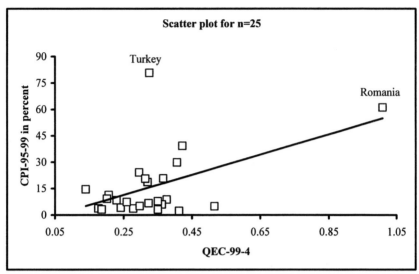

Figure 71: Scatter plot for QEC-99-4 versus CPI-95-99 (developing countries, n=25)

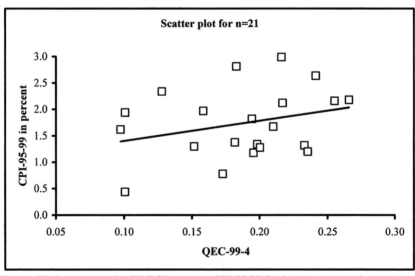

Figure 72: Scatter plot for QEC-99-4 versus CPI-95-99 (high income countries, n=21)

References

Alchian   Armen A. Alchian, Property Rights, in: John Eatwell, Murray
(1992)   Milgate and Peter Newman (editors), *The New Palgrave
               Dictionary of Money and Finance*, Macmillan: London, Vol.
               3, 1992, p. 223-226.

Alesina &   Alberto Alesina & Lawrence H. Summers, Central Bank
Summers   Independence and Macroeconomic Performance: Some
(1993)   Comparative Evidence, *Journal of Money, Credit, and
               Banking*, Vol. 25, No. 2, 1993, pp. 151–62.

Arnone *et al.*   Marco Arnone, Bernard J. Laurens and Jean-François
(2006a)   Segalotto, The Measurement of Central Bank Autonomy:
               Survey of Models, Indicators, and Empirical Evidence,
               International Monetary Fund Working Paper No. 06/227,
               October 2006.

Arnone *et al.*   Marco Arnone, Bernard J. Laurens and Jean-François
(2006b)   Segalotto, Measures of Central Bank Autonomy: Empirical
               Evidence for OECD, Developing, and Emerging Market
               Economies, *International Monetary Fund Working Paper No.
               06/228*, October 2006.

Bagehot   Walter Bagehot, *Lombard Street. A Description of the Money
(1873)   Market*, published by Frank C. Genovese, Hyperion Print:
               Westport, 1979.

Bailey (1998) Martin J. Bailey, Property Rights in Aboriginal Societies, in:
               Peter Newman (editor), *The New Palgrave Dictionary of
               Economics and the Law*, Macmillan: London, 1998, p. 155-
               158.

Bank of   Bank of Japan, The Bank of Japan's Eligible Collateral
Japan (2003)   Framework and Recently Accepted Collateral, in: *Bank of
               Japan Quarterly Bulletin*, May 2003, p. 1-9.

Bank of   Bank of Japan, Guidelines on Eligible Collateral, as of 16th of
Japan (2004)   March 2004, Internet:
               http://www.boj.or.jp/en/about/basic/yoryo/yoryo18.htm.

247

Barro & Gordon (1983a)	Robert J. Barro & David B. Gordon, A Positive Theory of Monetary Policy in a Natural Rate Model, in: *Journal of Political Economy*, Vol. 91, No. 4, 1983, p. 589-610.
Barro & Gordon (1983b)	Robert J. Barro & David B. Gordon, Rules, Discretion and Reputation in a Model of Monetary Policy, in: *Journal of Monetary Economics*, Vol. 12, No. 1, 1983, p. 101-121.
Barro (1976)	Robert J. Barro, The Loan Market, Collateral, and Rates of Interest, in: *Journal of Money, Credit, and Banking*, Vol. 8, 1976, p. 439-456.
Beckerman (1997)	Paul Beckerman, Central-Bank Decapitalization in Developing Economies, in: *World Development*, Vol. 25, No. 2, 1997, p. 167-178.
Begg *et al.* (1998)	David Begg, Paul de Grauwe, Francesco Giavazzi, Harald Uhlig and Charles Wyplosz, *The ECB: Safe at Any Speed?*, Center for Economic Policy Research: London, October 1998.
Berger & Udell (1990)	Allen N. Berger & Gregory F. Udell, Collateral, Loan Quality and Bank Risk, in: *Journal of Monetary Economics*, Vol. 25, No. 1, 1990, p. 21-42.
A. Berger *et al.* (2001)	Allen N. Berger, Leora F. Klapper, and Gregory F. Udell, The Ability of Banks to Lend to Informationally Opaque Small Businesses, in: *Journal of Banking and Finance*, Vol. 25, No. 12, 2001, p. 2127-2167.
Berger *et al.* (2003)	Allen N. Berger, Leora F. Klapper, Margaret J. Miller and Gregory F. Udell, Relationship Lending in the Argentine Small Business Credit Market, in: Margaret J. Miller (ed.), *Credit Reporting Systems and the International Economy*, Chicago Press: Chicago, 2003, p. 255-270.
Berger *et al.* (2001)	Helge Berger, Jakob de Haan and Sylvester C. W. Eijffinger, Central Bank Independence: An Update of Theory and Evidence, in: *Journal of Economic Surveys*, Vol. 15, No. 1, 2001, p. 3-40.

Bernanke & Blinder (1992)	Ben S. Bernanke & Alan S. Blinder, The Federal Funds Rate and the Channels of Monetary Transmission, in: *American Economic Review*, Vol. 82, No. 4, 1992, p. 901-921.
Bernanke & Gertler (1995)	Ben S. Bernanke & Mark Gertler, Inside the Black Box: The Credit Channel of Monetary Policy Transmission, in: *Journal of Economic Perspectives*, Vol. 9, No. 4, 1995, p. 27-48.
Bernanke & Mishkin (1997)	Ben S. Bernanke & Frederic S. Mishkin, Inflation Targeting: A New Framework for Monetary Policy?, in: *Journal of Economic Perspectives*, Vol. 11, No. 2, 1997, p. 97-116.
Bernanke et al. (1996)	Ben S. Bernanke, Mark Gertler and Simon Gilchrist, The Financial Accelerator and the Flight to Quality, in: *Review of Economics and Statistics*, Vol. 78, No. 1, 1996, p. 1-15.
Bigus et al. (2004)	Jochen Bigus, Thomas Langer and Dirk Schiereck, Wie werden Kreditsicherheiten in der Praxis eingesetzt? – Ein Überblick über empirische Befunde, in: *Zeitschrift für Bankrecht und Bankwirtschaft*, Vol. 16, 2004, p. 465-480.
Bigus et al. (2005)	Jochen Bigus, Thomas Langer and Dirk Schiereck, Warum gibt es Kreditsicherheiten?, in: *Kredit und Kapital*, Vol. 38, No. 4, 2005, p. 573-617.
Bindseil et al. (2004)	Ulrich Bindseil, Andres Manzanares and Benedict Weller, The Role of Central Bank Capital Revisited, *European Central Bank Working Paper No. 392*, September 2004.
BIS (2001)	Bank for International Settlements (BIS), *BIS Papers No. 9 Comparing Monetary Policy Operating Procedures Across the United States, Japan and the Euro Area*, December 2001.
Black (1998)	S. Black, Seigniorage, in: John Eatwell, Murray Milgate and Peter Newman (editors), *The New Palgrave A Dictionary of Economics*, Vol. 4, Paperback Edition, MacMillan: London, 1998, p. 287.
Blaug (1998)	Mark Blaug, The Disease of Formalism in Economics, or Bad Games That Economists Play, in: *Lectiones Jenenses*, Schriftenreihe des Max-Planck-Instituts zur Erforschung von Wirtschaftssystemen, issue 16, 1998.

Blejer & Schumacher (1998)	Mario I. Blejer & Liliana Schumacher, Central Bank Vulnerability and the Credibility of Commitments: A Value-at-Risk Approach to Currency Crises, *International Monetary Fund Working Paper 98/65*, 1998.
Blejer & Schumacher (2003)	Mario I. Blejer & Liliana Schumacher, Central bank use of contingent liabilities, in: Neil Courtis & Benedict Mander (editors), *Accounting Standards for Central Banks*, Central Banking Publications: London, 2003, p. 319-326.
Blenck *et al.* (2001)	Denis Blenck, Harri Hasko, Spence Hilton and Kazuhiro Masaki, The Main Features of the Monetary Policy Frameworks of the Bank of Japan, the Federal Reserve and the Eurosystem, in: *BIS Papers No. 9 Comparing Monetary Policy Operating Procedures Across the United States, Japan and the Euro Area*, December 2001, p. 23-56.
Blinder (1998)	Alan Stuart Blinder, *Central Banking in Theory and Practice*, MIT Press: London, 1998.
Blinder (2000)	Alan Stuart Blinder, Central-Bank Credibility: Why Do We Care? How Do We Build It?, in: *American Economic Review*, Vol. 90, No. 5, December 2000, p. 1421-1431.
Bofinger *et al.* (1996)	Peter Bofinger, Julian Reischle and Andrea Schächter, *Geldpolitik – Ziele, Institutionen, Strategien und Instrumente*, Franz Vahlen: Munich, 1996.
Bofinger *et al.* (2001)	Peter Bofinger, Julian Reischle and Andrea Schächter, Monetary Policy: Goals, Institutions, Strategies, and Instruments, Oxford University Press: Oxford, 2001.
Boland (1998)	Lawrence A. Boland, Methodology, in: John Eatwell, Murray Milgate and Peter Newman (editors), *The New Palgrave A Dictionary of Economics*, Vol. 3, Paperback Edition, MacMillan: London, 1998, p. 455-458.
Boot *et al.* (1991)	Arnoud W. A. Boot, Anjan V. Thakor and Gregory F. Udell, Secured Lending and Default Risk: Equilibrium Analysis, Policy Implications and Empirical Results, in: *The Economic Journal*, Vol. 101, No. 406, 1991, p. 458-472.

Borio (2001)   Claudio E. V. Borio, A Hundred Ways to Skin a Cat:
                Comparing Monetary Policy Operating Procedures Across the
                United States, Japan and the Euro Area, in: *BIS Papers No. 9
                Comparing Monetary Policy Operating Procedures Across the
                United States, Japan and the Euro Area*, December 2001, p. 1-
                22.

Bowen   Alex Bowen, Comment on Prudential Policy by Jean-Charles
(2005)   Rochet, in: *Bank of Japan Institute for Monetary and
                Economic Studies, Monetary and Economic Studies (Special
                Edition)*, Vol.23, No.S-1, 2005, p. 120-126.

Buiter (2004)   Willem H. Buiter, A Small Corner of Intertemporal Public
                Finance – New Developments in Monetary Economics: Two
                Ghosts, Two Eccentricities, a Fallacy, a Mirage and a Mythos,
                *National Bureau of Economic Research Working Paper No.
                10524*, May 2004.

Bürgerliches   *Bürgerliches Gesetzbuch*, 50th updated edition, as of 29th of
Gesetzbuch   November 2001, Deutscher Taschenbuch Verlag: Munich,
(2002)   2002.

Caballero *et* Ricardo J. Caballero, Takeo Hoshi, and Anil K. Kashyap,
al. (2006)   Zombie Lending and Depressed Restructuring in Japan,
                *National Bureau of Economic Research Working Paper No.
                12129*, April 2006.

Caldwell   Bruce J. Caldwell, Clarifying Popper, in: *Journal of Economic
(1991)   Literature*, Vol. 29, No. 1, 1991, p. 1-33.

Campillo &   Marta Campillo & Jeffrey A. Miron, Why Does Inflation
Miron (1997)   Differ across Countries?, in: Christina D. Romer and David H.
                Romer (editors), *Reducing Inflation. Motivation and Strategy*,
                University of Chicago Press: London, 1997, p. 335-357.

Cargill   Thomas F. Cargill, Is the Bank of Japan's Financial Structure
(2005)   an Obstacle to Policy?, in: *International Monetary Fund Staff
                Papers*, Vol. 52, Number 2, 2005, p. 311-334.

Cecchetti & Li (2005)	Stephen G. Cecchetti & Lianfa Li, Do Capital Adequacy Requirements Matter for Monetary Policy?, *National Bureau of Economic Research Working Paper No. 11830*, December 2005.
Chen *et al.* (2006)	Nan-Kuang Chen, Hsiao-Lei Chu, Jin-Tan Liu and Kuang-Hsien Wang, Collateral Value, Firm Borrowing, and Forbearance Lending: An Empirical Study of Taiwan, in: *Japan and the World Economy*, Vol. 18, No. 1, 2006 p. 49-71.
Chortareas *et al.* (2002a)	Georgios Chortareas, David Stasavage und Gabriel Sterne, Monetary Policy Transparency, Inflation and the Sacrifice Ratio, in: *International Journal of Finance and Economics*, Vol. 7, No. 2, 2002, p. 141-155.
Chortareas *et al.* (2002b)	Georgios Chortareas, David Stasavage und Gabriel Sterne, Does It Pay To Be Transparent? International Evidence from Central Bank Forecasts, in: *Federal Reserve Bank of St. Louis Review*, Vol. 84, No. 4, 2002, p. 99-118.
Coco (2000)	Giuseppe Coco, On the Use of Collateral, in: *Journal of Economic Surveys*, Vol. 14, No. 2, 2000, p. 191-214.
Córdoba & Ripoll (2004)	Juan Carlos Córdoba & Marla Ripoll, Credit Cycles Redux, *International Economic Review*, Vol. 45, No. 4, 2004, p.1011-1046.
Cossin & Hricko (2003)	Didier Cossin & Tomas Hricko, A Structural Analysis of Credit Risk With Risky Collateral: A Methodology for Haircut Determination, in: Economic Notes (Banca Monte dei Paschi di Siena SpA), Vol. 32, No. 2, 2003, p. 243-282.
Cossin *et al.* (2003)	Didier Cossin, Zhijiang Huang, Daniel Aunon-Nerin und Fernando González, A Framework for Collateral Risk Control Determination, *European Central Bank Working Paper No. 209*, January 2003.
Courtis & Mander (2003)	Neil Courtis & Benedict Mander, *Accounting Standards for Central Banks*, Central Banking Publications: London, 2003.

Cukierman (2002)	Alex Cukierman, Are Contemporary Central Banks Transparent About Economic Models and Objectives and What Difference Does it Make?, in: *Federal Reserve Bank of St. Louis Review*, Vol. 84, No. 4, 2002, p. 15-35.
Cukierman & Meltzer (1986)	Alex Cukierman & Allan H. Meltzer, A Theory of Ambiguity, Credibility, and Inflation under Discretion and Asymmetric Information, in: *Econometrica*, Vol. 54, No. 5, 1986, p. 1099-1128.
Cukierman et al. (1992a)	Alex Cukierman, Steven B. Webb and Bilin Neyapti, Measuring the Independence of Central Banks and Its Effect on Policy Outcomes, in: *World Bank Economic Review*, Vol. 6, No. 3, 1992, p. 353-398.
Cukierman et al. (1992b)	Alex Cukierman, Sebastian Edwards and Guido Tabellini, Seigniorage and Political Instability, in: *American Economic Review*, Vol. 82, No. 3, 1992, p. 537-555.
Dalton & Dziobek (2005)	John Dalton & Claudia Dziobek, Central Bank Losses and Experiences in Selected Countries, *International Monetary Fund Working Paper*, WP/05/72, April 2005.
Das et al. (2004)	Udaibir S. Das, Marc Quintyn and Kina Chenard, Does Regulatory Governance Matter for Financial System Stability? An Empirical Analysis, *International Monetary Fund Working Paper*, WP/04/89, May 2004.
Dekle & Kletzer (2002)	Robert S. Dekle & Kenneth Kletzer, Financial Intermediation, Agency and Collateral and the Dynamics of Banking Crises: Theory and Evidence for the Japanese Banking Crisis, *Federal Reserve Bank of San Francisco Pacific Basin Working Paper No. PB02-10*, September 2002.
Demsetz (1967)	Harold Demsetz, Toward a Theory of Property Rights, in: *American Economic Review,* Vol. 57, 1967, p. 347-59.
Demsetz (1998)	Harold Demsetz, Property Rights, in: Peter Newman (editor), *The New Palgrave Dictionary of Economics and the Law*, Macmillan: London, 1998, p. 144-155.

Dittus (1996)   Peter Dittus, Why East European banks don't want equity, in: *European Economic Review*, Vol. 40, No. 3-5, 1996, p. 655-662.

Dornbusch   Rudi Dornbusch, Exchange Rates and the Choice of Monetary
(2001)   Policy Regimes: Fewer Monies, Better Monies, in: *American Economic Review*, Vol. 91, No. 2, 2001, p. 238-242.

ECB (2001)   European Central Bank (ECB), The collateral framework of the Eurosystem, in: *European Central Bank Monthly Bulletin*, April 2001, p. 49-62.

ECB (2004)   European Central Bank (ECB), *Measures to Improve the Collateral Framework of the Eurosystem: Summary of the Answers to the Public Consultation*, 15th of January 2004, Internet: http://www.ecb.int/ecb/pdf/cons/impframew/ collateralframeworksummaryen.pdf.

ECB (2005)   European Central Bank (ECB), *The Implementation of Monetary Policy in the Euro Area: General Documentation on the Eurosystem Monetary Policy Instruments and Procedures*, February 2005 Internet: http://www.ecb.int/pub/pdf/other/gendoc2005en.pdf.

ECB (2006)   European Central Bank (ECB), *"Eligible Assets"*, 2006, Internet: http://www.ecb.int/mopo/implement/ assets/assets/html/eligible_info.en.html.

Economist   "Risk and the new financial order: Surviving the markets", in:
(2007a)   *The Economist*, Vol. 384, No. 8542, August 18th 2007, p. 9.

Economist   "Banks in trouble: The game is up", in: *The Economist*, Vol.
(2007b)   384, No. 8542, August 18th 2007, p. 59-60.

Economist   "A liquidity squeeze: Bankers' mistrust", in: *The Economist*,
(2007c)   Vol. 384, No. 8542, August 18th 2007, p. 60.

Elsas &   Ralf Elsas & Jan Pieter Krahnen, Collateral, Default Risk, and
Krahnen   Relationship Lending: An Empirical Study on Financial
(1999)   Contracting, *Center for Financial Studies Working Paper No. 1999/13*, 1999.

Elul (2005)   Ronel Elul, Collateral, Credit History, and the Financial
                     Decelerator, *Federal Reserve Bank of Philadelphia Working
                     Paper No. 05-23*, September 2005.

Ernhagen *et*   Tomas Ernhagen, Magnus Vesterlund and Staffan Viotti, How
al. (2002)   Much Equity Does a Central Bank Need?, in: *Sveriges
                     Riksbank Economic Review*, Vol. 2, 2002, p. 5-18.

Faig &   Miquel Faig & Gregory Gagnon, Scarce Collateral and Bank
Gagnon   Reserves, *University of Toronto Department of Economics
(2002)   Working Paper No. faig-03-01*, January 2002.

Faust &   Jon Faust & Lars E. O. Svensson, The Equilibrium Degree of
Svensson   Transparency and Control in Monetary Policy, in: *Journal of
(2002)   Money, Credit, and Banking*, Vol. 34, No. 2, 2002, p. 520-539.

Fischer   Stanley Fischer, Long-Term Contracts, Rational Expectations,
(1977)   and the Optimal Money Supply Rule, in: *Journal of Political
                     Economy*, Vol. 85, No. 1, 1977, p. 191-205.

Forder (2000)   James Forder, Central Bank Independence and Credibility: Is
                     there a Shred of Evidence?: Review, in: *International
                     Finance*, Vol. 3, No. 1, 2000, p. 167-185.

Freixas *et al.*   Xavier Freixas, Curzio Giannini, Glenn Hoggarth and Farouk
(2002)   Soussa, Lender of Last Resort: A Review of the Literature, in:
                     Charles A. E. Goodhart and Gerhard Illing (editors), *Financial
                     Crises, Contagion, and the Lender of Last Resort*, Oxford
                     University Press: Oxford, 2002, p. 27-53.

Friedman   Benjamin M. Friedman, The Use and Meaning of Words in
(2003)   Central Banking: Inflation Targeting, Credibility and
                     Transparency, in: Paul Mizen (editors), *Central Banking,
                     Monetary Theory and Practice*, Edward Elgar: Cheltenham,
                     2003, p. 111-124.

Friedman &   Milton Friedman & Anna J. Schwartz, Has Government Any
Schwartz   Role in Money?, in: *Journal of Monetary Economics*, Vol. 17,
(1986)   No. 1, 1986, p. 37-62.

Fry (1993)	Maxwell J. Fry, The Fiscal Abuse of Central Banks, *International Monetary Fund Working Paper No. WP/93/58*, 1993.
Fry (1998)	Maxwell John Fry, Assessing Central Bank Independence in Developing Countries: Do Actions Speak Louder Than Words?, in: *Oxford Economic Papers*, Vol. 50, No. 3, 1998, p. 512-529.
Fry *et al.* (1996)	Maxwell John Fry, Charles A. E. Goodhart and Alvaro Almeida, *Central Banking in Developing Countries. Objectives, Activities and Independence*, Routledge: London, 1996.
Fry *et al.* (2000)	Maxwell John Fry, DeAnne Julius, Lavan Mahadeva, Sandra Roger and Gabriel Sterne, Key Issues in the Choice of Monetary Policy Framework, in: Levan Mahadeva and Gabriel Sterne (editors), *Monetary Policy Frameworks in a Global Context,* Routledge: London, 2000, p. 1-216.
Fuhrer (1997)	Jeffrey C. Fuhrer, Central Bank Independence and Inflation Targeting: Monetary Policy Paradigms for the Next Millennium?, in: *New England Economic Review*, Vol. 3, No. 1-2, 1997, p. 19-36.
Fujiki (1996)	Hiroshi Fujiki, Central Bank Independence Indexes in Economic Analysis: A Reappraisal, *Monetary and Economic Studies*, Bank of Japan, Vol. 14 , 1996, pp. 79–101.
Gelos & Werner (2002)	R. Gaston Gelos & Alejandro M. Werner, Financial Liberalization, Credit Constraints, and Collateral: Investment in the Mexican Manufacturing Sector, in: *Journal of Development Economics*, Vol. 67, No. 1, 2002, p. 1-27.
Geraats (2002)	Petra M. Geraats, Central Bank Transparency, in: *Economic Journal*, Vol. 112, 2002, p. F532-F565.
Geraats (2005)	Petra M. Geraats, Transparency and Reputation: The Publication of Central Bank Forecasts, *Topics in Macroeconomics*, Vol. 5, No. 1, Article 1, 2005.

| Goldberg & Klein (2005) | Linda S. Goldberg & Michael W. Klein, Establishing Credibility: Evolving Perceptions of the European Central Bank, *Federal Reserve Bank of New York Staff Report No. 231*, November 2005. |

| Goldstone *et al.* (2000) | Jack A. Goldstone, Ted Robert Gurr, Barbara Harff, Marc A. Levy, Monty G. Marshall, Robert H. Bates, David L. Epstein, Colin H. Kahl, Pamela T. Surko, John C. Ulfelder, Jr. and Alan N. Unger, *State Failure Task Force Report: Phase III Findings*, McLean, Va.: Science Applications International Corporation, 2000. |

| Gonas *et al.* (2004) | John S. Gonas, Michael J. Highfield and Donald J. Mullineaux, When Are Commercial Loans Secured?, in: *The Financial Review*, Vol. 39, No. 1, 2004, p. 79-99. |

| Goodfriend (1986) | Marvin Goodfriend, Monetary Mystique: Secrecy and Central Banking, in: *Journal of Monetary Economics*, Vol. 17, No. 1, 1986, p. 63-92. |

| Goodhart (1985) | Charles A. E. Goodhart, The Evolution of Central Banks. A Natural Development?, *STICERD (Suntory-Toyota International Centre for Economics and Related Disciplines) Occasional Paper No. 8*, London School of Economics and Political Science: London, 1985. |

| Goodhart (1995) | Charles A. E. Goodhart, Some Regulatory Concerns, *Financial Marktets Group London School of Economics, Special Paper No. 79*, 1995. |

| Goodhart (1999) | Charles A. E. Goodhart, Myths about the Lender of Last Resort, in: *International Finance*, Vol. 2, No. 3, 1999, p. 339-360. |

| Gregory (1998) | C. A. Gregory, Gifts, in: John Eatwell, Murray Milgate and Peter Newman (editors), *The New Palgrave A Dictionary of Economics*, Vol. 2, Paperback Edition, MacMillan: London, 1998, p. 524-528. |

Gros (2004) Daniel Gros, Financial Aspects of Central Bank Independence and Price Stability: The Case of Turkey, Centre for European Policy Studies, *EU-Turkey Working Papers No. 12*, September 2004.

Hanser (2001) Frank Hanser, *Die Struktur von Kreditbeziehungen. Eine empirische Analyse zentraler Bestandteile von Kreditverträgen*, Gabler: Frankfurt am Main, 2001.

Hart (1998) Keith Hart, Barter, in: John Eatwell, Murray Milgate and Peter Newman (editors), *The New Palgrave A Dictionary of Economics*, Vol. 1, Paperback Edition, MacMillan: London, 1998, p. 196-198.

Hawkins (2004) John Hawkins, Central bank balance sheets and fiscal operations, in: *BIS Papers No. 20 – Fiscal issues and central banking in emerging economies*, 2004, p. 71-83.

Heinsohn & Steiger (1989) Gunnar Heinsohn & Otto Steiger, The Veil of Barter: The Solution to 'The Task of Obtaining Representations of an Economy in which Money is Essential', in: J. A. Kregel (editor), *Inflation and Income Distribution in Capitalist Crisis. Essays in Memory of Sidney Weintraub*, MacMillan: London, 1989, p. 175-201.

Heinsohn & Steiger (1996) Gunnar Heinsohn & Otto Steiger, *Eigentum, Zins und Geld: Ungelöste Rätsel der Wirtschaftswissenschaft*, Rowohlt: Reinbek, 1996; 3rd edition, Metropolis: Marburg, 2004.

Heinsohn & Steiger (2000a) Gunnar Heinsohn & Otto Steiger, The Property Theory of Interest and Money, in: John Smithin (editor), *What is Money?* Routledge: London, 2000, p. 67-100; corrected and updated reprint in: Geoffrey M. Hodgson (editor), *Recent Developments in Institutional Economics*, Edward Elgar: Cheltenham, 2003, p. 484-517.

Heinsohn & Steiger (2000b) Gunnar Heinsohn & Otto Steiger, Geldnote, Anleihe und Aktie: Gemeinsamkeiten und Unterschiede dreier Wertpapiere, *IKSF-Discussion Paper No. 22* (Universität Bremen), September 2000.

Heinsohn & Steiger (2002)	Gunnar Heinsohn & Otto Steiger, The Eurosystem and the Art of Central Banking, in: *Studi Economici: revista quadrimestrale* (Universität Neapel), Vol. 76, Nr. 1, 2002, p. 5-30.
Heinsohn & Steiger (2005a)	Gunnar Heinsohn & Otto Steiger, Alternative Theories of the Rate of Interest: A Reconsideration, in: Giuseppe Fontana & Riccardo Realfonzo (editors), *The Monetary Theory of Production – Tradition and Perspectives: Essays in Honour of Augusto Graziani*, Palgrave Macmillan: Basingstoke, 2005, p. 67-81.
Heinsohn & Steiger (2005b)	Gunnar Heinsohn & Otto Steiger, *Eigentumsökonomik*, Metropolis: Marburg, 2005.
Heinsohn & Steiger (2006)	Gunnar Heinsohn & Otto Steiger, Interest and Money: The Property Explanation, in: Philip Arestis & Malcolm C. Sawyer (editors), *A Handbook of Alternative Monetary Economics*. Edward Elgar: Cheltenham, UK and Northampton, MA, 2006, p. 490-507.
Heinsohn & Steiger (2007a)	Gunnar Heinsohn & Otto Steiger, Money, Markets and Property, in: Alberto Giacomin & Maria Cristina Marcuzzo (editors), *Money and Marktets: A Doctrinal Approach*, Routledge: London, 2007, p. 59-78.
Heinsohn & Steiger (2007b)	Gunnar Heinsohn & Otto Steiger, Collateral and Own Capital: The Missing Links in the Theory of the Rate of Interest and Money, in: Otto Steiger (editor), *Property Economics: Property Rights, Creditor's Money and the Foundations of the Economy*, Metropolis: Marburg, 2007, p. 181-222 (forthcoming).
Heinsohn & Steiger (2008)	Gunnar Heinsohn & Otto Steiger, *Property, Interest and Money: Foundations of Economic Theory*, Routledge: London, 2008 (forthcoming).
Holmström & Tirole (1997)	Bengt Holmström & Jean Tirole, Financial Intermediation, Loanable Funds, and the Real Sector, in: *Quarterly Journal of Economics*, Vol. 112, No. 3, 1997, p. 663-691.

Hubbard (1998)	R. G. Hubbard, Capital-market Imperfections and Investment, in: *Journal of Economic Literature*, Vol. 36, 1998, p. 193-225.
Hudson (1995)	John Hudson, The Case Against Secured Lending, in: *International Review of Law and Economics*, Vol. 15, No. 1, 1995, p. 47-63.
Igawa & Kanatas (1990)	Kazuhiro Igawa & George Kanatas, Asymmetric Information, Collateral, and Moral Hazard, in: *Journal of Financial and Quantitative Analysis*, Vol. 25, No. 4, 1990, p. 469-490.
IMF (1999)	International Monetary Fund, *Code of Good Practices on Transparency in Monetary and Financial Policies: Declaration of Principles*, 1999, Internet: http://www.imf.org/external/np/mae/mft/code/index.htm.
Inaba *et al.* (2005)	Nobuo Inaba, Takashi Kozu, Takashi Nagahata and Toshitaka Sekine, Non-performing loans and the real economy: Japan's experience, in: *Bank for International Settlements Papers No. 22 – Investigating the relationship between the financial and real economy*, April 2005, p. 106-127.
Ize (2005)	Alain Ize, Capitalizing Central Banks: A Net Worth Approach, *International Monetary Fund Staff Papers*, Vol. 52, Number 2, 2005, p. 269-310.
Jácome (2001)	Luis Ignacio Jácome Hidalgo, Legal Central Bank Independence and Inflation in Latin America During the 1990s, *International Monetary Fund Working Paper No. WP/01/212*, December 2001.
Jeanne & Svensson (2004)	Olivier Jeanne & Lars E.O. Svensson, Credible Commitment to Optimal Escape from a Liquidity Trap: The Role of the Balance Sheet of an Independent Central Bank, *National Bureau of Economic Research Working Paper No. 10679*, August 2004
Jiménez & Saurina (2004)	Gabriel Jiménez & Jesús Saurina, Collateral, Type of Lender and Relationship Banking as Determinants of Credit Risk, in: *Journal of Banking & Finance*, Vol. 28, No. 9, 2004, p. 2191-2212.

Jiménez *et al.* (2004)	Gabriel Jiménez, Vicente Salas and Jesús Saurina, Determinants of Collateral, *Banco de España Working Paper No. 0420*, 2004.
Jones (1976)	Robert A. Jones, The Origin and Development of Media of Exchange, in: *Journal of Political Economy*, Vol. 84, No. 4, 1976, p. 757-775.
Kanatas (1992)	George Kanatas, Collateral, in: *The New Palgrave Dictionary of Money and Finance*, Macmillan: London, 1992, Vol. 1, p. 381-383.
Kashyap & Stein (1995)	Anil K. Kashyap & Jeremy C. Stein, The Impact of Monetary Policy on Bank Balance Sheets, in: *Carnegie-Rochester Conference Series on Public Policy*, Vol. 42, 1995, p. 151-195.
Kaufmann *et al.* (2006)	Daniel Kaufmann, Aart Kraay and Massimo Mastruzzi, Governance Matters V: Governance Indicators for 1996-2005, *World Bank Policy Research Paper*, September 2006.
Keynes (1936)	John Maynard Keynes, *The General Theory of Employment, Interest, and Money*, in: Great Minds Paperback Series, Prometheus Books: New York, 1997.
Kim (1999)	Hyun E. Kim, Was Credit Channel a Key Monetary Transmission Mechanism Following the Recent Financial Crisis in the Republic of Korea?, *World Bank Policy Research Working Paper 3003*, April 1999.
Kiyotaki & Moore (1997)	Nobuhiro Kiyotaki & John Moore, Credit Cycles, in: *Journal of Political Economy*, Vol. 105, No. 2, 1997, p. 211–248.
Kocherlakota & Shim (2005)	Narayana Kocherlakota & Ilhyock Shim, Forbearance and prompt corrective action, *Bank for International Settlements Working Paper No. 177*, May 2005.
Koo (2001)	Richard C. Koo, The Japanese economy in balance sheet recession, in: *Business economics*, Vol. 36, No. 2, 2001, p.15-23.

Kopcke (2002)	Richard W. Kopcke, The Practice of Central Banking in Other Industrialized Countries, *New England Economic Review*, Second Quarter 2002, p. 3-9.
Kritikos & Vigenina (2005)	Alexander S. Kritikos & Denitsa Vigenina, Key Factors of Joint-Liability Loan Contracts: An Empirical Analysis, in: *Kyklos*, Vol. 58, No. 2, 2005, p. 213–238.
Kuhn (1970)	Thomas S. Kuhn, *The Structure of Scientific Revolutions*, University of Chicago Press: Chicago, 2nd enlarged edition, 1970.
Kurtzig (2003)	Joshua Kurtzig; Coping with Accounting Standards and Central Bank Transparency, in: Neil Courtis & Benedict Mander (editors), *Accounting Standards for Central Banks*, Central Banking Publications: London, 2003, p. 311-317.
Kurtzig & Mander (2003)	Joshua Kurtzig & Benedict Mander, Survey of Central Bank Accounting Practices, in: Neil Courtis & Benedict Mander (editors), *Accounting Standards for Central Banks*, Central Banking Publications: London, 2003, p. 21-46.
Kydland & Prescott (1977)	Finn E. Kydland & Edward C. Prescott, Rules Rather than Discretion: The Inconsistency of Optimal Plans, in: *Journal of Political Economy*, Vol. 85, No. 3, 1977, p. 473-491.
Lacker (2001)	Jeffrey M. Lacker, Collateralized Debt as the Optimal Contract, in: *Review of Economic Dynamics*, Vol. 4, No. 4, 2001, p. 842-859.
Lakatos (1970)	Imre Lakatos, Falsification and the Methodology of Scientific Research Programmes, in: Imre Lakatos and Alan Musgrave (editors), *Criticism and the Growth of Knowledge*, Cambridge University Press: Cambridge, 1970, p. 91-196.
Lehmbecker (2004)	Philipp Lehmbecker, *Eine empirische Untersuchung über den Einfluss der Güte von zentralbankfähigen Sicherheiten bei der Geldemission auf die Geldwertstabilität*, diploma thesis delivered at University of Kiel, December 2004.

Lehmbecker (2005)	Philipp Lehmbecker, On the Effect of the Quality of Eligible Collateral on Price Stability: An Empirical Analysis, *Institut für Konjunktur- und Strukturforschung Discussion Paper No. 33*, University of Bremen, June 2005.
Leone (1993)	Alfredo M. Leone, Institutional and Operational Aspects of Central Bank Losses, *Paper on Policy Analysis and Assessment of the International Monetary Fund (IMF)*, PPAA/93/14, September 1993.
Levine (1997)	Ross Levine, Financial Development and Economic Growth: Views and Agenda, in: *Journal of Economic Literature*, Vol. 35, No. 2, 1997, p. 688-726.
Loungani & Sheets (1997)	Prakash Loungani & Nathan Sheets, Central Bank Independence, Inflation, and Growth in Transition Economies, in: *Journal of Money, Credit, and Banking*, Vol. 29, No. 3, 1997, p. 381-399.
Lucas (1973)	Lucas, Robert E., Jr., Some International Evidence on Output-Inflation Tradeoffs, in: *American Economic Review*, Vol. 63, No. 3, June 1973, p. 326-334.
Maiangwa et al. (2004)	M. G. Maiangwa, S. A. Rahman, R. A. Omolehin and D. O. A. Phillip, A Review of Institutional Alternatives to Collateralized Lending, in: *African Development Review*, Vol. 16, No. 3, 2004, p. 472-491.
Manove & Padilla (1999)	Michael Manove & A. Jorge Padilla, Banking (conservatively) with optimists, in: *RAND Journal of Economics*, Vol. 30, No. 2, 1999, pp. 324–350.
Martínez-Resano (2004)	José Ramón Martínez-Resano, Central Bank Financial Independence, *Bank of Spain Occasional Paper No. 0401*, 2004.
McCallum (1997)	Bennett T. McCallum, Crucial Issues Concerning Central Bank Independence, in: *Journal of Monetary Economics*, Vol. 39, No. 1, 1997, p. 99-112.

McCloskey (1983)	Deidre N. (Donald) McCloskey, The Rhetoric of Economics, in: *Journal of Economic Literature*, Vol. 21, No. 2. 1983, p. 481-517.
Mishkin (1999)	Frederic S. Mishkin, International Experiences with Different Monetary Policy Regimes, in: *Journal of Monetary Economics*, Vol. 43, No. 3, 1999, p. 579-605.
Mishkin & Schmidt-Hebbel (2001)	Frederic S. Mishkin & Klaus Schmidt-Hebbel, One Decade of Inflation Targeting in the World: What Do We Know and What Do We Need to Know?, *National Bureau of Economic Research Working Paper No. 8397*, July 2001.
Muñoz (2007)	Sònia Muñoz, Central Bank Quasi-fiscal Losses and High Inflation in Zimbabwe: A Note, *International Monetary Fund Working Paper No. 07/98*, April 2007.
Nkurunziza (2005)	Janvier D. Nkurunziza, Reputation and Credit without Collateral in Africa's Formal Banking, *The Centre for the Study of African Economies Working Paper No. 236*, January 2005.
Ono & Uesugi (2005)	Arito Ono & Iichiro Uesugi, The Role of Collateral and Personal Guarantees in Relationship Lending: Evidence from Japan's Small Business Loan Market, *Research Institute of Economy, Trade and Industry (Ministry of Economy, Trade and Industry of Japan) Discussion Paper 05-E-027*, November 2005.
Peng (2005)	Wensheng Peng, Comment on Prudential Policy by Jean-Charles Rochet, in: *Bank of Japan Institute for Monetary and Economic Studies, Monetary and Economic Studies (Special Edition)*, Vol.23, No.S-1, 2005, p. 126-129.
Perraudin & Taylor (2004)	William Perraudin & Alex P. Taylor, On the consistency of ratings and bond market yields, in: *Journal of Banking & Finance*, Vol. 28, No. 11, 2004, p. 2769-2788.
Popper (2002)	Karl Popper, *Logik der Forschung*, Mohr Siebeck: Tübingen, jubilee edition, 2002, identical to the 10th edition from 1994.

Posen (1998)   Adam Simon Posen, Central Bank Independence and
                 Disinflationary Credibility: A Missing Link?, in: *Oxford
                 Economic Papers*, Vol. 50, No. 3, 1998, p. 335-359.

Posen (2002)   Adam Simon Posen, Commentary on "Does It Pay To Be
                 Transparent? International Evidence from Central Bank
                 Forecasts" by Georgios Chortareas, David Stasavage and
                 Gabriel Sterne, in: *Federal Reserve Bank of St. Louis Review*,
                 Vol. 84, No. 4, 2002, p. 119-126.

Posen (2003)   Adam Simon Posen, Six Practical Views of Central Bank
                 Transparency, in: Paul Mizen (editors), *Central Banking,
                 Monetary Theory and Practice: Essays in Honour of Charles
                 Goodhart, Volume One*, Edward Elgar: Cheltenham, 2003, p.
                 153-172.

Pozzolo   Alberto F. Pozzolo, The role of guarantees in bank lending,
(2004)   *Bank of Italy Working Paper No. 528*, December 2004.

Pringle   Robert Pringle, Why Central Banks Need Capital, in: *Central
(2003)   Banking*, Vol. 14, No. 1, 2003, p. 76-80.

Reichlin   Pietro Reichlin, Credit Markets, Intermediation, and the
(2004)   Macroeconomy: A Discussion, in: Sudipto Bhattacharya,
                 Arnoud W. A. Boot and Anjan V. Thakor (editors), *Credit,
                 Intermediation, and the Macroeconomy: Readings and
                 Perspectives in Modern Financial Theory*, Oxford: Oxford
                 University Press, 2004.

Reischle   Julian Reischle, *Die geldpolitische Strategie der Europäischen
(2004)   Zentralbank und alternative Strategien,* Presentation given on
                 the 4th summer workshop of Deutsche Bundesbank
                 „Europäische Geldpolitik in der Praxis" in Eltville
                 (28.06.2004 to 09.07.2004), 29. June 2004.

Ritter (1995)   Joseph A. Ritter, The Transition from Barter to Fiat Money,
                 in: *American Economic Review*, Vol. 85, No. 1, 1995, p. 134-
                 149.

Rochet (2005)	Jean-Charles Rochet, Prudential Policy, in: *Bank of Japan Institute for Monetary and Economic Studies, Monetary and Economic Studies (Special Edition)*, Vol.23, No.S-1, 2005, p. 93-119.
Rodríguez Palenzuela *et al.* (2003)	Diego Rodríguez Palenzuela, Gonzalo Camba-Méndez and Juan Ángel García, Relevant Economic Issues Concerning the Optimal Rate of Inflation, *European Central Bank Working Paper No. 278*, September 2003.
Rogoff (1985)	Kenneth Rogoff, The Optimal Degree of Commitment to an Intermediate Monetary Target, in: *Quarterly Journal of Economics*, Vol. 100, No. 4, 1985, p. 1169-1189.
Romer (1993)	David Romer, Openness and Inflation: Theory and Evidence, in: *Quarterly Journal of Economics*, Vol. 108, No. 4, 1993, p. 869-903.
Rudolph (1982)	B. Rudolph, Können die Banken ihre Kreditsicherheiten "vergessen"? in: *Kredit und Kapitel*, Vol. 15, 1982, p. 317-340.
Rudolph (1984)	B. Rudolph, Kreditsicherheiten als Instrumente zur Umverteilung und Begrenzung von Kreditrisiken, in: *Zeitschrift für betriebswirtschaftliche Forschung*, Vol. 36, 1984, p. 16-34.
Santoni (1984)	G. J. Santoni, A Private Central Bank: Some Olde English Lessons, in: *Federal Reserve Bank of St. Louis Review*, Vol. 66, April, 1984, p. 12-22.
Sargent & Wallace (1975)	Thomas J. Sargent & Neil Wallace, "Rational" Expectations, the Optimal Monetary Instrument, and the Optimal Money Supply Rule, in: *Journal of Political Economy*, Vol. 83, No. 2, 1975, p. 241-254.
Sargent & Wallace (1981)	Thomas J. Sargent & Neil Wallace, Some unpleasant monetarist arithmetic, in: *Federal Reserve Bank of Minneapolis Quarterly Review*, Vol. 5, Fall issue, p. 117-135.

Schumpeter   Joseph Alois Schumpeter, *Theorie der wirtschaftlichen*
(1911)   *Entwicklung. Eine Untersuchung über Unternehmergewinn,*
                Kapital, Kredit, Zins und den Konjunkturzyklus, Duncker &
                Humblot: Munich, 1926, 2nd edition.

Sekine *et al.*   Toshitaka Sekine, Keiichiro Kobayashi and Yumi Saita,
(2003)   Forbearance Lending: The Case of Japanese Firms, in:
                Monetary and Economic Studies (Institute for Monetary and
                Economic Studies, Bank of Japan), Vol. 21, No. 2, 2003, p.
                69-92.

Selgin &   George A. Selgin & Lawrence H. White, How Would the
White (1994)   Invisible Hand Handle Money? in: *Journal of Economic*
                Literature, Vol. 32, No. 4, 1994, p. 1718-1749.

Selgin &   George A. Selgin & Lawrence H. White, Credible Currency:
White (2005)   A Constitutional Perspective, *Constitutional Political*
                Economy, Vol.16, No. 1, 2005, p. 71–83.

Sims (2001)   Christopher Sims, Fiscal Aspects of Central Bank
                Independence, *CESifo Working Paper No. 547* (Munich:
                CESifo) 2001.

Smith (1776)   Adam Smith, An Inquiry into the Nature and Causes of the
                Wealth of Nations, in: R. H. Campbell and A. S. Skinner
                (editors), *Adam Smith. An Inquiry into the Nature and Causes*
                of the Wealth of Nations, Oxford University Press: Oxford,
                1976.

SNB (2004)   Swiss National Bank (SNB), *Richtlinien der SNB über das*
                geldpolitische Instrumentarium, (version as from 25th March
                2004), Internet:
                http://www.snb.ch/d/download/geldpol_instr_d.pdf.

Sonakul   M.R. Chatu Mongol Sonakul, *Keynote Address on the*
(2000)   *Occasion of the ADB Conference on Government Bond*
                Market and Financial Sector Development in Developing
                Asian Economies, based on a speech by Chatu Mongol
                Sonakul, Governor of the Bank of Thailand,Manila, 28-30
                March 2000, Internet: http://www.bot.or.th/BotHomepage/
                general/PressReleasesAndSpeeches/Speeches/english_version/
                Governor&DeputyGovernor/ADB_Mar00.htm

Spethmann & Steiger (2005)   Dieter Spethmann & Otto Steiger, The Four Achilles' Heels of the Eurosystem: Missing Central Monetary Institution, Different Real Rates of Interest, Nonmarketable Securities, and Missing Lender of Last Resort, in: *International Journal of Political Economy*, Vol. 34, No. 2, 2005, p. 46-68.

Stadermann (1994a)   Hans-Joachim Stadermann, *Die Fesselung des Midas. Eine Untersuchung über den Aufstieg und Verfall der Zentralbankkunst*, J. C. B. Mohr: Tübingen, 1994.

Stadermann (1994b)   Hans-Joachim Stadermann, *Geldwirtschaft und Geldpolitik. Einführung in die Grundlagen*, Gabler, Wiesbaden, 1994.

Stadermann (2000)   Hans-Joachim Stadermann, Aus Nichts wird Nichts. Commentary to H. Riese, in: *Ethik und Sozialwissenschaften: Streitforum für Erwägungskultur*, Vol. 11, No. 4, 2000, p. 534-537.

Stadermann (2002)   Hans-Joachim Stadermann, *Das Geld der Ökonomen, Ein Versuch über die Behandlung des Geldes in der Geldtheorie*, Mohr Siebeck, Tübingen, 2002.

Stadermann & Steiger (2001)   Hans-Joachim Stadermann & Otto Steiger, *Allgemeine Theorie der Wirtschaft. Erster Band Schulökonomik*, J. C. B. Mohr: Tübingen, 2001.

Steiger (2004)   Otto Steiger, Which Lender of Last Resort for the Eurosystem?, *Zentrum für Europäische Integrationsforschung Working Paper B23-04* (University of Bonn), September 2004.

Steiger (2005)   Otto Steiger, Schuldnergeld: Der Wunde Punkt in der keynesianischen Staatstheorie des Geldes, in: Gerhard Huber, Heinz D. Kurz and Hagen Krämer (editors), *Einkommensverteilung, technischer Fortschritt und struktureller Wandel: Festschrift für Peter Kalmbach*, Metropolis: Marburg, 2005, p. 169-188.

Steiger (2006a)   Otto Steiger, Property Economics *versus* New Institutional Economics: Alternative Foundations of How to Trigger Economic Development, in: *Journal of Economic Issues*, Vol. 40, No. 1, 2006, p. 183-208.

Steiger (2006b)	Otto Steiger, The Endogenity of Money and the Eurosystem: A Contribution to the Theory of Central Banking, in: Mark Setterfield (editor), *Complexity, Endogenous Money and Macroeconomic Theory: Essays in Honour of Basil J. Moore*, Edward Elgar: Cheltenham, 2006; prepublication as *ZEI Working Paper B24-04* (Universität Bonn), September 2004.
Stella (1987)	Peter Stella, Amalgamating Central Bank and Fiscal Deficits, *International Monetary Fund Working Paper No. 87/73*, October 1987.
Stella (1997)	Peter Stella, Do Central Banks Need Capital?, *International Monetary Fund Working Paper No. 97/83*, July 1997.
Stella (2002)	Peter Stella, Central Bank Financial Strength, Transparency, and Policy Credibility, *International Monetary Fund Working Paper No. 02/137*, August 2002.
Stella (2003)	Peter Stella, Why Central Banks Need Financial Strength, in: *Central Banking*, Vol. 14, No. 2, 2003, p.27-33.
Stella (2005)	Peter Stella, Central Bank Financial Strength, Transparency, and Policy Credibility, *International Monetary Fund Staff Papers*, Vol. 52, Number 2, 2005, p. 335-365.
Steuart (1767)	Sir James Steuart, *An Inquiry into the principles of political oeconomy: being an essay on the science of domestic policy in free nations, in which are particularly considered population, agriculture, trade, industry, money, coin, interest, circulation, banks, exchange, public credit and taxes*, Reprint; Oliver & Boyd: Edinburgh, 1966.
Stier (1996)	Winfried Stier, *Empirische Forschungsmethoden*, Springer: Berlin, 1996.
Stiglitz & Weiss (1981)	Joseph E. Stiglitz & Andrew Weiss, Credit Rationing in Markets with Imperfect Information, in: *American Economic Review*, Vol. 71, No. 3, 1981, p. 393-410.

Sullivan (2002)	Kenneth Sullivan, *Profits, Dividends and Capital – Considerations for Central Banks*, speech given at the IMF Seminar on Current Developments in Monetary and Financial Law, Washington, D.C., May 14, 2002, Internet: http://www.imf.org/external/np/leg/sem/2002/cdmfl/eng/sulliv.pdf
Sullivan (2005)	Kenneth Sullivan, Transparency in Central Bank Financial Statement Disclosures, *International Monetary Fund Working Paper 05/80*, 2005.
Svensson (1999)	Lars E. O. Svensson, Inflation Targeting as a Monetary Policy Rule, in: *Journal of Monetary Economics*, Vol. 43, No. 3, 1999, p. 607-654.
Taylor (1982)	John B. Taylor, Establishing Credibility: A Rational Expectations Viewpoint, in: *American Economic Review*, Vol. 72, No. 2, 1982, p. 81 – 85.
Taylor (1983)	John B. Taylor, Comment on "Rules, Discretion and Reputation in a Model of Monetary Policy" by Robert J. Barro & David B. Gordon, in: *Journal of Monetary Economics*, Vol. 12, No. 1, 1983, p. 123-125.
Tse & Leung (2002)	Chung Yi Tse & Charles Ka Yui Leung, Increasing Wealth and Increasing Instability: The Role of Collateral, in: *Review of International Economics*, Vol. 10, No. 1, 2002, p. 45-52.
Ueda (2003)	Kazuo Ueda, *The Role of Capital for Central Banks*, based on a speech by Kazuo Ueda, Member of the Policy Board Bank of Japan, 25th October 2003, Internet: http://www.boj.or.jp/en/press/04/ko0402b.htm.
Vaez-Zadeh (1991)	Reza Vaez-Zadeh, Implications and Remedies of Central Bank Losses, in: Patrick Downes and Reza Vaez-Zadeh (editors), *The Evolving Role of Central Banks*, International Monetary Fund: Washington D.C., 1991, p. 69-92.
van der Cruijsen & Demertzis (2005)	Carin van der Cruijsen & Maria Demertzis, The Impact of Central Bank Transparency on Inflation Expectations, *De Nederlandsche Bank Working Paper No. 031/2005*, March 2005.

Walsh (1995)   Carl E. Walsh, Optimal Contracts for Central Bankers, in:
                American Economic Review, Vol. 85, No.1, March 1995, p.
                150-167.

White (1980)   Halbert White, A Heteroscedasticity-Consistent Covariance
                Matrix Estimator and a Direct Test for Heteroscedasticity, in:
                Econometrica, Vol. 48, 1980, pp. 817-838.

White (1984)   Lawrence H. White, Competitive Payments Systems and the
                Unit of Account, in: *American Economic Review*, Vol. 74, No.
                4, 1984, p. 699-712.

Woodford   Michael Woodford, Central Bank Communication and Policy
(2005)   Effectiveness, *National Bureau of Economic Research
                Working Paper No. 11898*, December 2005.

World Bank   World Bank, *World Development Indicators on CD-ROM*,
(2006)   2006 (data CD-ROM).

World Bank   World Bank Analytical Classifications, *World Development
(2007)   Indicators*, February 2007, Internet:
                http://www.worldbank.org/.

Ralf Fendel

Monetary Policy, Interest Rate Rules, and the Term Structure of Interest Rates

Theoretical Considerations and Empirical Implications

Frankfurt am Main, Berlin, Bern, Bruxelles, New York, Oxford, Wien, 2007.
XIII, 187 pp., num. tab. and graphs
Studien zu internationalen Wirtschaftsbeziehungen. Edited by Michael Frenkel.
Vol. 8
ISBN 978-3-631-55894-2 · pb. € 39.–*

Interest rate rules play an important role in the empirical analysis of monetary policy as well as in modern monetary theory. Besides giving a comprehensive insight into this line of research the study incorporates the term structure of interest rates into interest rate rules. This is performed analytically as well as empirically. In doing so, state of the art techniques of modern finance for the analysis of the term structure of interest rates are introduced into the macroeconomic concept of interest rate rules. The study implies that from the theoretical perspective term structure effects are an important extension of interest rate rules. From an empirical perspective it shows that including term structure effects in interest rate reaction functions improves our understanding of the interest rate setting of the Deutsche Bundesbank and the European Central Bank.

Contents: Analysis of the monetary policy of the ECB and the Bundesbank · Derivation and estimation of interest rate rules · Special focus on the term structure of interest rates · Combination of the concept of interest rate rules with affine no-arbitrage term structure models

Frankfurt am Main · Berlin · Bern · Bruxelles · New York · Oxford · Wien
Distribution: Verlag Peter Lang AG
Moosstr. 1, CH-2542 Pieterlen
Telefax 00 41 (0) 32 / 376 17 27

*The €-price includes German tax rate
Prices are subject to change without notice
Homepage http://www.peterlang.de